Essays in Population History

Preface

ace those years that we thought the topic worthy of
tion. Our tentative reopening took the form of a
 at the symposium on socio-economic history at the
rnational Congress of Americanists, held in Mexico
ptember 1974. Although that paper excited consider-
st, it was not published in the proceedings because
f funds led the secretariat of the Congress to omit all
n papers. The content of that paper, here included in
ably extended essay, revises views we had published
e propose a theory of sustained undernutrition as the
e bulk of the population of central Mexico in late
times.
r III, on the registers of eight northern California
moves our focus from central Mexico and the Carib-
California. The shift was not a departure from our
ncern with the impact of the coming of the Europeans
 Indians of Mexico, but rather an extension of that
For Sherburne Cook, further, it meant returning to the
of many of his earlier studies. He had long wished to
the California mission registers the kinds of analysis we
ed for Mexican materials. When we found that the
funds available to us—modest indeed by present stan-
 demographic or social science research, but generous
erms we had had before—would cover the costs, we
 collect data to analyze the registers of the California
 Our plan was to start with those among the Costanoan
nd widen our scope gradually to include those of the
e state. We also hoped to complement materials from
ornia missions with study of one or two comparable
sewhere in the Southwest of the United States and the
 Mexico. At the time of Sherburne Cook's death, we
cted data for seven northern California missions, were
 off data on Mission Santa Clara, and were about to
gotiations for access to the registers of the other north-
ornia missions. Chapter III in this volume thus repre-
runcated implementation of our project; it covers the
ssions for which we had collected or were collecting
w that we have shown what can be done, others may
t similar, and perhaps better, work on the other mis-
ur essay indicates need for considerably more examina-
the functioning of the California missions; the potential
insight is far from exhausted.

Essays in Population History: *Mexico and California*

Sherburne F. Cook and Woodrow Borah

Volume Three

University of California Press
Berkeley • Los Angeles • London

University of California Press
Berkeley and Los Angeles, California

University of California Press, Ltd.
London, England

ISBN: 0-520-03560-7
Library of Congress Catalog Card Number: 75-123626
Printed in the United States of America

Preface and Acknowledg

This is the last volume of Cook
F. Cook died on November
forced changes in our plans. By
one essay near completion; it
two more essays, we were in
discussions that over the years
and creative. I have complete
California mission records, has
the scope of our original projec
A fourth inquiry, to identify t
the Indian population of cent
period, we had planned but not
Implementation would require
trained in physiology or med
partnership would have to be de

Accordingly, our third volur
locates the low point of the Ind
ico at the end of the long dec
Conquest. With that point finally
a reasonably complete outline of
tion since 1518 and to demonstr
introduced by the Europeans bro
central Mexico within a century
its 1518 value. The document
also gave much information on
we have analyzed in the same cha

Our second chapter, on food
central Mexico during the sixteen
turies, reopens inquiries that had
of anthropologists in the 1930's

to light s
new atte
paper rea
XLII Int
City in S
able inte
shortage
symposiu
a conside
earlier: V
lot of th
aborigina

Chapt
missions,
bean to
central c
upon th
concern.
territory
apply to
had lea
research
dards fc
by any
agreed t
missions
Indians
rest of t
the Cali
groups
North
had col
drawing
begin
ern Ca
sents a
eight
data.
carry c
sions.
tion of
for nev

In preparing the essays of this volume, as for those of the earlier ones, we have had much help and kindness, which we should want remembered. Film and permission freely to use the document basic to Chapter I, we owe to the gracious understanding of His Excellency, the Duque del Infantado; to the good offices of his sister, the Reverend Mother Cristina de la Cruz de Arteaga; and to the disinterested and generous wish to further scholarly inquiry of E. William Jowdy, then a graduate student working in the archives of Madrid. In the preparation of Chapter II, we have needed and have had much advice and help from colleagues on the various campuses of the University of California. They are, among others, Martin Baumhoff, Lincoln Constance, Robert Heizer, Jonathan Sauer, and John M. Tucker. For access to materials and assistance of other kinds for Chapter III, we are indebted to the officials of the diocesan archive of the Monterey-Salinas diocese; to the library of the University of Santa Clara; to the good will toward all scholars of Father Norman Martin, S.J., of the University of Santa Clara, and to the librarians and archivists, past and present, of that institution; to the Genealogical Society of Utah through its branch in Oakland, California; and to Father Stafford Poole, C.M. Finally, our work on California missions has been greatly aided by the assistance of Thomas Workman Temple III, Dr. María C. Puerta, and Dr. Harry Cross. Dr. Cross has served not merely as research assistant but also as statistical aide. His help has been indispensable in reducing a mass of data into comprehensive parallel tables. Finally, let me record my deep personal gratitude to my co-author for a quarter of a century of warm and stimulating partnership.   WOODROW BORAH

Contents

List of Figures

Maps

Abbreviations Used in Citations

AGI Archivo General de Indias, Seville, Spain.
AGN Archivo General de la Nación, Mexico City.
HMAI *Handbook of Middle American Indians.* General editor, Robert Wauchope. 16 vols. Austin, Texas, 1964–1976.
IA *Ibero-Americana.* University of California Publications, Berkeley and Los Angeles.
PNE Paso y Troncoso, Francisco del, comp. *Papeles de Nueva España: Segunda serie, geografía y estadística.* 6 vols. Mexico City, 1905–1906. Plus appendices and additional volumes published by Vargas Rea, Mexico City, 1944–1948.

A NOTE ON MONEY

Colonial Mexican money (silver pesos of 8 reales, each real of 12 granos) is written as in the old English system: 1/3/11. If there are no granos, the third grouping is omitted, but there is always a notation for the peso, as 1/ and 0/7.

Chapter I

Royal Revenues and Indian Population in New Spain, ca. 1620-1646

1. INTRODUCTION

In a series of earlier studies, we examined materials on the Indian population of central Mexico and made calculations of numbers based upon our analysis of those materials. We have thus been able to present estimates for various years in the sixteenth and the first decade of the seventeenth centuries. For the convenience of the reader we list them:

1518	25.2 million	1585	1.9 million
1532	16.8 million	1595	1.375 million
1548	6.3 million	1605	1.075 million
1568	2.65 million		

These are based upon samples whose extent and ease of interpretation vary considerably. The estimate for 1568, the most firmly based, derives from a sample of perhaps 90% of the towns in central Mexico, which were newly counted in terms of a reformed and relatively uniform classification of tributaries and half-tributaries. That for 1605 is based upon a small sample of towns whose populations had shrunk so badly that they were relocated in new larger towns under the policy of *congregación*. [1]

At the other end of the colonial period, calculations of Indian population are comparatively simple for various years of the eighteenth century, since tribute counts for that century are

---

1. Sherburne F. Cook and Woodrow Borah, *The Indian Population of Central Mexico, 1531–1610 (IA* 44), pp. 47–49 and correction at end; Borah and Cook, *The Aboriginal Population of Central Mexico on the Eve of the Spanish Conquest (IA* 45), p. 88; Borah and Cook, *The Population of Central Mexico in 1548: An Analysis of the* Suma de visitas de pueblos *(IA* 43), *passim.* The discussion of sources is found throughout all three works.

frequent and careful, and the viceregal administration was making the first attempts at general civil censuses. So for the eighteenth century, scholars have abundant material, subject to the new problems that arise from the increasing number of racial mixtures in the population and the growing confusion in the application of social and racial criteria to them.[2]

The span of years from 1610 to perhaps 1700, in contrast, has presented a gap in evidence. Yet those years contain the point at which the Indian population of central Mexico reached its nadir and began to recover from the long decline unleashed by the European Conquest. Our difficulty, like that of other students, has been to find materials that under treatment could provide evidence. In recent years a number of papers have appeared that offer partial or regional approaches to the problem. In August 1962, in a paper read at the XXXV International Congress of Americanists in Mexico City, José Miranda presented comparisons of prevailing tribute assessments for a number of towns in the bishoprics of Mexico, Puebla, and Michoacán for two periods in the seventeenth century: 1644-1657 and 1692-1698. He found them in accounts of the half-real for cathedral construction *(medio real de fábrica)* levied annually on every Indian tributary and directly convertible to the prevailing tribute assessment. There was no indication of the precise year when the assessments were made. Miranda's material showed a substantial increase in Indian population, on the order of 28%, between assessments in force in 1644-1657 and in 1692-1698. He conjectured that the low point of the Indian population came in the 1620's or 1630's.[3]

Subsequently, in our study of the historical demography of one small region in central Mexico, the Mixteca Alta, published in 1968, we made use of the Montemayor y Córdova de Cuenca count of that region in 1661, found in the Archivo General de Indias, in Seville. Analysis of the count indicated that the nadir of Indian population in the Mixteca Alta probably came in the decades 1600-1620 at a value of from 20% to 25% of the population in 1569, and as little as 3% or 4% of the pre-Con-

2. Cook and Borah, *Essays in Population History,* I and II, *passim,* but esp. chap. 1 of vol. I.

3. José Miranda, "La población indígena de México en el siglo XVII," pp. 182–189. See also Miranda, "La población indígena de Ixmiquilpan y su distrito en la época colonial."

quest level. The Montemayor y Córdova de Cuenca report also gave the dates of the previous counts and so provided the first clear evidence of the extent to which prevailing accounts should be adjusted to an average year some time back.[4]

Another study, which we published in 1971, of the population of west-central Mexico, 1548-1960, indicates.that the low point of Indian numbers in that region occurred around 1650, with a value of slightly over 12% of that for 1548 and 33% of that for 1570.[5] Much of west-central Mexico, however, was conquered and settled later than central Mexico. Moreover, it remained essentially a frontier area until late in the colonial period. Accordingly, the experience of west-central Mexico cannot be extrapolated directly, without adjustment, to central Mexico.

More recently, a study by Günter Vollmer on Indian towns in southern Puebla sets the low point of the Indian population at approximately 1650, when he estimates it to have been 27% of the value for 1570.[6] Another study, by Claude Morin, of Santa Inés Zacatelco in the Puebla basin suggests also that the low point of population in central Mexico occurred around 1650, with perhaps 816,000 Indians.[7] A more general study of central Mexico in the seventeenth century, by J. I. Israel, holds that "the Indian population of central Mexico, having fallen to a level of between 1½ and 2 million in 1607, continued to decline at least until the middle of the century." Increase did not become manifest until 1671.[8] So the effort to fill the gap has continued, with fair agreement that the low point of the Indian population came in the seventeenth century, although there has

4. Cook and Borah, *The Population of the Mixteca Alta, 1520-1960 (IA* 50), pp. 33-38 and 71-75.

5. Cook and Borah, *Essays,* I, chap. 5, esp. p. 310.

6. Günter Vollmer, "La evolución cuantitativa de la población indígena en la región de Puebla (1570-1810)."

7. Claude Morin, "Population et épidémies dans une paroisse mexicaine: Santa Inés Zacatelco, XVIIe-XIXe siècles," esp. p. 70.

8. J.I. Israel, *Race, Class and Politics in Colonial Mexico, 1610-1670,* pp. 27-28. Israel cites the estimate of Landeras de Velasco, 10 January 1607, that there were 344,000 full tributaries, presumably in the Audiencia of Mexico without Yucatan. Israel must be using a multiplicative factor of close to 5.0 to estimate total Indian population, for at the factor we have established on the basis of very careful inspection of evidence (2.8), the total Indian population would be 963,200. Even with adjustment to include the Indians of Nueva Galicia, the total, using the factor of 2.8, would not reach a million. See Cook and Borah, *Essays,* I, p. 309, for estimates of Nueva Galicia.

been no agreement on a more exact placing of the point within
that span of years nor on the value to be assigned to the Indian
population at that point. Our own two studies, it will be
noticed, differ on placement of the point, admittedly for two
very different regions.

Clearly the resolution of this question required more data in
the form of counts of Indian population in the early and middle
decades of the seventeenth century. Since there had been available as yet almost no tribute counts for that period, we turned
to another possible source of information in the records of the
pastoral inspections of bishops, some of them published, others
unpublished but available in manuscripts. Unfortunately, those
for the seventeenth century did not give adequate information
on numbers of Indian tributaries, total population, or some
group in the population that would give a clue to total number.[9]
So this attempt met a dead end.

Ideally, we wanted a set of counts taken in a relatively short
period of time and covering all of central Mexico, either like the
Montemayor y Córdova de Cuenca count for the Mixteca Alta
or those of the tribute reform of the 1560's. In the absence of
the ideal, we could use a statement of prevailing assessments, like
those in the encomenderos' petition of 1597, but would have to
understand that the data referred to the time when each count
was made and that an average year should be calculated to
adjust for the lag in the set as a whole. In 1958–59 Woodrow
Borah spent a sabbatical year in Spain for the purpose *inter alia*
of hunting for just such material. The search turned up the
Córdova de Cuenca count and a great deal of eighteenth-century
data, but only a few scattered town counts for the rest of
central Mexico. After that and searches in Mexico, we had
decided that the hunt would have to be left to the next
generation of scholars exploring as yet ill-known reaches of the
Archivo General de Indias, the *bodega* of the Archivo General
de la Nación in Mexico City, or the largely unknown private
archives of Spanish noble families, few of which in 1958–59
were open to scholars. Then, literally out of the blue, an
airgram dated October 24, 1971, came to Woodrow Borah from
E. William Jowdy, then a graduate student at the University of
Michigan and doctoral candidate under the guidance of Charles

9. Many records of pastoral inspections are valuable sources of demographic
data. See Cook and Borah, *Essays,* I, chap. 1, esp. pp. 47–48.

Gibson, doing archival research in Madrid. Jowdy reported finding a document in the archive of the Duques del Infantado which gave much information on royal revenues and tribute assessments in the Audiencia of Mexico in 1646. A reply by return mail indicating that the find might be very important brought a generous offer to try to secure a film copy for our use. Jowdy brought the matter to the attention of the Duque del Infantado through the good offices of the latter's sister, the Reverend Mother Cristina de la Cruz de Arteaga, whereupon the duke graciously gave full permission to film the document and use it in any way.

The document of thirty-three folios is found among the papers of the Conde de Salvatierra, viceroy of New Spain from November 1642 to May 1648, when he moved to Peru. It forms folios 148-180 in volume 54 of the archive, the entire volume being correspondence and reports of various kinds of the Conde de Salvatierra for the years 1645-46.[10] The document consists of a one-folio letter of transmittal and thirty-two folios of report, both dated at Mexico City 4 September 1646, and signed by Juan de Cervantes Casaus, Contador Mayor of the Tribunal de Cuentas.[11] It is addressed merely to an *excelentísimo señor,* who could be either the viceroy or the visitador-general, Juan de Palafox y Mendoza, but since the closing paragraph of the report states that it was prepared at the express command of the visitador-general, it seems probable that the report and covering letter are addressed to him. On the other hand, since the document is among the Salvatierra papers, it may be that we deal here with a second clean, signed copy prepared for the viceroy as well. The personal papers of both men have become part of the archive of the Duques del Infantado.

It is worth recalling here that the Palafox visita, a remarkably stormy one, occurred during years of unusual strain for the monarchy in Spain—continuation of the Thirty Years' War, the dissolution of the Crown Union with Portugal, and the revolts

10. The published description is as follows: "Libro LIV. Correspondencia, informes y otros papeles referentes a América del conde de Salvatierra, 1645-6." Spain, Dirección General de Archivos y Bibliotecas, *Guía de fuentes para la historia de Ibero-América conservadas en España,* II, p. 90.

11. Genealogical details may be found in Guillermo Lohmann Villena, *Los americanos en las órdenes nobiliarias,* I, pp. 103-105 and 173-174. Juan de Cervantes Casaus was an important Creole figure in the early and middle seventeenth century. See Israel, *passim.*

of Catalonia and Naples—and of perhaps the low point of decay and inefficiency in royal administration in New Spain. The royal government was in ever greater need of funds just when the treasury in the Audiencia of Mexico found that local costs absorbed almost all local revenues. New taxes, such as stamped paper, were imposed, but were just coming into yield in 1646. On royal command Palafox removed one viceroy, the Marqués de Villena, a relative of the Duke of Braganza and new King of Portugal, through fear of disloyalty, and governed the colony until the arrival of the Conde de Salvatierra. In the end, the political storms arising from attempts at church reform delayed attempts at reforming civil administration, despite the cooperation of Salvatierra and Palafox in finding funds for remittance to Spain. Salvatierra was promoted to be viceroy of Peru; Palafox was recalled to Spain shortly afterward and left Mexico in June 1649.[12] A normal element in any general inspection would have been a review of the royal finances; in the special circumstances of the Castilian monarchy in the 1640's, one was especially necessary and incumbent upon both visitador-general and viceroy. The report of 1646 was at least part of such a review.

The closing paragraph of the report clearly states that the review was ordered by Palafox, at what date we have no clear indication. The covering letter asks pardon for delay in preparing the report, blaming the delay upon burden of work and upon the difficulty of obtaining precise figures, since collections of royal revenues in the provinces (alcaldías mayores) were sometimes placed in charge of the governors and sometimes entrusted to others at the decision of the Comptroller of Tributes and Sales Tax. The report, therefore, must have been asked for some months or even years before the date it bears. Preparation, even in terms of the leisurely processes of that period, was delayed and made difficult by the complex subdivision of administration of royal finance, which defeated any attempt at centralized supervision and accounting. The amounts due as royal tribute, one of the principal sources of revenue, could be ascertained by consulting the assessments of the Indian towns; but, without resort to the Comptroller of Tributes and Sales Tax, there was no way of determining amounts paid and in

12. Israel, p. 247.

arrears, the latter a considerable sum. The yield of taxes leased out could be ascertained easily, and averages estimated for some revenues of variable yield, directly administered by the Crown, such as the state monopoly of mercury and other taxes upon mining. Even so, the clerks collecting the material worked with surprising negligence, since, as we shall see, they passed over the folios of tribute assessments for a large number of Indian towns. The report is a substantial sample rather than a full statement. It is, nevertheless, a remarkable view of the royal finances in the Audiencia of Mexico for what were probably the years of most corrupt and inefficient fiscal administration during the entire colonial period. In the 1650's there was a drastic overhaul of the administration of Indian tributes and the royal monopoly of mercury after a quarter-century of virtual paralysis.

We now discuss the report under the rubrics of data on Indian population and the royal fiscal system.

2. INDIAN POPULATION

The initial determinations that must be made are how complete is the coverage of the data on Indian tributaries—i.e., how many towns are represented in the report and what is their proportion to the total number in the Audiencia of Mexico at the time; and further, what year should be set as the average date for the counts on which the assessments were based, since all of them must have been made some time before the formal tribute was set and an even longer interval before the listing in the report. Let us start with the second matter.

In terms of mid-sixteenth-century town boundaries, there are approximately 740 towns in the 1646 list. The statements of tribute for towns held by the Crown give the amounts due under the standard tribute assessment of money, maize, cacao, cotton cloth, etc.; the amount of money due as *servicio real,* an additional tax of four reales per tributary; and usually an additional statement on the number of tributaries found at the count on which the assessment was based. For example, the statement on Atoyac finishes "respecto de tener ciento y quarenta y tres tributarios" ["since it has 143 tributaries"]. For towns held partly by the Crown and partly by an encomendero, the statement of standard tribute usually covers only the share of the Crown, and so it is the servicio real and statement of

number of tributaries that provide the data. For towns held
entirely by encomenderos, there is usually no statement of
standard tribute or number of tributaries; but the servicio real,
which was levied on all Indian tributaries whether in Crown or
encomienda towns, is given, and since it had a standard relation
to the number of tributaries, is directly convertible to the
number in the prevailing assessment.

There is unfortunately no statement in the report on the date
when the assessments were made. Nor is it likely that the
interval between the date of the count and the report was so
short that we may ignore the matter. For, in the closing years of
the sixteenth century, the rhythm of recounts and reassessments began to slacken and the intervals between counts to
lengthen. In the neighboring Audiencia of Nueva Galicia, a
survey of tributes in 1594 reported that in that treasury jurisdiction, Crown towns were paying under assessments made an
average of nine years five months earlier, and that for the six
towns reassessed in 1594 the average interval to the preceding
count was fourteen years one month.[13] Nueva Galicia was a
separate treasury jurisdiction, although in general it followed
the lead of the Audiencia of Mexico. Accordingly, its experience is no more than an indication. We do know that in the
second quarter of the seventeenth century the administration of
tributes in the Audiencia of Mexico was under an unusually
fraudulent and inept administration. In 1653 charges were
brought against the Comptroller, and the entire administration
eventually was shaken up and reorganized. One of the failures
of the Contaduría General de Tributos in that period was in
carrying out recounts and reassessments—some indeed were
made, but few.

The most useful testimony we have for the Audiencia of
Mexico is that of Montemayor y Córdova de Cuenca about the
Mixteca Alta in 1661. His reporting gave the dates of previous
tribute counts, and *inter alia* has enabled us to determine that
the 1646 report embodies the latest count up to 1646 for the
towns of the Mixteca Alta. The average interval between time of
assessment and the reassessment by Montemayor y Córdova de
Cuenca in 1661 was thirty and a half years.[14] One cannot

13. Woodrow Borah, "Los tributos y su recaudación en la Audiencia de la Nueva
Galicia durante el siglo XVI," pp. 40–42.
14. Cook and Borah, *The Population of the Mixteca Alta,* pp. 33–35.

subtract fifteen years (1661-1646) from this average and apply it without further adjustment, for in the reporting for the Mixteca Alta there are a number of towns counted and reassessed after 1646 which bring down the average. The intervals between those counts and the preceding ones would raise it. Neither can we apply the thirty and a half years without downward adjustment, for Indian towns nearer Spanish centers may well have been counted and reassessed more frequently than those in the Mixteca Alta; and the lag in recounts must have built up at some time after the period in the second half of the sixteenth century when recounts were frequent. An average lag of thirty and a half years probably represents the low point of tribute administration. The adjustment we must make is thus fifteen years plus another term of years ranging from five to ten, a total of twenty to twenty-five. The average date of the assessments in the 1646 list should be set somewhere between 1620 and 1625. If the reader demands a single year, 1622 or 1623.

The other matter to be determined here is the extent to which the 1646 list covers the Indian towns of the Audiencia of Mexico. Our basis for comparison is the assessments of the tribute reform with an average date of 1568, which give us our fullest list with least adjustment. Indian towns in the Audiencia of Nueva Galicia would automatically be excluded because they lay in another treasury jurisdiction, that of Guadalajara. Similarly, Tabasco would be excluded because it lay in the subordinate but separate government of Yucatán. Its Indian tributes were administered by the *subcaja* of Santa María de la Victoria, reporting to the *caja* of Mérida, for Yucatán was also a separate treasury jurisdiction. These automatic exclusions remove from either list some hundreds of towns of the approximately 2,000 which existed in the early sixteenth century in central Mexico as we have defined it. Another group of towns on neither list is those that went out of existence in the first half-century of Spanish rule. In all, the 2,000 towns would come down to perhaps 1,400.

Comparing the two lists is also complicated by the changes of the nearly eighty years separating them. During that long interval, shrunken towns were consolidated through congregación; settlement shifted within the territory of towns remaining formally intact; within other towns dependent units *(sujetos)* became autonomous, for they saw no reason to continue in a status of dependency forced upon them by former rulers when the current overlords were willing to annul it; in some regions where population almost vanished, new towns were created; and in the zone to the north which had been the territory of nomadic Indians in 1520, the Spanish founded new settlements.[15] The identification of relationships and shifts has been a detective job of considerable difficulty. One surprise has been the uncovering of a substantial number of towns on the 1646 list which we knew existed in the first half of the sixteenth century, but thought had gone out of existence by the 1560's. In terms of number of towns, we may tabulate our findings:

On both lists	648
On the 1646 list but not the 1568 one, or impossible to match	89
On the 1646 list but could not be located	3
Subtotal	740
On the 1568 list but not the 1646 one	630
Total	1,370

Relative to the 1568 list there is, then, a coverage of approximately 50%; in terms of the number of towns in the district of the royal treasury of Mexico City, the 1646 list gives information on 54%.

Another way of approaching this determination is in terms of proportion of aggregate population involved in coverage and omission. The best approach here is to compare the aggregate population reported by the 1646 list with that calculated by ratio through comparison with the 1568 list. (We jump to our results here; the detail is in Table 1.2, part C.) For the plateau, the omission is 18.6%; for the coasts, 37.0%; for the district of the caja of Mexico City as a whole, 24.1%. In other words, the 1646 list reports 75.9% of the reconstructed total population, and in these terms is an even better sample. The difference in the findings by number of towns and aggregate population is easily explainable as due to a tendency to pass over smaller rather than larger towns in preparing the 1646 list.

The omissions from the 1646 list cast further light on the way the Contaduría de Tributos kept its records of Indian tribute counts and assessments. We know through the discovery

15. On the shifts in town jurisdictions and relationships, see Peter Gerhard, *A Guide to the Historical Geography of New Spain, passim.* This volume is an invaluable and now indispensable guide to a remarkably intricate local history.

and publication of a substantial part of the second colonial set of such records that they were kept in looseleaf fashion. The records of a single town, especially if important; of towns held initially by one encomendero, even if dispersed geographically; or of contiguous towns were entered on a single folio or group of folios. We do not know how these were filed in relation to each other, for the present alphabetical order of the records, manuscript and printed, reflects a recent arrangement of the scattered folios discovered. The second colonial *matrícula de tributos* was superseded in the 1570's, presumably by copying off the latest assessments on fresh folios to form a new set of records.[16] The 1646 list may have been taken from the third colonial matrícula de tributos, or even a fourth one, although the slowing down of tribute reassessments suggests that the creation of a fourth set by 1646 was unlikely. The 1646 list indicates that there was a tendency to file together the folios of town assessments for a single region. The partial listing together of towns in the Zapotecas, the Veracruz coast, Colima, etc., can only have come about in this way. We may surmise that the tribute records of many towns in 1646 were filed together by alcaldía mayor, but that systematic grouping by province was to wait until the eighteenth century. The order of towns in the 1646 report, as well as the omissions in it, must arise either directly or at one remove from the perhaps hasty work of a scribe taking off the information from the folios of the Contaduría de Tributos. It was easy to miss folios, especially if the assessments for any group of towns ran to more than one folio so that it was necessary to locate the end of one set of records and the beginning of the next.

Let us turn now to our procedure in taking off and using the information in the 1646 report for calculating Indian population. Our first step was to identify the towns one by one, ascertain their geographical location and their identity or relation to towns on the 1568 list, include data for 1595 where possible, and prepare working charts by region. The regions were automatically those we had laid out for our calculations of population in the sixteenth century.[17] The data for Indian population in 1568 and 1595 had been segregated previously

16. Mexico, AGN, *El libro de las tasaciones de pueblos de la Nueva España,* passim.

17. A full description with map may be found in Cook and Borah, *The Indian Population of Central Mexico, 1531–1610,* pp. 33–36.

and published for those regions.[18] As we have already suggested, identification of the towns involved a long series of
problems in detection. Many towns in Mexico have identical
names; others have nearly identical ones, which in the more
haphazard spelling of the seventeenth century become identical.
Here the tendency of the 1646 report to list together contiguous towns or towns of one region helped very greatly.
Changes brought by the nearly eighty years between 1568 and
1646 also created serious problems of identification, for many
towns had changed their names, or moved the location of the
main settlement within their territory, sometimes keeping the
name and sometimes taking on the name associated with the
new site; others had become consolidated; others were sujetos
of towns in 1568, but had since become autonomous and dealt
directly with Spanish authorities; others represented new settlement on abandoned land—a phenomenon particularly of the
lower altitudes; yet others were new settlements within what
had been nomadic Chichimec territory in 1520, but was being
brought under control by the Spaniards. In all probability, the
task of identification would have been impossible for at least a
quarter to a third of the names if we had not been able to use
the newly published *A Guide to the Historical Geography of
New Spain* by Peter Gerhard. This remarkable volume, organized by the alcaldías mayores of the eighteenth century,
permits tracing the territorial history and changes of towns in
the district of the treasury of Mexico City. It even gives the
history of encomiendas and parishes. In the end, we were
unable to identify and locate just three of the towns in the
1646 list.

Once towns in the 1646 report were segregated by region and
listed with information, where possible, on population in 1568
and 1595 and numbers of tributaries in 1646, the second step
was to convert tributaries into total population. We have explored at considerable length elsewhere the problems and evidence for arriving at appropriate multiplicative factors for
various years in order to convert tributary number into total
Indian population.[19] There is accordingly no need to repeat the

18. *Ibid.*, pp. 59–109.
19. Borah and Cook, *The Population of Central Mexico in 1548*, pp. 75–102;
Cook and Borah, *The Indian Population of Central Mexico, 1531–1610*, pp. 59–109;
Cook and Borah, *The Population of the Mixteca Alta*, pp. 39–47; Cook and Borah,
Essays, I, chaps. 3 and 4.

exploration here. For 1568 and 1595, our data already applied the factor of 2.8 (which implies a factor of 3.3 for a married man or *casado*). That value, although low, is derived from a substantial mass of evidence and must be regarded as solidly based. It is, however, clearly inapplicable to a later period when the number of tributaries reached nadir but demographic changes within the Indian population were preparing the way for the fairly steady increase that was characteristic from some time in the first half of the seventeenth century to the end of the colonial period. Equally, the relatively high factors necessary for conversion of eighteenth-century tributary numbers to total Indian population, although they are very firmly based on a substantial mass of data—some of the best we have for Mexico at any time—cannot be applied to the years in the seventeenth century when the population was in transition from one demographic pattern to another. Accordingly we returned to our explanation and the graph in our study of the population of the Mixteca Alta and chose 3.4 as the most appropriate value for application to the data in the 1646 report, understanding that the data should be regarded as falling in the years 1620–1625.

We had hoped to verify our calculations further by a comparison of the data in the 1646 report with the tribute counts of the early eighteenth century, approximately 1715–1733, for which there survives an unusually full series of new counts for the treasury district of Mexico. The appropriate factor for converting tributaries to total Indian population for those data would be 3.8. Unfortunately for our needs in this study, the eighteenth-century tribute counts and assessments were made under a new system which handled a province at a time. Comparison on any extensive basis with earlier counts and assessments by individual towns accordingly required so much adjustment that we abandoned the attempt.

Our next steps were to rearrange the regional data on new worksheets, breaking down the regional division into further categories which we applied uniformly to the eleven regions (which are numbered from I to X, with a IIA). For each region, Table 1.1, part A for that region lists all towns or other places which occur on both the 1568 and 1646 lists. From the total of these we have calculated the ratio of the two populations 1646/1568. Table 1.1, part B for the region gives the names of places which occur in the 1646 reporting but are not on the 1568 list. The aggregate of these populations must be added to

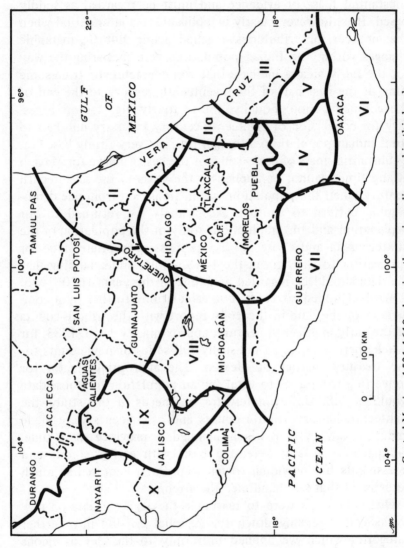

Central Mexico, 1531-1610, showing the regions discussed in this book.

the regional total in order to calculate the percentage of deficiency in the 1646 reporting for the region. Table 1.1, part C for each region gives the names of places for which only the 1568 list has a value, i.e., they are missing from the 1646 list. We have not included towns or places for which we had calculated hypothetical populations for 1568 on the basis of information of earlier date. The numerical weight of places with a population value in 1568, but not in the 1646 reporting, can be estimated by dividing the total of their population by that of the entire region. The resulting value, expressed as a percentage, gives an index to the degree of deficiency found in the 1646 reporting for the region.

Since the population reported in the 1646 list is deficient in all regions, the probable true population must be calculated. An estimate may be obtained by the use of simple proportions based upon the logical assumption that the mean ratio found for each region from the paired values for places in Table 1.1, part A holds equally for each region for the towns in Table 1.1, part C for which we have no information in the 1646 reporting. Since the proportion of places for which we have information in each region is large—for some regions very large—the ratios, although not absolutely precise, are reasonably close to the true value. We then applied the ratio for each region of the population reported in the 1568 data for that region to the totals in parts A and C. The resulting value is the reconstructed Indian population of the region in 1620–1625 (our adjusted average date for the tribute assessments).

As a check upon the results secured by comparing the data in the 1568 and 1646 reporting, we have turned to the data of average date of 1595. For each region, Table 1.1, part D shows the towns for which we have data in the 1568 and 1595 reporting, together with the ratios 1595/1568. We determine the mean ratio and apply it to the total Indian population of the region in 1568, a procedure which yields an estimated population for the entire region in 1595. A similar operation is performed with those towns of each region for which we have population figures in both the 1595 and 1646 reporting. The numerical values and ratios of 1646/1595 are in Table 1.1, part E for each region. In all cases, the populations in 1595 calculated from those in 1646 are smaller than the populations calculated from the 1568 data. This difference, or deficiency, in the values calculated from 1646 confirms the result of direct, town-by-town comparison of 1568 and 1646.

We turn now to the analysis of the data region by region. Our explanation is deliberately arranged to be as uniform as possible for each region, in accordance with the uniform organization of the data.

Region I. The Central Plateau, a culturally homogeneous area that was the core of ancient Mexico at the time of the Spanish Conquest and still has substantial unity today. On the north, the boundary is the Chichimec frontier of 1550. On the east, it is the Atlantic escarpment at approximately the contour line of 1200 meters to the meeting point of the state boundaries of Veracruz, Oaxaca, and Puebla. On the south, the boundary runs along the Balsas River, including the south bank, as far as Michoacán. From there it runs north along the Mexico-Michoacán state line and then east along the Hidalgo-Querétaro state line to the Moctezuma River.

We find 206 places, not necessarily towns, which occur on both the 1568 and 1646 lists. In 1568 the population of these 206 places is 1,321,329; in 1646 it is 303,717. The ratio 1646/1568 is 0.230. (See Table 1.1, Region I, part A.)

TABLE 1.1, REGION I, PART A

Towns Found on Both 1568 and 1646 Lists

Name	Loc.	Population in 1568	Population in 1646	Ratio 1646/1568
Acamixtla	Gro.	1,264	213	.169
Acatlán	Hid.	2,352	122	.052
Acatlán and Totoltepec	Pue.	2,612	892	.341
Acayuca	Hid.	2,288	92	.040
Actopan	Hid.	20,295	3,090	.152
Ahuatlán	Pue.	112	44	.393
Ajuchitlán	Gro.	3,780	578	.153
Alahuixtlán	Gro.	825	342	.414
Atempan	Pue.	1,129	508	.450
Amatepec and Sultepec and Almoloya	Mex.	3,440	889	.258
Amecameca	Mex.	4,976	1,182	.238
Apaxco	Mex.	3,814	286	.075

TABLE 1.1, REGION I, PART A (Cont.)

Name	Loc.	Population in 1568	Population in 1646	Ratio $\dfrac{1646}{1568}$
Atenango	Gro.	1,823	877	.481
Atengo	Hid.	1,860	158	.085
Atitalaquia	Hid.	4,673	275	.059
Atlacomulco and Xocotitlán and Temascalingo	Mex.	13,959	3,325	.238
Atlapulco	Mex.	3,478	472	.136
Atlatlauca and Xochiac	Mex.	1,125	298	.265
Atotonilco	Hid.	4,735	241	.051
Atotonilco	Hid.	12,672	358	.028
Atzcapotzalco	D.F.	5,082	1,482	.291
Axacuba	Hid.	13,398	315	.024
Axapuxco and Zaguala	Mex.	3,699	241	.065
Ayotzingo	Mex.	1,278	22	.017
Calimaya	Mex.	5,379	1,391	.259
Calpan	Pue.	13,761	2,795	.203
Calpulalpan	Tlax.	3,666	177	.048
Capulhuac	Mex.	1,653	742	.448
Coatepec	Mex.	1,419	1,275	.899
Coatepec	Mex.	3,947	206	.052
Coatlán and Aquitlapan	Gro.	1,177	439	.373
Coatzingo	Pue.	139	46	.331
Coxcatlán	Pue.	1,472	554	.376
Coyoacán	D.F.	13,629	5,457	.400
Coyotepec	Mex.	1,591	141	.089
Cuatinchán	Pue.	5,874	3,009	.513
Cuautitlán and Xalascan	Mex.	9,587	3,531	.369
(Cuautla) Amilpas and Ahuehuepan and Tetelcingo	Mor.	4,184	914	.218
Cuernavaca	Mor.	39,336	6,967	.177
Culhuacán	Mex.	2,864	404	.141
Cutzamala	Gro.	2,805	503	.179
Chapa de Mota	Mex.	8,118	456	.056
Chapantongo	Hid.	5,808	145	.025
Chapulco	Pue.	565	308	.546
Chapulhuacán	Hid.	2,618	517	.198

TABLE 1.1, REGION I, PART A (Cont.)

Name	Loc.	Population in 1568	Population in 1646	Ratio $\frac{1646}{1568}$
Chiautla	Pue.	9,488	1,413	.149
Chiconautla	Mex.	1,688	214	.127
Chicoloapan	Mex.	789	116	.147
Chichicastla	Hid.	3,366	150	.045
Chietla and Atzala	Pue.	2,567	1,080	.421
Chila	Pue.	1,564	278	.178
Chila	Pue.	1,690	498	.295
Chilcuautla	Hid.	3,409	107	.031
Chimalhuacán	Mex.	2,541	262	.103
Chimalhuacán	Mex.	5,854	2,081	.362
Chinantla	Pue.	2,690	272	.101
Cholula and sujetos	Pue.	35,772	9,768	.273
Ecatepec and Coacalco and Coacalco, No. 2	Mex.	7,333	573	.079
Eloxochitlán	Pue.	825	353	.428
Epatlán	Pue.	1,907	668	.350
Epazoyuca	Hid.	5,481	173	.032
Huauchinango	Pue.	11,312	2,775	.245
Huaquechula	Pue.	10,329	2,922	.283
Huatlauca	Pue.	1,766	986	.558
Huayacocotla and Zontecomatlán and Tlachichilco	Ver.	6,237	2,446	.392
Huazalingo	Hid.	2,254	646	.287
Huejotzingo	Pue.	26,285	5,651	.215
Huexotla	Mex.	8,250	515	.062
Hueyapan	Mor.	1,851	65	.035
Hueypoxtla	Mex.	8,036	619	.077
Huitzitzilapan	Mex.	1,594	286	.179
Huitzuco	Gro.	4,406	170	.039
Ilamatlán and Tehuitzila	Ver.	5,300	1,225	.231
Istapaluca	Mex.	1,805	388	.215
Ixcuinquitlapilco	Hid.	20,988	624	.030
Ixmiquilpan	Hid.	6,056	2,360	.390
Ixtacamaxtitlán and Tustepec	Pue.	3,214	2,585	.805

TABLE 1.1, REGION I, PART A (Cont.)

Name	Loc.	Population in 1568	Population in 1646	Ratio 1646/1568
Ixtapalapa	D.F.	1,972	257	.130
Ixtapan de la Sal	Mex.	1,693	289	.171
Ixtlahuaca	Mex.	4,079	1,549	.380
Ixtepec	Pue.	564	172	.305
Izucar and Cuylucan and Tlatectla	Pue.	5,247	1,957	.372
Jalacingo	Ver.	3,020	1,153	.382
Jalatlaco and Tianguistengo	Mex.	4,498	2,195	.448
Jicotepec	Pue.	4,950	999	.202
Jilotepec de Abasolo	Mex.	19,471	4,950	.254
Jilotzingo	Mex.	566	265	.468
Jipiquilco	Mex.	9,389	1,131	.120
Jonacatlán	Pue.	3,241	1,036	.320
Jonotla	Pue.	2,624	519	.198
Jumiltepec	Mor.	3,062	317	.104
Malinalco	Mex.	7,046	2,251	.320
Mexicalcingo	D.F.	621	257	.414
México, San Juan	D.F.	52,000	16,369	.315
Michimaloya	Mex.	4,402	75	.017
Mizquiahuala	Hid.	3,851	345	.090
Molango and Malila	Hid.	11,705	639	.055
Necoxtla	Pue.	320	243	.759
Nextlalpan	Mex.	2,541	61	.024
Nopaluca	Pue.	789	617	.782
Noxtepec	Gro.	2,694	177	.066
Oaxtepec	Mor.	17,870	333	.019
Ocuituco	Mor.	4,458	427	.096
Ostuma	Gro.	849	359	.423
Otumba	Mex.	16,368	449	.027
Papaloticpac	Pue.	1,247	173	.139
Piaxtla	Pue.	1,848	549	.297
Puebla, Barrios	Pue.	2,168	761	.351
Pungarabato	Gro.	2,960	150	.051
Quicholac	Pue.	14,603	3,260	.223
Quetzala and Tlacotepec and Xochicuautla	Mex.	3,838	1,524	.397

TABLE 1.1, REGION I, PART A (Cont.)

Name	Loc.	Population in 1568	Population in 1646	Ratio 1646/1568
San Salvador	Pue.	3,383	122	.036
Soyanaquilpan	Mex.	1,752	44	.025
Suchitlán	Pue.	845	389	.460
Sultepec	Tlax.	2,343	83	.035
Tacuba	D.F.	13,266	2,670	.201
Talasco	Mex.	1,521	510	.355
Tasco, total partido	Gro.	7,306	1,454	.199
Tecali	Pue.	14,735	7,860	.534
Tecama	Mex.	1,782	37	.021
Tehuacán	Pue.	7,788	4,828	.620
Tejupilco	Mex.	1,782	850	.477
Teloloapan	Gro.	2,303	428	.186
Temascaltepec	Mex.	1,211	1,112	.918
Temoac	Mor.	2,260	221	.098
Tenancingo	Mex.	3,310	437	.132
Tenango and Ayapango and Guazacongo	Mex.	8,154	3,054	.375
Tenayuca	D.F.	2,671	476	.178
Teoloyucan	Mex.	2,967	876	.295
Teopantlán	Pue.	1,482	503	.339
Teotenango	Mex.	3,154	410	.130
Teotihuacán	Mex.	4,689	510	.109
Teotlalpa	Hid.	5,854	2,283	.380
Tepapayeca	Pue.	4,356	1,352	.310
Tepeaca	Pue.	21,879	8,220	.376
Tepeapulco	Hid.	17,408	359	.021
Tepeji de la Seda	Pue.	7,409	4,185	.552
Tepetitlán	Hid.	2,162	167	.077
Tepezoyuca	Mex.	1,013	236	.233
Tepotzotlán	Mex.	8,900	1,080	.121
Tequisistlán	Mex.	1,244	537	.432
Tetela de Ocampo	Pue.	1,396	575	.412
Tetela del Volcán	Mor.	4,726	495	.105
Tetepango	Hid.	1,386	112	.081
Tetipac	Gro.	1,320	248	.188
Texaluca	Pue.	141	48	.340

TABLE 1.1, REGION I, PART A (Cont.)

Name	Loc.	Population in 1568	Population in 1646	Ratio 1646/1568
Texcaltitlán and Ixtapa	Mex.	1,408	719	.511
Texcoco and Tezoyuca and Chiautla and Coatlinchán	Mex.	25,212	4,825	.191
Teyuca	Pue.	2,538	194	.077
Tezontepec	Hid.	1,607	214	.133
Tezontepec	Hid.	2,267	63	.028
Teziutlán	Pue.	3,442	1,182	.343
Tianguistengo	Hid.	1,690	437	.259
Tilapa	Pue.	1,225	291	.238
Tizayuca	Hid.	3,433	177	.052
Tlacotepec	Mex.	1,441	297	.206
Tlacotepec	Mor.	1,409	138	.098
Tlahuac (Cuevas)	D.F.	3,887	578	.149
Tlahuelilpa	Hid.	2,501	372	.149
Tlamaco	Hid.	2,244	85	.038
Tlamanalco and Chalco Atengo	Mex.	19,067	2,275	.120
Tlanalapan	Hid.	2,115	126	.060
Tlaquilpan and Guaquilpa	Hid.	2,402	134	.056
Tlaquiltenango	Mor.	13,959	1,530	.110
Tlatelolco	D.F.	14,982	4,255	.283
Tlatlauquitepec	Pue.	4,231	1,542	.364
Tlatzintla	Hid.	3,332	253	.076
Tlaxcala, province	Tlax.	165,000	54,400	.330
Tlayacac	Mor.	726	85	.117
Tlayacapan	Mor.	4,241	2,263	.534
Tochimilco	Pue.	4,521	1,161	.257
Tolcayuca	Hid.	2,970	109	.037
Toluca and Atengo	Mex.	16,550	6,398	.386
Tonatico	Mex.	763	282	.370
Tornacustla	Hid.	2,330	37	.016
Totimehuacán	Pue.	2,822	1,257	.445
Totolapan and Atlatlauca	Mor.	10,659	2,853	.268
Tula and estancias	Hid.	14,593	943	.065
Tultitlán	Mex.	4,686	1,710	.365

TABLE 1.1, REGION I, PART A (Cont.)

Name	Loc.	Population in 1568	Population in 1646	Ratio 1646/1568
Tututepec	Hid.	10,643	4,165	.392
Tuzantla	Gro.	1,340	299	.223
Xalostoc	Mor.	536	32	.060
Xipacoya (Jaso)	Hid.	6,155	379	.062
Xochimilco and Milpa Alta	D.F.	31,008	8,257	.266
Yahualica	Hid.	2,228	992	.445
Yautepec	Mor.	13,352	1,632	.122
Yecapistla	Mor.	14,240	624	.044
Yetecomac	Hid.	1,047	117	.112
Zacango	Gro.	190	168	.885
Zacatlán	Pue.	8,465	2,980	.352
Zacualpan and Malinaltenango	Mex.	1,974	343	.174
Zacualpan	Mor.	706	226	.320
Zapotitlán	Pue.	6,056	1,530	.253
Zapotlán	Hid.	1,106	20	.018
Zempoala	Hid.	3,571	109	.305
Zicapuzalco	Gro.	564	124	.220
Zinacántepec	Mex.	6,056	2,775	.459
Zinguilucan	Hid.	2,402	105	.044
Zitlaltepec	Mex.	1,934	143	.074
Zoquitlán	Pue.	798	529	.664
Zoyatitlanapa	Pue.	548	343	.626
Zumpahuacán and Joquitzingo	Mex.	3,392	1,296	.382
Zumpango	Gro.	1,475	862	.584
Zumpango	Mex.	6,369	1,006	.158
Las Tlalnaguas				
Jantetelco, Amayuca, Jonacatepec, Tetela, Amacuitlapilco, Axochapan, Chalcacingo, Atotonilco, Atlicahualoya, Amayuca, Jonacatepec, Jantetelco, Tepancingo, Tetela, Tlalistac	Mor.	13,706	1,843	.134
Total		1,321,329	303,717	0.230
Number of cases	206			

Part B of the table for Region I shows 21 places found on the 1646 list which had to be omitted from part A because the name did not appear on the 1568 list, because the place was part of another town for which no population was given, or for various other reasons. The total population of these 21 places is 9,662, making the total for the 1646 list 313,379. Of this, the population deleted (9,662) is only 3.1%, an insignificant amount. We conclude, therefore, that the 1646 reporting for Region I, within plus or minus 3%, can be found in the 1568 list, and that the population ratio of 0.230 *for these places* is valid.

TABLE 1.1, REGION I, PART B

Towns on the 1646 list for which there is no corresponding figure for 1568, or which should be omitted from Part A, for various reasons. Starred populations are omitted from the total.

Name	Loc.	Population in 1040	Comment
Acapetlahuacán	Pue.	2,637	
Ajoloapan	Mex.	63	
Atzala	Pue.	1,032	
Capulalcolulco	Gro.	60	
Cocula	Gro.	198	
Huasco	Hid.	97	
Jalatlaco	Mex.	517*	Duplication
Miltepec	Mex.	87	
Mizantla	Ver.	459*	To Region IIA
Querétaro	Que.	2,620	Settled after 1568
Suchitepec	Mex.	94	
Suchitonalá	Gro.	199*	To Region VI
Tecajique	Hid.	49	
Tizahuapan	Hid.	29	
Tizayuca	Hid.	63*	Duplication
Tulistlahuaca	Mex.	99	
Tuzantlalpa	Hid.	48	
Utlaspa	Mex.	445	
Xochitlán	Hid.	287	
Yautepec	Mor.	109	Extravagantes
Zacapoastla	Pue.	1,807	
Total		9,662	
Number of cases	21		

Table 1.1, Region I, part C gives the names of 125 places which occur in the 1568 list but are not found in the 1646 reporting. Some of these are of considerable size and cannot possibly have been depopulated or lost in congregation between the two dates; for example, Metztitlán and Tulancingo in Hidalgo; Acolmán, Amecameca, and Oxtotipac in the state of México; Tacubaya and Churubusco in the Distrito Federal; and Tecamachalco in Puebla. The only explanation is that the 1646 reporting is incomplete and that a relatively large number of towns has been omitted. The total population in 1568 of the 125 places which are missing from the 1646 reporting is 396,306. The aggregate for 1568 would be 1,321,329 plus 396,306, or 1,717,635, of which the towns missing in the 1646 report would account for about 23%.

TABLE 1.1, REGION I, PART C

Towns on the 1568 list for which a population is given but which are not found on the 1646 list. Towns on the list for which no separate population is given are omitted.

Name	Loc.	Population in 1568
Acalhuacán	Mex.	448
Acapuzalco	Gro.	158
Acatzingo	Pue.	8,950
Acaxuchitlán	Mex.	1,974
Acaxuchitlán	Hid.	2,540
Acolman	Mex.	10,085
Alfajajuca	Hid.	6,765
Aljojuca	Pue.	462
Alpatlahuac	Pue.	3,020
Amecameca	Mex.	4,976
Anecuchtla	Pue.	310
Axiotepec	Hid.	3,948
Aztotoacán	Pue.	2,538
Calmeca	Pue.	358
Calmecatitlán	Pue.	391
Coatepec	Pue.	168
Coatepec	Mex.	3,947
Coatitlán	Mex.	654
Colucan	Pue.	528

TABLE 1.1, REGION I, PART C (Cont.)

Name	Loc.	Population in 1568
Coyotepec	Pue.	627
Coyuca	Gro.	1,475
Cuahualulco	Pue.	1,610
Cuahuequasco	Mor.	863
Cuapanoya	Mex.	423
Cuetzala	Gro.	5,151
Cuimixtlán	Pue.	85
Cuitlapilco	Mex.	300
Chalchicomula	Pue.	1,782
Chalma	Pue.	677
Chilpopocatlán	Hid.	1,302
Churubusco	D.F.	1,320
Guatepeque	Mex.	239
Huaculco	Mor.	406
Huehuetlán	Pue.	2,254
Huehuetoca	Mex.	5,755
Hueoquilpan	Hid.	523
Hueytlalpan	Pue.	5,660
Huichapan	Hid.	14,520
Huixtac	Gro.	1,455
Iguala	Gro.	2,795
Ixcalpa	Pue.	226
Ixitlán	Pue.	1,056
Ixquilpan	Hid.	3,670
Ixtapa	Gro.	650
Ixtayucan	Pue.	6,770
Jalostoc	Mor.	627
Jojupango	Pue.	2,475
Jolalpan	Pue.	262
Malacatepec	Mex.	2,079
Matalcingo	Mex.	1,742
Matlaquetonatico	Pue.	638
Mecatlán	Pue.	2,538
Metepec	Mex.	6,640
Metztitlán	Hid.	24,638
Mexicalcingo	Pue.	4,349

TABLE 1.1, REGION I, PART C (Cont.)

Name	Loc.	Population in 1568
Mimiapan	Mex.	243
Mixquic	Mex.	2,363
Mixtepec	Pue.	2,934
Mauquilpan	Hid.	990
Ocotelulco	Pue.	449
Ocoyoacac	Mex.	1,016
Ocuilan	Mex.	5,214
Oxtotipac	Mex.	10,907
Oztutla	Pue.	423
Pachuca	Hid.	6,079
Pahuatlán	Pue.	6,346
Patlalcingo	Pue.	422
Quapanoaya	Mex.	423
Sayula	Hid.	993
Setusco	Ver.	44
Suchitlán	Pue.	845
Tacubaya	D.F.	1,521
Tamacasapa	Gro.	1,113
Tatetla	Pue.	924
Teacalco	Mex.	564
Tecamachalco	Pue.	17,688
Tecoloapan	Mex.	8,234
Telitlazingo	Pue.	1,168
Tenango	Hid.	3,070
Tenochtitlán	Pue.	258
Teotlalcó	Pue.	4,359
Teotlalzingo	Pue.	1,128
Tepanco	Pue.	6,392
Tepatetpec	Hid.	564
Tepecuacuilco	Gro.	6,468
Tepeitic	Hid.	700
Tepetlaostoc	Mex.	9,867
Tepexi del Río	Hid.	11,267
Tepexpan	Mex.	1,548
Tepoztlán	Mor.	7,498
Tequepilpa	Pue.	1,165

TABLE 1.1, REGION I, PART C (Cont.)

Name	Loc.	Population in 1568
Tequixquiac	Mex.	6,616
Tetela del Río	Gro.	1,818
Teuzan	Pue.	365
Texaquique	Mex.	1,308
Texcatepec	Hid.	8,663
Texmelucan	Pue.	2,258
Texcatepec	Hid.	393
Tilcuautla	Hid.	2,046
Tlacachique	Hid.	359
Tlacotepec	Pue.	·8,062
Tlacotlapilco	Hid.	2,254
Tlacuilotepec	Pue.	2,696
Tlachichilpa	Mex.	4,165
Tlalnepantla	Mex.	9,587
Tlanacopan	Hid.	1,690
Tlapanala	Pue.	1,591
Tlapanaloya	Mex.	610
Tlaxcoapan	Pue.	5,075
Tlaxmalac	Gro.	3,346
Tonalá	Pue.	6,336
Tuchitlán	Pue.	423
Tulancingo	Hid.	15,510
Tultepec	Gro.	657
Uzizila	Pue.	541
Verde	Pue.	1,128
Xalpantepec	Pue.	864
Xaltocan	Mex.	1,518
Xicotepec	Pue.	2,822
Xiutetelco	Pue.	5,078
Xochicoatlán	Hid.	4,607
Xoquicingo	Mex.	612
Zacotlán	Pue.	2,822
Ziotepec	Mex.	392
Zultepec	Mex.	5,075
Total		396,306
Number of cases	125	

We may calculate the probable true population of Region I in 1620–1625 (our estimated average date) simply by using proportions and assuming that the ratio between the two sets of data was the same for all towns alike (in totals). This would mean that 1,717,635 × 0.230 = 395,056. The latter figure should be taken as the population of Region I in 1620–1625.

The data in the 1595 list may serve to verify our calculations for the other two dates and, in turn, may be verified by them. Table 1.1, part D shows the population of 119 places in 1568 and 1595. The total of the former is 668,867 and of the latter 332,256. The ratio 1595/1568 is 0.497. By proportion, the entire population of Region I in 1595 would be 1,709,793 × 0.497 = 849,767. Table 1.1, Region I, part E shows similar data for 1595 and 1646, with 81 places. Here the totals are respectively 231,140 and 93,572, and the ratio 1646/1595 is 0.405. The entire population of Region I in 1595, calculated from the total in the 1646 reporting (313,379 as above), would be 773,775. The two results differ by 10% but, allowing for omissions in the 1646 list, are remarkably close.

TABLE 1.1, REGION I, PART D

Towns Found in Both 1568 and 1595 Lists

Name	Loc.	Population in 1568	Population in 1595	Ratio 1595 / 1568
Acamixtlahuaca	Gro.	1,264	766	.607
Acaxuchitlán	Mex.	1,974	1,007	.511
Acaxuchitlán	Hid.	2,540	1,493	.588
Acolman	Mex.	10,085	3,345	.332
Actopan	Hid.	20,295	10,770	.531
Acuitlapan	Gro.	613	847	1.317
Apaxco	Mex.	3,814	934	.245
Atlapulaco	Mex.	3,478	1,242	.357
Atotonilco	Hid.	12,672	5,445	.430
Atotonilco and Zacamul	Hid.	4,735	968	.205
Axacuba	Hid.	13,398	2,110	.157
Calimaya	Mex.	5,379	2,724	.507
Capulhuac	Mex.	1,653	2,406	1.455
Coyoacán	D.F.	13,639	9,420	.705

TABLE 1.1, REGION I, PART D (Cont.)

Name	Loc.	Population in 1568	Population in 1595	Ratio $\frac{1595}{1568}$
Cuatinchán	Pue.	5,874	4,115	.701
Cuernavaca	Mor.	39,336	21,780	.553
Cuevas	Mex.	3,887	2,574	.662
Culhuacán	Mex.	2,864	1,750	.611
Cutzamala	Gro.	2,805	1,131	.403
Chapa de Mota	Mex.	8,118	2,751	.339
Chapulco	Pue.	565	983	1.685
Chapulhuacán	Hid.	2,618	1,375	.525
Chichicaxtla	Hid.	3,366	2,080	.618
Chila	Pue.	1,690	815	.482
Chimalhuacán	Mex.	2,541	1,188	.467
Churubusco	D.F.	1,320	697	.528
Ecatepec	Mex.	7,333	1,270	.173
Eloxochitlán	Pue.	825	728	.882
Epazoyuca	Hid.	5,481	1,945	.355
Huaculco	Mor.	406	260	.640
Huauchinango	Pue.	11,312	7,450	.658
Huaquechula	Pue.	10,329	5,625	.545
Huazalingo	Hid.	2,254	1,252	.555
Huehuetlán	Pue.	2,254	1,368	.602
Hueypoxtla	Mex.	8,036	2,225	.277
Huizuco	Gro.	4,406	1,563	.355
Ilamatlán	Ver.	5,300	5,820	1.098
Ixitlán	Pue.	1,056	262	.248
Ixtacamaxtitlán	Pue.	3,214	2,665	.829
Ixtapaluca	Mex.	1,805	708	.392
Jantetelco	Mor.	2,680	833	.311
Jicotepec	Pue.	4,950	3,470	.701
Jojupango	Pue.	2,475	2,050	.828
Jonacatepec	Mor.	55,640	1,425	.252
Jonacatlán	Pue.	3,241	1,185	.366
Jumiltepec	Mor.	3,062	812	.265
Malinalco	Mex.	7,046	6,660	.945
Metepec	Mex.	6,640	3,765	.567
Metztitlán	Hid.	24,638	20,450	.830

TABLE 1.1, REGION I, PART D (Cont.)

Name	Loc.	Population in 1568	Population in 1595	Ratio 1595/1568
Mexicalcingo	Pue.	4,349	2,717	.624
Michimaloya	Mex.	4,402	702	.159
Mimiapan	Mex.	243	383	1.575
Mixquic	Mex.	2,363	1,744	.738
Mixtepec	Pue.	2,934	1,073	.365
Mizquiahuala	Hid.	3,851	2,468	.641
Nextlalpan	Mex.	2,541	705	.277
Oaxtepec	Mor.	17,870	5,700	.319
Ocuilan	Mex.	5,214	1,668	.320
Oxtotipac	Mex.	10,907	2,975	.273
Pahuatlán	Pue.	6,346	2,288	.360
Papaloticpac	Pue.	1,247	1,433	1.149
Petlalcingo	Pue.	422	319	.756
Piaxtla	Pue.	1,848	1,664	.902
Quecholac	Pue.	14,603	4,950	.339
Sultepec	Tlax.	2,343	1,170	.495
Tacuba	D.F.	13,266	5,460	.411
Tacubaya	D.F.	2,016	1,805	.896
Tecalco	Pue.	14,735	11,400	.775
Tecamachalco	Pue.	17,688	14,400	.815
Temoac	Mor.	2,260	1,207	.535
Tenancingo	Mex.	3,310	866	.262
Teotenango	Mex.	3,154	2,220	.704
Teotihuacán	Mex.	4,689	2,896	.617
Tepapayeca	Pue.	4,356	2,763	.635
Tepecuacuilco	Gro.	6,468	2,650	.410
Tepeojuma	Pue.	2,538	1,311	.517
Tepetitlán	Hid.	2,162	919	.425
Tepetlaoxtoc	Mex.	9,867	4,525	.458
Tepexi del Río	Hid.	11,237	3,740	.333
Tepexpan	Mex.	1,548	1,353	.875
Tepoztlán	Mor.	7,498	4,890	.653
Tequisistlán	Mex.	1,244	1,555	1.250
Tetipac	Gro.	1,320	804	.610
Texcatepec	Hid.	8,663	808	.093
Tezontepec	Hid.	1,607	550	.342

TABLE 1.1, REGION I, PART D (Cont.)

Name	Loc.	Population in 1568	Population in 1595	Ratio 1595/1568
Tianguistengo	Hid.	1,690	1,486	.880
Tlacotepec	Mor.	1,409	302	.214
Tlacotepec	Mex.	1,441	1,148	.797
Tlacuilotepec	Pue.	2,696	1,846	.685
Tlachichilpa	Mex.	4,165	2,703	.649
Tlalnepantla	Mex.	9,587	3,275	.342
Tlatelolco	D.F.	14,982	513	.034
Tlanalapa	Mex.	2,115	592	.280
Tlapanaloya	Mex.	610	770	1.262
Tlaquilpan	Hid.	2,402	1,359	.565
Tlaxmalac	Gro.	3,346	1,420	.424
Tlayac	Mor.	726	364	.502
Tolcayuca	Hid.	2,970	558	.188
Toluca	Mex.	16,550	6,220	.376
Tornacustla	Hid.	2,330	414	.178
Totimehuacán	Pue.	2,822	1,455	.515
Tulancingo	Hid.	15,510	6,535	.421
Tultitlán	Mex.	4,686	3,456	.738
Tututepec	Hid.	10,643	6,110	.574
Xalatlaco	Mex.	4,498	2,740	.609
Xalostoc	Mor.	536	344	.642
Xilozingo	Mex.	566	420	.742
Xilotzingo	Mex.	1,550	1,013	.654
Xiquipilco	Mex.	9,389	3,640	.388
Yautepec	Mor.	13,352	6,585	.493
Yecapixtla	Mor.	14,240	4,560	.320
Zacatlán	Pue.	8,465	5,945	.703
Zacualpan	Mex.	1,974	900	.456
Zacualpan	Mor.	706	305	.432
Zapotitlán	Pue.	6,056	4,945	.817
Zicapuzalco	Gro.	564	649	1.151
Zinacantepec	Mex.	6,056	3,360	.555
Zoquitlán	Pue.	798	880	1.103
Zumpahuacán	Mex.	3,392	1,856	.547
Total		668,867	332,256	0.497
Number of cases	119			

TABLE 1.1, REGION I, PART E

Towns Found in Both 1595 and 1646 Lists

Name	Loc.	Population in 1595	Population in 1646	Ratio 1646/1595
Acatlán	Hid.	707	122	.173
Actopan	Hid.	10,770	3,090	.287
Apaxco	Mex.	934	286	.306
Atengo	Hid.	766	158	.205
Atlapulco	Mex.	1,242	472	.380
Atotonilco	Hid.	968	241	.249
Atotonilco	Hid.	5,445	358	.066
Axacuba	Hid.	2,110	315	.149
Calimaya	Mex.	2,724	1,391	.511
Capulhuac	Mex.	2,406	742	.308
Coyoacán	D.F.	9,420	5,457	.579
Cuatinchán	Pue.	4,115	3,009	.732
Cuernavaca	Mor.	21,780	6,967	.320
Culhuacán	Mex.	1,750	404	.231
Cutzamala	Gro.	1,131	503	.444
Chapa de Mota	Mex.	2,751	456	.166
Chapulco	Pue.	983	308	.314
Chapulhuacán	Hid.	1,375	517	.376
Chichicastla	Hid.	2,080	150	.072
Chila	Pue.	815	498	.612
Chimalhuacán	Mex.	1,188	262	.221
Ecatepec	Mex.	1,270	573	.451
Eloxochitlán	Pue.	728	353	.485
Epazoyuca	Hid.	1,945	173	.089
Huaquechula	Pue.	5,625	2,922	.520
Huauchinango	Pue.	7,450	2,775	.373
Huazalingo	Hid.	1,252	646	.518
Hueypoxtla	Mex.	2,225	619	.278
Huitzuco	Gro.	1,563	170	.109
Ilamatlán	Ver.	5,820	1,225	.210
Ixtacamaxtitlán	Pue.	2,665	2,585	.971
Ixtapaluca	Mex.	708	388	.548
Jalatlaco	Mex.	2,740	2,195	.801
Jicotepec	Pue.	3,470	999	.288
Jilocingo	Mex.	420	265	.631

TABLE 1.1, REGION I, PART E (Cont.)

Name	Loc.	Population in 1595	Population in 1646	Ratio 1646/1595
Jilotzingo	Mex.	1,013	506	.500
Jiquipilco	Mex.	3,640	1,131	.307
Jonacatlán	Pue.	1,185	1,036	.875
Malinalco	Mex.	6,660	2,251	.338
Michimaloya	Mex.	702	75	.117
Mizquiahuala	Hid.	2,468	345	.140
Nextlalpan	Mex.	705	61	.086
Oaxtepec	Mor.	5,700	333	.058
Papaloticpac	Pue.	1,433	173	.121
Piaxtla	Pue.	1,664	549	.330
Quecholac	Pue.	4,950	3,260	.659
Tacuba	D.F.	5,460	2,670	.489
Tecali	Pue.	11,400	7,860	.689
Temoac	Mor.	1,207	221	.183
Tenancingo	Mex.	866	437	.505
Teotenango	Mex.	2,220	410	.185
Teotihuacán	Mex.	2,896	510	.176
Tepapayeca	Pue.	2,763	1,352	.489
Tepetitlán	Hid.	919	167	.182
Tequisistlán	Mex.	1,555	537	.345
Tetipac	Gro.	804	248	.309
Teyuca	Pue.	1,311	194	.148
Tezontepec	Hid.	550	214	.389
Tianguistengo	Hid.	1,486	437	.294
Tlacotepec	Mex.	1,148	297	.259
Tlacotepec	Mor.	302	138	.457
Tlahuac (Cuevas)	D.F.	2,574	578	.225
Tlanalapan	Hid.	592	126	.213
Tlaquilpan	Hid.	1,359	134	.099
Tlayacac	Mor.	364	85	.234
Tolcayuca	Hid.	588	109	.185
Toluca	Mex.	6,220	6,398	1.025
Tornacustla	Hid.	414	37	.089
Totimehuacán	Pue.	1,455	1,257	.864
Tultitlán	Mex.	3,456	1,710	.495
Tututepec	Hid.	6,110	4,165	.682

TABLE 1.1, REGION I, PART E (Cont.)

Name	Loc.	Population in 1595	Population in 1646	Ratio 1646/1595
Xalostoc	Mor.	344	32	.093
Yautepec	Mor.	6,585	1,632	.248
Yecapistla	Mor.	4,560	624	.137
Zacatlán	Pue.	5,945	2,980	.502
Zacualpan	Mor.	305	226	.742
Zacualpan and Malinalco	Mex.	900	343	.381
Zapotitlán	Pue.	4,925	1,530	.310
Zinacantepec	Mex.	3,360	2,775	.826
Zoquitlán	Pue.	880	529	.601
Zumpahuacán and Zoqui	Mex.	1,856	1,296	.699
Total		231,140	93,572	0.405
Number of cases	81			

Region II. Valles–Pánuco. This is the coastal plain and foot-hills of the Huaxteca from southern Tamaulipas to northern Veracruz as far south as latitude 20°N. There are 28 places which occur in both the 1568 list and the 1646 list. In 1568 the population of these 28 places is 35,316; in 1646 it is 8,559. The ratio 1646/1568 is 0.242. The data are given in detail in Table 1.1, Region II, part A. Part B shows 9 places found in the 1646 report which had to be omitted from part A. The total population of these 9 places is 353, making the total for the 1646 list 8,912. Part C shows 122 places which occur in the 1568 list but which are not found in that for 1646. The total 1568 population of these 122 places is 37,818. The aggregate for 1568 would be 35,316 plus 37,818, or 73,134, of which the towns missing in the 1646 list would account for 52.2%.

We may calculate the probable true population of Region II by using proportions and assuming that the ratio between the two sets of data was the same for all towns alike (in totals). This would mean that 73,134 × 0.242 = 17,698. The difference be-tween this value and that of the 1646 list (8,912) is very great and may invalidate the assumption. It may be necessary to assume additionally that many of the places on the 1568 list disappeared before 1646.

Table 1.1, Region II, part D shows the population of 22 places in 1568 and 1595. The total of the former is 26,991 and of the latter 23,752. The ratio 1595/1568 is 0.880. By proportion, the entire population of Region II in 1595 would be 73,134 × 0.880 = 64,358. Part E shows similar data for 1595 and 1646, with only 5 places. Here the totals are respectively 14,087 and 5,039, and the ratio 1646/1595 is 0.358. The entire population of Region II in 1595, calculated from the total in the 1646 data (8,912 ÷ 0.358), would be 24,894. The two results are discrepant, a fact probably referable to the disappearance of many small towns in the region.

TABLE 1.1, REGION II, PART A

Towns Found in Both 1568 and 1646 Lists

Name	Loc.	Population in 1568	Population in 1646	Ratio 1646/1568
Alcececa	Ver.	554	83	.150
Atlán	Ver.	350	94	.268
Chaltitlán, Picula, Chalchicuautla	Ver.	2,015	428	.212
Chicontepec	Ver.	1,693	1,336	.790
Chichilintla	Ver.	3,416	950	.278
Huejutla	Hid.	2,881	330	.115
Mecatlán	Ver.	608	105	.173
Metatepec and Tantoyuca	Ver.	3,290	223	.068
Metateyuca	Ver.	125	23	.184
Nexpa, Huehuetlán, Tauzán	Ver.	1,181	209	.177
Ozuluama and Moyutla	Ver.	282	197	.699
Tamahol	S.L.P.	47	0	.000
Tamohí	S.L.P.	644	221	.343
Tamalol and Suacacasco	S.L.P.	336	146	.434
Tamoxol	S.L.P.	36	107	2.972
Tamiutla and Las Laxas	Ver.	91	114	1.253
Tampamolón	S.L.P.	822	289	.351
Tanbaca	Ver.	161	119	.739
Tancuayalab	S.L.P.	403	71	.177
Tanchinamol	Ver.	99	121	1.222
Tancuiche	Ver.	825	138	.167
Tancuiname	Ver.	58	71	1.223

TABLE 1.1, REGION II, PART A (Cont.)

Name	Loc.	Population in 1568	Population in 1646	Ratio 1646/1568
Tenampulco	Pue.	495	248	.501
Tezapotitlán	Ver.	213	44	.207
Tlacolula (de Busto)	S.L.P.	55	68	1.236
Tlaculula and Magueyes	Ver.	601	171	.285
Tlanchinol and Acuimantla	Hid.	12,474	2,308	.185
Tonatico, Zozocolco	Ver.	1,561	345	.221
Total		35,316	8,559	0.242
Number of cases	28			

TABLE 1.1, REGION II, PART B

Towns on the 1646 list for which there is no corresponding figure for 1568, or which should be omitted from Part A, for various reasons. Starred populations are omitted from the total.

Name	Loc.	Population in 1646	Comment
Acultzingo	Ver.	158*	In Region IIA
Nexpa	Hid.	143*	Duplicate
Tanbeate	S.L.P.	61	Not on the 1568 list
Tancajual	S.L.P.	0	Not on the 1568 list
Tancalicoche	?	95	Not on the 1568 list
Tanleón	S.L.P.	0	No assessment
Tantima	?	112	No assessment
Tesontlal	?	5	Not on the 1568 list
Zayula	Ver.	80	With Tamoz in 1568
Total		353	
Number of cases	9		

TABLE 1.1, REGION II, PART C

Towns on the 1568 list for which a population is given but which are not found on the 1646 list. Towns on the 1568 list for which no separate population is given are omitted.

Name	Loc.	Population in 1568
Acatlán	S.L.P.	185
Ahuatipan	Hid.	3,070
Amatlán	S.L.P.	48
Ameluca	Pue.	56
Apaztlán	Ver.	55
Axtla	S.L.P.	825
Calixlantongo	Pue.	113
Calpan	Ver.	141
Cihuala	Ver.	44
Coxcatlán	S.L.P.	2,584
Coyutla	Ver.	254
Culuama	Ver.	282
Chacual	Ver.	42
Chachapala	Ver.	64
Chiconamel	Ver.	56
Guzahapa	Ver.	143
Huatzpaltepec	Ver.	9
Huautla	Ver.	282
Huezco	Ver.	109
Huitzila	Pue.	226
Ixcatepec	Ver.	39
Jalpan	Quer.	776
Jicayán	Ver.	45
Macatlán	S.L.P.	630
Macolutla	Ver.	128
Macuilxóchitl	Hid.	1,875
Mezuntlán	Ver.	18
Nanahuatla	Ver.	174
Nanahuatlán	Ver.	170
Ojitipa	S.L.P.	2,396
Pantepec	Ver.	185
Pánuco	Ver.	990
Papantla	Ver.	423
Piaxtla	Ver.	57

TABLE 1.1, REGION II, PART C (Cont.)

Name	Loc.	Population in 1568
Puxutlán	Ver.	248
Tabuco	Ver.	42
Taculilla	Ver.	49
Tamacolite	S.L.P.	88
Tamacuiche	S.L.P.	99
Tamacuil	Ver.	186
Tamahol	S.L.P.	47
Tamaholipa	Tamps.	2,310
Tamahu	S.L.P.	33
Tamalaguaco	S.L.P.	141
Tamalocuco	Ver.	183
Tamalol	Ver.	282
Tamatao	Ver.	170
Tamateque	Ver.	110
Tamazunchale	S.L.P.	1,399
Tamazunchale	Ver.	99
Tameci	S.L.P.	114
Tamiahua	Ver.	990
Tamole	Ver.	62
Tamontao	Ver.	54
Tamos	Ver.	66
Tampaca	Ver.	27
Tampacal	Ver.	56
Tampacán	Ver.	25
Tampacayal	Ver.	1,690
Tampayal	S.L.P.	62
Tampico	Ver.	340
Tamposque	S.L.P.	282
Tampuche	Ver.	182
Tampucho	Tamps.	86
Tampulen	Ver.	36
Tamu	Ver.	42
Tancamalmonco	S.L.P.	144
Tancanhuitz	S.L.P.	705
Tancaxan	S.L.P.	92
Tancaxual	S.L.P.	79

TABLE 1.1, REGION II, PART C (Cont.)

Name	Loc.	Population in 1568
Tancazneque	Tamps.	36
Tancelete	Ver.	58
Tancetuco	Ver.	492
Tancolón	S.L.P.	72
Tancolul	Ver.	44
Tancoxual	Tamps.	213
Tancoyol	Quer.	165
Tancuy	S.L.P.	88
Tanchaba	S.L.P.	85
Tanchicuy	Ver.	29
Tanchicuy	Ver.	49
Tanchilabe	Tamps.	29
Tanchipa	Tamps.	330
Tanchipa	S.L.P.	152
Tanchoy	Tamps.	88
Tanhuizin	Ver.	163
Tanistla	Ver.	337
Tanlocuque	S.L.P.	93
Tanlocoten	Ver.	299
Tanquián	S.L.P.	825
Tanta	Ver.	85
Tantamol	Ver.	142
Tantamol	Ver.	226
Tantay	Tamps.	36
Tantoin	S.L.P.	72
Tantoyetla	Ver.	22
Tantoyeque	Ver.	85
Tantoyuca	Tamps.	165
Tantuana	S.L.P.	141
Tanxohol	S.L.P.	68
Tanzacana	Tamps.	72
Tanzaquila	Ver.	416
Tanzomonoco	Tamps.	83
Tanzulupe	Ver.	274
Tanzumonoco	S.L.P.	133
Taxicui	S.L.P.	85

TABLE 1.1, REGION II, PART C (Cont.)

Name	Loc.	Population in 1568
Temapache	S.L.P.	845
Tempoal	Ver.	756
Tenacusco	Ver.-	1,026
Texupexpa	Ver.	40
Tlacocoatla	Ver.	178
Tlapahuantla	Ver.	86
Tlapotongo	Pue.	30
Tomomolo	Ver.	6
Topila	Ver.	33
Topla	Ver.	183
Totonchal	Ver.	6
Tuxpan	Ver.	423
Tuzapan	Ver.	423
Valles	S.L.P.	132
Xilitla	S.L.P.	1,700
Xocutla	Ver.	85
Total		37,818
Number of cases	122	

TABLE 1.1, REGION II, PART D

Towns Found in Both 1568 and 1595 Lists

Name	Loc.	Population in 1568	Population in 1595	Ratio 1595/1568
Calpan	Ver.	141	133	.944
Coxcatlán	S.L.P.	2,584	1,027	.397
Coyutla	Ver.	254	226	.890
Chiconamel	Ver.	56	141	2.528
Chicontepec	Ver.	1,693	1,953	1.147
Chichilintla	Ver.	3,416	2,610	.765
Huautla	Ver.	282	657	2.328
Huehuetlán	S.L.P.	564	963	1.710
Moyutla	Ver.	282	293	1.038
Tamalaguaco	S.L.P.	141	175	1.240

TABLE 1.1, REGION II, PART D (Cont.)

Name	Loc.	Population in 1568	Population in 1595	Ratio 1595/1568
Tamalol	Ver.	282	457	1.621
Tamazunchale	S.L.P.	1,399	1,438	1.028
Tamazunchale	Ver.	99	169	1.707
Tamiahua	Ver.	990	834	.843
Tampucho	Tamps.	86	17	.198
Tancaxán	S.L.P.	92	90	.978
Tancetuco	Ver.	492	71	.144
Tanchipa	Tamps.	330	377	1.143
Tanzaquila	Ver.	416	437	1.063
Tenampulco	Pue.	495	206	.416
Tlanchinol	Hid.	12,474	8,995	.722
Tuzapan	Ver.	423	2,483	5.870
Total		26,991	23,752	0.880
Number of cases	22			

TABLE 1.1, REGION II, PART E

Towns Found in Both 1595 and 1646 Lists

Name	Loc.	Population in 1595	Population in 1646	Ratio 1646/1595
Chichilintla	Ver.	2,610	950	.364
Chicontepec	Ver.	1,983	1,336	.685
Ozuluama	Ver.	293	197	.673
Tenampulco	Pue.	206	248	1.204
Tlanchinol and Acuimantla	Hid.	8,995	2,308	.257
Total		14,087	5,039	0.358
Number of cases	5			

Region II-A. Central Veracruz. This is a small homogeneous area embracing the clusters of towns around present-day Jalapa and Orizaba. Although in part the region is coastal plain, most of the towns are at fairly high elevations. The region, in general, resembles the interior plateau more than Pánuco to the north or the region of the Alvarado River to the south. There are 25 places which occur on both the 1568 and 1646 lists. In 1568 the population of these 25 places is 22,394; in 1646 it is 10,065. The ratio 1646/1568 is 0.449. (See part A of Table 1.1, Region II-A.) Part B shows 8 places found on the 1646 list which had to be omitted from part A. The population of these 8 places is 1,684, making the total for the 1646 list 11,749. Part C shows 20 places which are found in the 1568 list but are not in the 1646 report. The total 1568 population of these 20 places is 10,306. The aggregate for 1568 would be 22,394 plus 10,306, or 32,700, of which the towns missing in the 1646 list would account for 31.5%.

We may calculate the probable true population of Region II-A in 1620–1625 by using proportions and assuming that the ratio between the two sets of data was the same for all towns alike (in totals). This would mean that 32,700 × 0.449 = 14,682. The difference between this value and that of the actual list (11,749) is not large and supports the assumption.

We verify by use of data in the 1595 list. Part D of Table 1.1 for the region shows the population of 6 places in 1568 and in 1595. The total of the former is 2,950 and of the latter 1,762. The ratio 1595/1568 is 0.597. By proportion, the entire population of Region II-A in 1595 would be 32,700 × 0.597 = 19,522. Part E of Table 1.1, Region II-A, gives similar data for 1595 and 1646, with only 3 places. Here the totals are respectively 492 and 530, and the ratio 1646/1595 is 1.077. The entire population of Region II-A, calculated from the total in the 1646 report (11,749 ÷ 1.077), would be 10,909. The two results are discrepant, but the numbers of cases are too small for adequate calculation.

TABLE 1.1, REGION IIA, PART A

Towns Found in Both 1568 and 1646 Lists

Name	Loc.	Population in 1568	Population in 1646	Ratio 1646/1568
Actopan	Ver.	237	206	.869
Acultzingo	Ver.	990	158	.178
Almolonga	Ver.	69	26	.377
Coacoazintla	Ver.	422	173	.410
Coatepec	Ver.	781	292	.267
Chapultepec and Tonayan	Ver.	462	428	.926
Chichiquila and Quimixtlan	Pue.	3,478	1,114	.320
Chicocentepec	Ver.	148	53	.358
Chiconquiaco and Miahuatlán	Ver.	495	374	.756
Chiltoyac	Ver.	282	141	.500
Chocamán	Ver.	571	316	.554
Huatusco	Ver.	1,029	968	.942
Ixhuatlán	Ver.	493	282	.572
Jalapa	Ver.	3,651	631	.173
Jilotepec	Ver.	1,403	447	.319
Maltrata	Ver.	1,047	903	.862
Maxtlatlán	Ver.	115	41	.357
Mizantla	Ver.	2,082	459	.221
Naolingo, Colipa and Jalcomulco	Ver.	604	793	1.313
Tepetlán	Ver.	291	107	.368
Tepetlaxco	Ver.	141	148	1.050
Tequila	Ver.	1,059	1,098	1.037
Zempoala	Ver.	34	27	.794
Zintla	Ver.	141	77	.546
Zongolica	Ver.	2,369	976	.412
Total		22,394	10,065	0.449
Number of cases	25			

TABLE 1.1, REGION IIA, PART B

Towns on the 1646 list for which there is no corresponding
figure for 1568, or which should be omitted from Part A, for
various reasons. Starred populations are omitted from the total.

Name	Loc.	Population in 1646	Comment
Huatusco and sujetos	Ver.	104*	Duplicates Huatusco
Ixhuacán	Ver.	927	Not on the 1568 list
Papalote	Ver.	61	Congregated
Tlacotepec	Ver.	77	Not on 1568 list
Tlateca	Ver.	226	With Ozumatzintla in 1568
Tlaltetela	Ver.	213*	In Region III
Tomatlán	Ver.	136	Not on 1568 list
Xicochimalco	Ver.	257	Not on 1568 list
Total		1,684	
Number of cases	8		

TABLE 1.1, REGION IIA, PART C

Towns on the 1568 list for which a population is given but
which are not found on the 1646 list. Towns on the 1568 list
for which no separate population is given are omitted.

Name	Loc.	Population in 1568
Acatlán	Ver.	272
Almería	Ver.	130
Anilicapa	Ver.	338
Atlán	Ver.	846
Catusco	Ver.	78
Coatlatepec	Ver.	101
Cuzamasernaca	Ver.	845
Chico	Ver.	1,115
Icapacingo	Ver.	29
Ixtepec	Ver.	870
Orizaba	Ver.	554
Ozpicha	Ver.	967
Ozumacintla	Ver.	139
Quetzalcoatl	Ver.	194

TABLE 1.1, REGION IIA, PART C (Cont.)

Name	Loc.	Population in 1568
Tecoautla	Ver.	334
Texhuacán	Ver.	846
Tlacolula	Ver.	1,921
Tustenec	Ver.	97
Utila	Ver.	280
Yahuatlán	Ver.	350
Total		10,306
Number of cases	20	

TABLE 1.1, REGION IIA, PART D

Towns Found in Both 1568 and 1595 Lists

Name	Loc.	Population in 1568	Population in 1595	Ratio 1595/1568
Acatlán	Ver.	272	250	.919
Acultzingo	Ver.	990	282	.285
Coacoatzintla	Ver.	442	189	.448
Chocomán	Ver.	571	262	.459
Orizaba	Ver.	554	677	1.222
Tepetlaxco	Ver.	141	102	.724
Total		2,950	1,762	0.597
Number of cases	6			

TABLE 1.1, REGION IIA, PART E

Towns Found in Both 1595 and 1646 Lists

Name	Loc.	Population in 1595	Population in 1646	Ratio 1646/1595
Coacoatzintla	Ver.	189	173	.916
Chocomán	Ver.	262	316	1.205
Maxtlatlán	Ver.	41	41	1.000
Total		492	530	1.077
Number of cases	3			

Region III. Alvarado-Coatzcoalcos. This region embraces
southern Veracruz and the coast of Tabasco and Campeche to
the Laguna de Términos. The part of Campeche included in the
region was populous in aboriginal times, but by the seventeenth
century was deserted. The region includes the lowland basins of
the Alvarado-Papaloapan drainage, the northwest portion of the
Usumacinta drainage, and the small part of northeastern Oaxaca
which is in the basins of the Papaloapan and Coatzacoalcos
systems.

There are 33 places which occur on both the 1568 and 1646
lists. In 1568 the population of these 33 places is 20,751; in
1646 it is 5,183. The ratio 1646/1568 is 0.250. (See Table 1.1,
Region III, part A.) Part B shows 11 places found on the 1646
list which had to be omitted from part A. The total population
of these places is 1,463, making the total for the 1646 list
6,646. In part C there are 41 places which occur in the 1568 list
but are not found in the 1646 report. The total 1568 population of these 41 places is 26,928. The aggregate for 1568 would
be 20,751 plus 26,928, or 47,679, of which the towns omitted
in the 1646 report would account for 56.5%.

We calculate the probable true population of Region III in
1620-1625 by using proportions and assuming that the ratio
between the two sets of data was the same for all towns alike
(in totals). This would mean that 47,679 × 0.250 = 11,920. The
difference between this value and that of the 1646 list is
considerable. The condition resembles that obtaining in Region
II and indicates the disappearance of numerous towns between
1568 and 1646.

TABLE 1.1, REGION III, PART A

Towns Found on Both 1568 and 1646 Lists

Name	Loc.	Population in 1568	Population in 1646	Ratio 1646/1568
Acalapa	Ver.	86	29	.337
Agualulco, Mecatepec and Otiliacac	Tab.	1,214	343	.282
Atoco, Otepa and Tenantitlán	Tab.	942	124	.132
Ayautla	Oax.	224	163	.728
Cachultenango	Ver.	56	34	.607

TABLE 1.1, REGION III, PART A (Cont.)

Name	Loc.	Population in 1568	Population in 1646	Ratio 1646/1568
Cosamaloapan	Ver.	330	143	.433
Cotaxtla	Ver.	66	82	1.242
Chicoacan	Tab.	209	153	.733
Chilapa	Ver.	649	53	.082
Chinameca	Ver.	621	15	.024
Guazuilapa	Ver.	377	39	.104
Huatzpaltepec	Oax.	710	165	.232
Hueytlán	Ver.	70	19	.271
Ixcatlán	Oax.	700	183	.261
Jalapa	Oax.	422	292	.692
Jaltipan, Acayuca, Olutla, Chacalapa, Zayultepec, Tequistepec, Tiquipipa, Tepozuntlán	Ver.	2,822	337	.119
Jotlapa	Ver.	282	148	.525
Macayapa and Cihuatlán	Chis.	1,177	116	.098
Michoacán	Tab.	226	66	.292
Minzapa	Ver.	1,690	61	.036
Moloacán and Uliacán	Ver.	141	93	.655
Ocoapa	Ver.	148	87	.588
Ojitlán	Oax.	303	126	.416
Ozolotepec	Ver.	110	58	.527
Puctla (Acula)	Ver.	485	231	.476
Putlancingo	Oax.	58	48	.828
Tapalan	Ver.	264	26	.099
Tanango	Oax.	450	102	.227
Teotalco, Huestepec and Cuitlatlán	Ver.	1,129	388	.344
Tepeapa	Oax.	155	100	.645
Teutila	Oax.	3,630	937	.258
Tlacotalpan	Ver.	825	258	.313
Tuxtepec and Chiltepec	Oax.	192	164	.854
Total		20,751	5,183	0.250
Number of cases	33			

48   Essays in Population History

TABLE 1.1, REGION III, PART B

Towns on the 1646 list for which there is no corresponding
figure for 1568, or which should be omitted from Part A, for
various reasons. Starred populations are omitted from the total.

Name	Loc.	Population in 1646	Comment
Acatlán	Oax.	167	Not on 1568 list
Amatlán	Ver.	184	Encomendero doubtful
Atecolotepec	Oax.	324	Not on 1568 list
Hueylutla	Ver.	151	Not on 1568 list
Ixcalpan	Ver.	203	Location doubtful
Mezapa, Santiago	Ver.	41*	Duplicates Minzapa, not on 1568 list
Mitlancuautla	Ver.	41	Not on 1568 list
Ostotitlán	Tab.	104	Not on 1568 list
Tequipac	?	39	Not on 1568 list
Teutalco	?	37	Not on 1568 list
Tlaltetela	Ver.	213	From Region IIA, position doubtful
Total		1,463	
Number of Cases	11		

TABLE 1. 1, REGION III, PART C

Towns on the 1568 list for which a population is given but
which are not found on the 1646 list. Towns on the 1568 list
for which no separate population is given are omitted.

Name	Loc.	Population in 1568
Agutaco	Ver.	71
Amascalapa	Ver.	38
Amatlán	Ver.	254
Amatlán	Ver.	705
Ataco	Ver.	25
Atiquipaque	Oax.	168
Coaquilpa	Ver.	211
Coatzacoalcos (province)	Ver.	9,900
Cotatlán	Ver.	1,414

TABLE 1.1, REGION III, PART C (Cont.)

Name	Loc.	Population in 1568
Chalcholoacán	Ver.	313
Chicaloacán	Ver.	85
Huachapa	Ver.	60
Huaquilpa	Ver.	960
Huatusco	Ver.	169
Huestepec	Ver.	986
Ixhuatlán	Oax.	449
Ixtayuca	Ver.	225
Ixtayuca	Ver.	1,119
Jicayan	Ver.	1,580
Miahuatlán	Ver.	113
Miahuatlán	Ver.	235
Micaostoc	Ver.	85
Ostopa	Ver.	105
Otlatitlán	Ver.	987
Papalote	Ver.	16
Pigualulco	Tab.	1,025
Quitatán	Ver.	294
San Juan Ulúa	Ver.	452
Soyaltepec	Oax.	113
Tacotalpa	Tab.	525
Taquilpas	Ver.	306
Tilzapuapa	Ver.	330
Tlaliscoyan	Ver.	294
Tlatlatelco	Ver.	135
Tonela	Ver.	284
Totutla	Ver.	94
Tuchitepec	Ver.	226
Tuxtla	Ver.	1,815
Uxitem	Oax.	254
Zapotitlán	Ver.	367
Zinacamostoc	Oax.	141
Total		26,928
Number of cases	41	

In parts D and E of Table 1.1, Region III, we use the data for 1595 for verification. Part D shows the population of 12 places in 1568 and 1595, the ones for which there are data in both lists. The total of the former is 10,686 and of the latter 6,442. The ratio 1595/1568 is 0.603. By proportion, the entire population of Region III in 1595 would be 47,679 × 0.604 = 28,750. Part E shows similar data for 1595 and 1646, with only 5 places. Here the totals are respectively 1,496 and 925, and the ratio 1646/1595 is 0.618. The entire population of Region III, calculated from the total of the 1646 list for this region (6,646 ÷ 0.618), would be 10,754. The two results are discrepant. The numbers of places are small, but there may also be a difference due to the disappearance of towns between 1595 and 1646.

TABLE 1.1, REGION III, PART D

Towns Found in Both 1568 and 1595 Lists

Name	Loc.	Population in 1568	Population in 1595	Ratio 1595/1568
Amatlán	Ver.	705	250	.355
Cotaxtla	Ver.	66	96	1.454
Huatzpaltepec	Oax.	710	547	.771
Huestepec	Ver.	986	295	.299
Jalapa	Oax.	422	446	1.057
Jaltipan	Ver.	2,822	801	.284
Jicayán	Ver.	1,580	1,478	.935
Jotlapa	Ver.	282	99	.351
Micaostoc	Ver.	85	56	.658
Michoacán	Tab.	226	54	.239
Otlatitlán	Ver.	987	474	.481
Tuxtla	Ver.	1,815	1,846	1.017
Total		10,686	6,442	0.603
Number of cases	12			

TABLE 1.1, REGION III, PART E

Towns Found in Both 1595 and 1646 Lists

Name	Loc.	Population in 1595	Population in 1646	Ratio 1646/1595
Cotaxtla	Ver.	96	82	.855
Jalapa	Oax.	446	292	.655
Jaltipan	Ver.	801	337	.421
Jotlapa	Ver.	99	148	1.495
Michoacán	Tab.	54	66	1.221
Total		1,496	925	0.618
Number of cases	5			

Region IV. Northwestern Oaxaca. This region embraces the Mixteca Alta and Baja (but not the Mixteca of the coast), the central valleys of Oaxaca, and some peripheral territory. Most of the region is plateau or of intermediate altitude, and resembles the Central Plateau.

Table 1.1, Region IV, part A gives the names of 87 places which occur in both the 1568 and 1646 reporting. In 1568 the population of these 87 places is 183,601; in 1646 it is 60,785. The ratio 1646/1568 is 0.331. According to part B, the 1646 list contains 8 places which had to be omitted from part A. The total population of these places is 1,289, making the total for the 1646 list 62,074. Part C shows 39 places which are in the 1568 list but are not found in that of 1646. The aggregate for 1568 would be 183,601 plus 39,732, or 223,333, of which the towns missing in the 1646 reporting would account for 17.8%.

We calculate the probable true population of Region IV in 1620–1625 by using proportions and assuming that the ratio between the two sets of data was the same for all towns alike (in totals). This would mean that 223,333 × 0.331 = 73,923. The difference between this value and that of the actual list (62,074) is relatively small. The smallness of the discrepancy indicates that most of the towns remained in existence, and that relatively little disturbance occurred between 1568 and 1646 in this area.

TABLE 1.1, REGION IV, PART A

Towns Found in Both 1568 and 1646 Lists

Name	Loc.	Population in 1568	Population in 1646	Ratio 1646/1568
Achiutla	Oax.	3,238	774	.239
Amoltepec	Oax.	181	136	.752
Apoala	Oax.	1,478	292	.198
Atlatlauca	Oax.	282	189	.670
Atoyaquillo	Oax.	707	122	.173
Coatlahuistla	Oax.	703	223	.317
Coatepec	Oax.	1,178	92	.078
Coixtlahuaca	Oax.	8,250	1,780	.216
Coyotepec	Oax.	974	966	.992
Cuautitlán	Oax.	85	53	.623
Cuicatlán	Oax.	1,020	366	.358
Cuilapan	Oax.	20,246	3,350	.165
Cuquila	Oax.	338	157	.465
Chachoapan	Oax.	1,409	116	.082
Chalcatongo	Oax.	1,995	1,367	.686
Chicahuaxtla	Oax.	1,198	720	.601
Chichicapa and Amatlán	Oax.	3,352	1,663	.496
Elotepec	Oax.	706	362	.513
Estetla	Oax.	564	228	.404
Etla	Oax.	4,696	2,153	.458
Etlatongo	Oax.	904	126	.139
Huajuapan	Oax.	1,650	782	.474
Huajolotitlán	Oax.	282	88	.312
Huajolotitlán	Oax.	3,346	1,564	.468
Huapanapa	Oax.	195	357	1.831
Huautla	Oax.	297	83	.279
Huautla	Oax.	541	275	.508
Huautla	Oax.	845	486	.576
Igualtepec	Oax.	1,185	1,107	.587
Ixcatlán	Oax.	2,152	258	.120
Ixcuintepec	Oax.	522	316	.606
Ixpatepec	Oax.	1,089	619	.569
Ixtatepec and Chicahuastepec	Oax.	732	194	.265
Ixtepec	Oax.	1,937	1,394	.720

TABLE 1.1, REGION IV, PART A (Cont.)

Name	Loc.	Population in 1568	Population in 1646	Ratio 1646 / 1568
Jaltepec	Oax.	4,402	274	.062
Jaltepetongo	Oax.	568	29	.051
Jocotipac	Oax.	379	274	.723
Justlahuaca	Oax.	935	352	.377
La Magdalena	Oax.	966	173	.179
Macuilxóchil	Oax.	792	541	.684
Malinaltepec	Oax.	706	197	.279
Mitla	Oax.	2,376	1,265	.532
Mitlantongo, Santiago and Santa Cruz	Oax.	845	299	.354
Nanacatepec, Tequiztepec and Alpizahua	Oax.	1,501	711	.474
Nanahuaticpac	Oax.	198	179	.904
Nochistlán	Oax.	2,950	179	.061
Oaxaca, Villa	Oax.	1,129	675	.598
Papaloticpac	Oax.	1,680	323	.192
Putla	Oax.	706	173	.245
Quiotepec	Oax.	891	294	.330
Sosola	Oax.	1,409	643	.457
Suchitepec	Oax.	436	235	.539
Talistaca	Oax.	1,366	847	.620
Tamazola	Oax.	1,000	160	.160
Tamazulapan	Oax.	4,472	2,010	.449
Tanatepec	Oax.	350	73	.208
Tataltepec	Oax.	282	117	.415
Tecomaxtlahuaca	Oax.	734	1,275	1.740
Tecomavaca	Oax.	413	66	.160
Tejupan	Oax.	3,063	571	.186
Tenexpa	Oax.	708	177	.250
Teotitlán del Camino	Oax.	2,798	1,508	.539
Teozacoalco	Oax.	1,828	971	.532
Tepeucila	Oax.	618	507	.821
Tepezimatlán	Oax.	2,630	170	.065
Teposcolula	Oax.	11,418	4,070	.356
Tequecistepec	Oax.	3,607	1,540	.427
Tetiquipa	Oax.	2,086	961	.461

TABLE 1.1, REGION IV, PART A (Cont.)

Name	Loc.	Population in 1568	Population in 1646	Ratio 1646/1568
Tetiquipa, San Mateo	Oax.	2,086	1,268	.608
Tilantongo	Oax.	2,845	281	.099
Tiltepec	Oax.	846	211	.249
Tlacolula	Oax.	1,191	529	.444
Tlacochahuaya	Oax.	1,552	1,034	.667
Tlapacoyan	Oax.	282	138	.489
Tlaxiaco and Chilapa	Oax.	11,372	2,296	.202
Tonalá	Oax.	6,108	3,072	.503
Tonaltepec and Soyaltepec	Oax.	885	180	.203
Totomachapa	Oax.	257	122	.475
Tuchitlapilco	Oax.	199	240	1.206
Tutla	Oax.	845	388	.459
Tututepetongo	Oax.	304	139	.457
Yanhuitlán and Coyotepec	Oax.	17,160	3,062	.174
Yolotepec	Oax.	1,056	666	.630
Zaachila	Oax.	3,594	1,562	.434
Zacatepec	Oax.	2,006	141	.070
Zimatlán	Oax.	1,709	750	.439
Zoyatepec	Oax.	85	109	1.282
Total		183,601	60,785	0.331
Number of cases	87			

TABLE 1.1, REGION IV, PART B

Towns on the 1646 list for which there is no corresponding figure for 1568, or which should be omitted from Part A, for various reasons. Starred populations are omitted from the total.

Name	Loc.	Population in 1646	Comment
Amoltepec	Oax.	136	Duplication
Amusgos	Oax.	620*	In Region VI
Atoyac	Oax.	65	Position doubtful
Atoyaquillo	Oax.	122	Not on 1568 list
Huajolotitlán	Oax.	78	Duplication or position doubtful

TABLE 1.1, REGION IV, PART B (Cont.)

Name	Loc.	Population in 1646	Comment
Tejotepec	Oax.	46	Not on 1568 list
Tlacolula	Oax.	672	Duplication
Tulistlahuaca	Oax.	170	Not on 1568 list
Total		1,289	
Number of cases	8		

TABLE 1.1, REGION IV, PART C

Towns on the 1568 list for which a population is given but which are not found on the 1646 list. Towns on the 1568 list for which no separate population is given are omitted.

Name	Loc.	Population in 1568
Alupancingo	Oax.	564
Atoyac	Oax.	2,363
Atoyaque	Oax.	71
Axomulco	Oax.	182
Calihuala	Oax.	466
Coatlán	Oax.	141
Coculco	Oax.	112
Cuitepec	Oax.	293
Cuyotepexi	Oax.	564
Cuytlaguiztlán	Oax.	846
Chazumba	Oax.	564
Chiagualtepec	Oax.	705
Chimatlán	Oax.	56
Ixcatlán	Oax.	564
Justepec	Oax.	130
Manalcatepec	Oax.	564
Michiapa	Oax.	282
Miquitla	Oax.	1,518
Nextepec	Oax.	225
Oaxaca (Antequera)	Oax.	3,010
Ocotlán	Oax.	5,693
Patanala	Oax.	705
Paxtlahuaca	Oax.	931

TABLE 1.1, REGION IV, PART C (Cont.)

Name	Loc.	Population in 1568
Petlaquistlahuaca	Oax.	918
San Miguel Grande	Oax.	1,128
Silacayoapan	Oax.	789
Suchitepec	Oax.	845
Tecaxic	Oax.	440
Teitipac	Oax.	2,948
Teotitlán del Valle	Oax.	1,125
Teozatlán	Oax.	1,409
Tequixtepec	Oax.	707
Titicapa	Oax.	4,944
Tlacotepec	Oax.	1,550
Tlapancingo	Oax.	660
Utlancingo	Oax.	56
Yepatepel	Oax.	846
Yucucuí	Oax.	254
Yucuxaco	Oax.	564
Total		39,732
Number of cases	39	

Verification of our calculations is supplied by the data in parts D and E of Table 1.1, Region IV. Part D gives values for 31 places in 1568 and 1595. The total of the former is 92,517 and of the latter 49,655. The ratio 1595/1568 is 0.537. By proportion, the entire population of Region IV in 1595 would be 223,333 × 0.537 = 119,930. Part E gives similar data for 1595 and 1646, with 29 places. Here the totals are respectively 48,561 and 24,919, and the ratio 1646/1595 is 0.513. The entire Indian population of Region IV, calculated from the total in 1646 (62,074 ÷ 0.513), would be 121,002. The two results are almost incredibly close, and indicate that for this region the data are as accurate as could ever be expected.

TABLE 1.1, REGION IV, PART D

Towns Found in Both 1568 and 1595 Lists

Name	Loc.	Population in 1568	Population in 1595	Ratio 1595/1568
Achiutla	Oax.	3,238	1,652	.510
Apoala	Oax.	1,478	635	.429
Atoyaque	Oax.	71	102	1.436
Cotahuistla	Oax.	703	402	.572
Coyotepec	Oax.	974	491	.504
Cuilapan	Oax.	20,246	8,470	.418
Chalcatongo	Oax.	1,995	1,131	.567
Chicahuaxtla	Oax.	1,198	934	.780
Etla	Oax.	4,696	3,210	.683
Etlatongo	Oax.	904	336	.372
Huautla	Oax.	845	434	.513
Huautla	Oax.	297	657	2.210
Igualtepec	Oax.	1,885	2,680	1.421
Jaltepec	Oax.	4,402	1,410	.320
Jaltepetongo	Oax.	568	322	.567
Jocotipac	Oax.	379	325	.857
Mitlantongo	Oax.	845	494	.585
Oaxaca (Antequera)	Oax.	3,010	1,740	.578
Petlaquistlahuaca	Oax.	918	401	.437
Sosola	Oax.	1,409	820	.582
Tamazola	Oax.	1,000	288	.288
Tamazulapan	Oax.	4,472	2,920	.653
Tecomaxtlahuaca	Oax.	734	1,481	2.018
Tenexpa	Oax.	708	203	.287
Tiltepec	Oax.	846	412	.487
Tlacochahuaya	Oax.	1,552	1,050	.677
Tlacotepec	Oax.	1,550	880	.568
Tlaxiaco	Oax.	11,372	4,730	.416
Yanhuitlán	Oax.	17,160	9,460	.551
Yolotepec	Oax.	1,056	553	.523
Zacatepec	Oax.	2,006	1,032	.516
Total		92,517	49,655	0.537
Number of cases	31			

TABLE 1.1, REGION IV, PART E

Towns Found in Both 1595 and 1646 Lists

Name	Loc.	Population in 1595	Population in 1646	Ratio 1646/1595
Achiutla	Oax.	1,652	774	.468
Apoala	Oax.	635	292	.460
Coatlahuistla	Oax.	402	223	.555
Coyotepec	Oax.	491	966	1.967
Cuilapan	Oax.	8,470	3,350	.395
Chalcatongo	Oax.	1,131	1,367	1.208
Chicahuaxtla	Oax.	934	720	.771
Etla	Oax.	3,210	2,153	.671
Etlatongo	Oax.	336	126	.375
Huautla	Oax.	434	486	1.120
Huautla	Oax.	657	83	.126
Igualtepec	Oax.	2,680	1,107	.413
Jaltepec	Oax.	1,410	274	.194
Jaltepetongo	Oax.	322	29	.090
Jocotipac	Oax.	325	274	.843
Mitlantongo	Oax.	494	299	.606
Oaxaca (Villa)	Oax.	1,740	675	.388
Sosola	Oax.	820	643	.785
Tamazola	Oax.	288	160	.555
Tamazulapan	Oax.	2,920	2,010	.686
Tecomaxtlahuaca	Oax.	1,481	1,275	.861
Tejotepec	Oax.	289	46	.159
Tenexpa	Oax.	203	177	.873
Tiltepec	Oax.	412	211	.512
Tlacochahuaya	Oax.	1,050	1,034	.985
Tlaxiaco	Oax.	4,730	2,296	.485
Yanhuitlán	Oax.	9,460	3,062	.324
Yolotepec	Oax.	553	666	1.204
Zacatepec	Oax.	1,032	141	.137
Total		48,561	24,919	0.513
Number of cases	29			

Region V. The Zapotecas, the term used by the Spaniards. This region is the home territory of the northern Mountain Zapotecs, the Mijes, and several smaller adjacent linguistic groups. In elevation it ranges from high mountain to relatively low foothill and coast, with considerable ecological variation. The area was distinct in the sixteenth century in terms of culture and territorial arrangements. It was penetrated and dominated relatively slowly by the Spaniards, in part because of the difficult terrain, in part because of political fragmentation. On the whole, the region is warm country descending at points to coastal elevations.

We work with the data for the region in Table 1.1, parts A–E. In part A, we are able to identify 72 places as occurring on both the 1568 and 1646 lists. In 1568 the population of these 72 places is 37,142; in 1646 it is 22,774. The ratio 1646/1568 is 0.613. According to part B, the 1646 reporting gives the names of 20 places which had to be omitted from part A. The total population of these 20 places is 4,277, making the total for places reported in the 1646 list 27,051. Part C shows 68 places which are found in the 1568 list but not in that of 1646. The total 1568 population of these 68 places is 32,427. The aggregate for 1568 would be 37,142 plus 32,427, or 69,569, of which the towns missing in the 1646 reporting would account for 46.7%.

TABLE 1.1, REGION V, PART A

Towns Found in Both 1568 and 1646 Lists

Name	Loc.	Population in 1568	Population in 1646	Ratio 1646/1568
Alotepec	Oax.	338	60	.178
Amaltepec	Oax.	155	100	.645
Atepeque and Analco	Oax.	1,020	554	.543
Ayacastepec	Oax.	339	204	.602
Cacalotepec	Oax.	169	160	.946
Cacalotepec	Oax.	281	87	.310
Camotlán	Oax.	71	77	1.085
Chicomesuchil	Oax.	1,742	631	.362
Chichicastepec	Oax.	254	65	.256

TABLE 1.1, REGION V, PART A (Cont.)

Name	Loc.	Population in 1568	Population in 1646	Ratio 1646/1568
Choapan	Oax.	676	1,554	2.300
Comaltepec	Oax.	423	456	1.081
Huayastepec	Oax.	254	119	.469
Huazcomaltepec	Oax.	509	269	.529
Huitepec	Oax.	422	82	.194
Ixcuintepec	Oax.	1,694	1,312	.775
Ixtepeji	Oax.	749	814	1.087
Ixtlán	Oax.	1,129	340	.301
Jaltepec	Oax.	460	20	.044
Jaltianguis	Oax.	375	49	.131
Jilotepec	Oax.	153	488	3.190
Lachichivia	Oax.	478	105	.220
La Hoya	Oax.	225	43	.191
Lalopa	Oax.	423	167	.395
Malinaltepec	Oax.	283	226	.799
Maxcaltepec	Oax.	201	783	3.890
Metepec	Oax.	141	97	.688
Mexitlán	Oax.	85	99	1.165
Nanacatepec	Oax.	495	141	.285
Nejapa	Oax.	1,742	576	.331
Nobaá	Oax.	395	250	.633
Ocotepec	Oax.	522	241	.462
Pazoltepec	Oax.	493	177	.359
Petlalcatepec	Oax.	1,198	75	.063
Quezalapa	Oax.	169	88	.521
Sogocho	Oax.	742	504	.679
Suchitepec	Oax.	215	313	1.457
Tagui	Oax.	142	310	2.183
Tagui and Lazagaya	Oax.	266	168	.632
Tava	Oax.	338	570	1.685
Tecomaltepec	Oax.	423	167	.395
Tecpanzacualco	Oax.	2,254	116	.051
Tehuilotepec	Oax.	254	1,002	3.944

TABLE 1.1, REGION V, PART A (Cont.)

Name	Loc.	Population in 1568	Population in 1646	Ratio $\frac{1646}{1568}$
Teococuilco	Oax.	680	347	.510
Teotalcingo	Oax.	2,268	745	.329
Teotlaxco	Oax.	168	122	.726
Tepetolutla	Oax.	1,409	908	.645
Tetepetongo	Oax.	141	43	.305
Ticatepec	Oax.	337	253	.751
Tiltepec	Oax.	622	352	.566
Tlacoatzintepec	Oax.	565	774	1.369
Tlahuilotepec	Oax.	564	590	1.046
Tlapanala	Oax.	706	473	.670
Tlazoltepec	Oax.	378	39	.103
Tonagoyotepec	Oax.	218	185	.844
Tonaguía	Oax.	282	235	.834
Totolinga	Oax.	155	88	.568
Totontepec	Oax.	405	294	.726
Usila	Oax.	1,385	343	.248
Xareta	Oax.	254	54	.212
Yacoche	Oax.	168	92	.547
Yagavila	Oax.	407	400	.983
Yagayo	Oax.	169	206	1.220
Yalalag	Oax.	169	306	1.812
Yao	Oax.	282	495	1.755
Yatao	Oax.	169	85	.503
Yatobe	Oax.	163	163	1.000
Yavago	Oax.	282	136	.482
Yaxila	Oax.	169	166	.982
Yolox	Oax.	916	177	.193
Zapotequilla	Oax.	338	129	.382
Zoochila	Oax.	338	789	2.333
Zoquiapan	Oax.	338	126	.373
Total		37,142	22,774	0.613
Number of cases	72			

TABLE 1.1, REGION V, PART B

Towns on the 1646 list for which there is no corresponding figure
for 1568, or which should be omitted from Part A, for various reasons.

Name	Loc.	Population in 1646	Comment
Ayacastla	Oax.	330	Not in 1568 list
Camotlán	Oax.	292	"
Coatlán	Oax.	138	"
Chimaltepec	Oax.	337	"
Huixtepec	Oax.	75	"
Ixcuintepec	Oax.	184	"
Lobani	Oax.	117	"
Macihuixi	Oax.	43	"
Malacatepec	Oax.	253	"
Petlapa	Oax.	864	"
Quiaecuza	Oax.	541	"
Quilacohe	Oax.	168	"
Tianguillo Achate	Oax.	26	"
Tlacotepec	Oax.	73	"
Totolinga	Oax.	41	"
Xossa	Oax.	44	"
Yachiuc	Oax.	138	"
Yagalaci	Oax.	48	"
Yahuitzi	Oax.	204	"
Yatzilam	Oax.	361	"

Total		4,277	
Number of cases	20		

TABLE 1.1, REGION V, PART C

Towns on the 1568 list for which a population is given but
which are not found on the 1646 list. Towns on the 1568 list
for which no separate population is given are omitted.

Name	Loc.	Population in 1568
Atlatlauca	Oax.	2,171
Ayotepec	Oax.	71
Cacatepec	Oax.	169
Calajo	Oax.	423
Calpulalpan	Oax.	564

TABLE 1.1, REGION V, PART C (Cont.)

Name	Loc.	Population in 1568
Citlaltepec	Oax.	247
Comaltepec	Oax.	423
Comatlán	Oax.	124
Cuezcomaltepec	Oax.	564
Chicome	Oax.	279
Chichiapa	Oax.	160
Chisme	Oax.	141
Chontales bravos	Oax.	4,514
Eltianguillo	Oax.	113
Esuchicala	Oax.	282
Huatenicamanes	Oax.	4,231
Hucitepec	Oax.	113
Itacatepec	Oax.	112
Ixcocan	Oax.	655
Ixtacatepec	Oax.	141
Jalahui	Oax.	113
Jaltepec	Oax.	1,007
Macuiltianguis	Oax.	1,409
Madoxoya	Oax.	113
Malinaltepec	Oax.	380
Maltepec	Oax.	131
Mayana	Oax.	613
Metepec	Oax.	2,257
Metlaltepec	Oax.	169
Miahuatlán	Oax.	218
Moctun	Oax.	113
Ocotepec	Oax.	1,551
Santa Cruz	Oax.	282
Tacatepec	Oax.	123
Taeta	Oax.	169
Talea	Oax.	113
Tecianzacualco	Oax.	141
Temascalapa	Oax.	168
Tepequepacagualco	Oax.	185
Tepuxtepec	Oax.	170
Tiquini	Oax.	169
Tlapalcatepec	Oax.	845

TABLE 1.1, REGION V, PART C (Cont.)

Name	Loc.	Population in 1568
Tlaxuca	Oax.	1,075
Tochitepec	Oax.	141
Toltepec	Oax.	395
Tualilapa	Oax.	351
Tutlaco	Oax.	185
Tzaindan	Oax.	339
Vichinaguía	Oax.	163
Villa Alta	Oax.	85
Xacobo	Oax.	169
Xayatepec	Oax.	225
Xicaltepec	Oax.	127
Xilotepec	Oax.	165
Xocochi	Oax.	141
Xuquila	Oax.	338
Yacastla	Oax.	593
Yachinicingo	Oax.	113
Yagoni	Oax.	141
Yaquiza	Oax.	141
Yaviche	Oax.	85
Yolotepec	Oax.	191
Yotepec	Oax.	452
Yoveo	Oax.	169
Zaiutepec	Oax.	135
Zentecomaltepec	Oax.	282
Zoquío	Oax.	149
Zultepec	Oax.	141
Total		32,427
Number of cases	68	

We calculate the probable true population of Region V in 1620-1625 (our estimated average date) by using proportions and assuming that the ratio between the two dates was the same for all towns alike (in totals). This would mean that 69,569 × 0.613 = 42,646. The difference between this value and that of the actual list (27,051) is considerable, and may be

due to the disappearance of many small places through congregación and extinction of the entire population. Further, the
Huatenicamanes and the Chontales Bravos, for which the 1568
values are only a vague estimate, account for 8,750 souls. If
these are deducted from the 1568 total, the values for the
calculated and the actual population, according to the 1646
reporting, come quite close together.

Resort to the 1595 data for verification yields further discrepancy. Part D of Table 1.1, Region V, shows the population
of 24 places in 1568 and 1595. The total of the former is
16,120 and of the latter 10,309. The ratio 1595/1568 is 0.639.
By proportion, the entire population of Region V in 1595
would be 69,569 × 0.639 = 44,455. Similar data for 1595 and
1646 are given in part E, with 23 places. Here the totals are
respectively 6,862 and 7,184; the ratio 1646/1595 is 1.047. The
entire Indian population of Region V, calculated from the total
in 1646 (27,051 ÷ 1.047), would be 25,837. These results are
widely apart. In connection with this discrepancy, it should be
noted that for the 23 towns the population in 1646 is actually
greater than in 1595. There may have been a real increase in
population, the extension of Spanish control may have come
later than has been generally assumed, or there may be a factor
of selection in the data whereby the more important towns are
represented at the expense of those which disappeared. The
Zapotecas may have constituted a special case which deserves
further examination.

TABLE 1.1, REGION V, PART D

Towns Found in Both 1568 and 1595 Lists

Name	Loc.	Population in 1568	Population in 1595	Ratio 1595 1568
Alotepec	Oax.	338	254	.751
Atlatlauca	Oax.	2,171	3,039	1.400
Ayacastepec	Oax.	339	443	1.307
Cacalotepec	Oax.	281	164	.584
Chicomesúchil	Oax.	1,742	674	.387
Chichicastepec	Oax.	254	127	.500
Ixtlán	Oax.	1,129	421	.373
Lachichivia	Oax.	478	220	.461

TABLE 1.1, REGION V, PART D (Cont.)

Name	Loc.	Population in 1568	Population in 1595	Ratio 1595/1568
Ocotepec	Oax.	522	699	1.340
Ocotepec	Oax.	1,551	547	.353
Sococho	Oax.	742	206	.278
Suchitepec	Oax.	215	180	.837
Tecianzacualco	Oax.	141	96	.681
Tepetolutla	Oax.	1,409	863	.613
Tiltepec	Oax.	622	336	.540
Tlahuilotepec	Oax.	564	268	.475
Tlapanala	Oax.	706	392	.556
Tlazoltepec	Oax.	378	96	.253
Totolinga	Oax.	155	206	1.330
Xareta	Oax.	254	127	.500
Yacastla	Oax.	593	282	.476
Yao	Oax.	282	93	.330
Yolox	Oax.	916	234	.256
Zochila	Oax.	338	342	1.012
Total		16,120	10,309	0.639
Number of cases	24			

TABLE 1.1, REGION V, PART E

Towns Found in Both 1595 and 1646 Lists

Name	Loc.	Population in 1595	Population in 1646	Ratio 1646/1595
Alotepec	Oax.	254	60	.236
Ayacastepec	Oax.	443	204	.460
Ayacastla	Oax.	281	330	1.174
Cacalotepec	Oax.	164	87	.531
Chicomesúchil	Oax.	674	631	.950
Chichicastepec	Oax.	127	65	.512
Ixtlán	Oax.	421	340	.807
Lachichivia	Oax.	220	105	.478
Ocotepec	Oax.	699	241	.345
Sococho	Oax.	206	504	2.438

TABLE 1.1, REGION V, PART E (Cont.)

Name	Loc.	Population in 1595	Population in 1646	Ratio 1646/1595
Suchitepec	Oax.	180	313	1.740
Tepetolutla	Oax.	863	908	1.051
Tiltepec	Oax.	336	352	1.048
Tlahuilotepec	Oax.	268	590	2.202
Tlapanala	Oax.	392	473	1.207
Tlazoltepec	Oax.	96	39	.407
Totolinga	Oax.	206	88	.427
Yachiuc	Oax.	123	138	1.122
Yahuitzi	Oax.	113	204	1.805
Yao	Oax.	93	495	5.325
Yolox	Oax.	234	177	.756
Xareta	Oax.	127	54	.425
Zochila	Oax.	342	789	2.306
Total		6,862	7,184	1.047
Number of cases	23			

Region VI. Oaxaca Coast. This region is the coast of the present state of Oaxaca, a strip extending inland from sixty to eighty miles. Although, as in the Zapotecas, the region includes high mountains, its ecology is coastal. In aboriginal times the states of Tehuantepec, Huatulco, and Tututepec were included within the region.

We here work with the data presented in Table 1.1, Region VI, parts A- E. According to part A, 45 places occur in both the 1568 and 1646 lists. In 1568 the population of these 45 places is 50,316; in 1646 it is 30,106. The ratio 1646/1568 is 0.600. Part B gives the name of the only place found on the 1646 list which is not in the 1568 reporting. The population of this place is 22, making the total for the 1646 list 30,128. According to part C, the 1568 list has 28 places which are not found in the 1646 report. The total population in 1568 of these 28 places is 13,680. The aggregate for 1568 would be 50,316 plus 13,680, or 62,996, of which the towns missing in the 1646 list would account for 21.7%.

TABLE 1.1, REGION VI, PART A

Towns Found in Both 1568 and 1646 Lists

Name	Loc.	Population in 1568	Population in 1646	Ratio 1646/1568
Amusgos	Oax.	845	620	.734
Atoyac	Oax.	419	389	.929
Ayoquesco	Oax.	469	180	.394
Ayutla	Oax.	67	44	.657
Coatlán	Oax.	3,947	1,840	.466
Colotepec	Oax.	150	170	1.133
Cozoaltepec	Oax.	99	97	.980
Ejutla	Oax.	1,033	332	.322
Huamelula	Oax.	1,561	357	.229
Huatulco	Oax.	776	85	.110
Ixpuchtepec	Oax.	696	682	.980
Ixtacoya	Oax.	611	162	.265
Ixtayutla	Oax.	495	107	.216
Jalapa del Marqués	Oax.	2,736	1,340	.490
Jicayán	Oax.	677	163	.241
Jicayán and partido	Oax.	677	383	.566
Lapaguía	Oax.	380	515	1.355
Mazatlán	Oax.	86	48	.558
Miahuatlán, Suchitepec Tamascalapa	Oax.	3,802	1,313	.345
Necotepec	Oax.	426	136	.319
Olintepec	Oax.	168	105	.625
Pilcintepec	Oax.	221	204	.924
Pinotepa Nacional	Oax.	211	306	1.450
Pochutla	Oax.	103	43	.417
Potutla	Oax.	31	41	1.323
Sola	Oax.	2,261	789	.349
Tecpa, Xilotepequillo	Oax.	282	269	.954
Tehuantepec	Oax.	8,910	7,201	.808
Tepalcatepec, Xolotepec	Oax.	875	638	.729
Tepextepec	Oax.	332	808	2.432
Topiltepec	Oax.	419	111	.265
Tequixistlán	Oax.	2,115	422	.199
Tetepec	Oax.	231	112	.485
Tizatepec	Oax.	466	756	1.621
Tlacamama	Oax.	264	201	.762

TABLE 1.1, REGION VI, PART A (Cont.)

Name	Loc.	Population in 1568	Population in 1646	Ratio 1646/1568
Tlacolula	Oax.	185	462	2.500
Tlahuiltoltepec	Oax.	240	95	.396
Totolapan	Oax.	1,198	388	.324
Totolapilla	Oax.	169	93	.551
Tututepec, Nopala, Juquila	Oax.	9,075	6,887	.759
Yautepec	Oax.	564	119	.211
Yeytepec	Oax.	564	271	.481
Zentecomaltepec	Oax.	282	78	.276
Zenzontepec	Oax.	634	452	.713
Zoquitlán	Oax.	564	292	.518
Total		50,316	30,106	0.600
Number of cases	45			

TABLE 1.1, REGION VI, PART B

Towns on the 1646 list for which there is no corresponding figure for 1568.

Name	Loc.	Population in 1646	Comment
Totoltepec	Oax.	22	Not in 1568 list
Total		22	
Number of cases	1		

TABLE 1.1, REGION VI, PART C

Towns on the 1568 list for which a population is given but which are not found on the 1646 list. Towns on the 1568 list for which no separate population is given are omitted.

Name	Loc.	Population in 1568
Amatlán	Oax.	423
Amatlán	Oax.	313
Astata	Oax.	508
Azuntepec	Oax.	564

TABLE 1.1, REGION VI, PART C (Cont.)

Name	Loc.	Population in 1568
Cacalotepec	Oax.	169
Cahuitlán	Oax.	1,158
Coahuitlán	Oax.	67
Comaltepec	Oax.	249
Cuaquezpaltepec	Oax.	140
Chayuco	Oax.	377
Ecatepec	Oax.	180
Ixtepec	Oax.	176
Jamiltepec	Oax.	384
Malinaltepec	Oax.	84
Mixtepec	Oax.	94
Mixtepec	Oax.	282
Ozoltepec	Oax.	2,534
Pinotepa la Chica	Oax.	795
Río Hondo	Oax.	1,973
Suchiopan	Oax.	58
Temascaltepec	Oax.	577
Tepexi	Oax.	212
Tequecistepec	Oax.	96
Tiquipa	Oax.	897
Tonameca	Oax.	99
Tuxtla	Oax.	122
Xochitepec	Oax.	1,043
Zimatlán	Oax.	106
Total		13,680
Number of cases	28	

We calculate the probable true population of Region VI for the 1646 data by using proportions and assuming that the ratio between the two sets of data was the same for all towns alike (in totals). This would mean that $62{,}996 \times 0.600 = 37{,}798$. The difference between this value and that of the actual list, 30,128, is only moderate. This coastal region, therefore, was much more stable with respect to retention of towns than the inland Zapotecas.

Verification of our calculations through resort to the data for 1595 is in parts D and E. Part D shows the population of 19 places in 1568 and 1595. The total of the former is 33,684 and of the latter 28,197. The ratio 1595/1568 is 0.837. By proportion, the entire population of Region VI in 1595 would be 62,996 × 0.838 = 52,728. Part E gives similar data for 1595 and 1646, with 17 places. Here the totals are respectively 23,345 and 16,407, and the ratio 1646/1595 is 0.703. The entire Indian population of Region VI, calculated from the total in the 1646 data (30,128 ÷ 0.703), would be 42,856. This is moderately different from the value obtained by proportion from the population in 1568.

TABLE 1.1, REGION VI, PART D

Towns Found in Both 1568 and 1595 Lists

Name	Loc.	Population in 1568	Population in 1595	Ratio 1595/1568
Amusgos	Oax.	845	866	1.026
Azuntepec	Oax.	564	1,006	1.784
Coatlán	Oax.	3,947	2,855	.724
Ejutla	Oax.	1,033	274	.264
Ixpuchtepec	Oax.	696	1,278	1.835
Ixtacoya	Oax.	611	285	.466
Ixtayutla	Oax.	495	86	.174
Jalapa	Oax.	2,736	2,196	.803
Jicayán	Oax.	677	135	.200
Miahuatlán	Oax.	3,802	2,576	.678
Necotepec	Oax.	426	212	.498
Olintepec	Oax.	168	209	1.245
Ozolotepec	Oax.	2,534	3,846	1.518
Sola	Oax.	2,261	1,385	.613
Tepexistepec	Oax.	332	378	1.139
Tequixistlán	Oax.	2,115	1,283	.606
Totolapan	Oax.	1,198	570	.476
Totolapilla	Oax.	169	257	1.522
Tututepec	Oax.	9,075	8,500	.937
Total		33,684	28,197	0.837
Number of cases	19			

TABLE 1.1, REGION VI, PART E

Towns Found in Both 1595 and 1646 Lists

Name	Loc.	Population in 1595	Population in 1646	Ratio 1646/1595
Amusgos	Oax.	866	620	.716
Coatlán	Oax.	2,855	1,840	.645
Ejutla	Oax.	274	332	1.211
Ixpuchtepec	Oax.	1,278	682	.534
Ixtacoya	Oax.	285	162	.569
Ixtayutla	Oax.	86	107	1.245
Jalapa	Oax.	2,196	1,340	.611
Jicayán and partido	Oax.	135	383	2.836
Miahuatlán	Oax.	2,576	1,313	.510
Necotepec	Oax.	212	136	.642
Olintepec	Oax.	209	105	.502
Sola	Oax.	1,385	789	.570
Tepextepec	Oax.	378	808	2.138
Tequixistlán	Oax.	1,283	422	.329
Totolapan	Oax.	570	388	.681
Totolapilla	Oax.	257	93	.362
Tututepec	Oax.	8,500	6,887	.811
Total		23,345	16,407	0.703
Number of cases	17			

Region VII. Zacatula- Guerrero. This region includes two natural areas grouped together because of similarity. The first is the long coastal strip extending from the Oaxaca- Guerrero state line, past Acapulco, to the western extremity of the old province of Zacatula in the southwestern corner of Michoacán. The second area is the inland group of towns south of the Balsas basin centering around Tlapa, Chilapa, and Tixtla. In a strict sense, the area is neither coastal nor plateau but, rather like similar areas in Oaxaca, ranges from *tierra templada* toward *tierra caliente.* The Balsas basin here constitutes a natural dividing line; to the south there is no such boundary.

Our data are in Table 1.1, Region VII, parts A- E. Part A lists the names of 51 places which occur in both the 1568 and 1646 reporting. In 1568 the population of these 51 places is 58,403; in 1646 it is 20,036. The ratio 1646/1568 is 0.343. According to part B, 5 places found in the 1646 report had to be omitted from part A. The population of these 5 places is 470, making the total for the 1646 report 20,506. Conversely, part C shows 101 places which occur in the 1568 list but are not in the 1646 report. The total 1568 population of these 101 places is 52,376. The aggregate for 1568 would be 58,403, plus 52,376, or 110,779, of which the towns omitted in the 1646 list would account for 47.3%.

TABLE 1.1, REGION VII, PART A

Towns Found in Both 1568 and 1646 Lists

Name	Loc.	Population in 1568	Population in 1646	Ratio 1646/1568
Acapulco (province) Incl. Zitlaltomagua, Tepesuchil, Tesca	Gro.	8,470	491	.058
Acatlán, San Luis	Gro.	145	65	.458
Anacuilco	Gro.	69	117	1.695
Arimao	Mich.	439	255	.581
Atenchancaleca	Gro.	98	114	1.163
Atlan	Mich.	79	10	.116
Ayutla	Gro.	591	394	.668
Ayutla (A855), Chiuli, Azolo, Guexulutla	Gro.	121	184	1.520
Borona	Mich.	142	31	.218
Cacahuatepec	Gro.	1,042	143	.137
Cayaco	Gro.	129	56	.434
Chacala	Mich.	87	14	.161
Chilapa	Gro.	12,111	3,817	.315
Ciutlán, Tepeapulco, Puchitlán, Zacatula	Mich.	459	114	.248
Copalitas	Gro.	69	37	.537
Coyuca	Gro.	528	112	.212
Coyuca and Lacoaba	Gro.	1,624	408	.251
Cuaucayulichan	Gro.	106	31	.292
Cuautepec	Gro.	189	92	.487
Cuitlatenamic	Gro.	2,214	513	.232
Cuilutla	Gro.	233	58	.249

TABLE 1.1, REGION VII, PART A (Cont.)

Name	Loc.	Population in 1568	Population in 1646	Ratio $\frac{1646}{1568}$
Huitziltepec	Gro.	341	62	.182
Iguala	Gro.	1,128	175	.155
Igualapa	Gro.	1,924	1,280	.666
Ihuitlán	Mich.	25	36	1.440
Ixcateopan	Gro.	940	156	.166
Ixtapa	Mich.	168	39	.232
Jalapa	Gro.	106	56	.529
Mechia	Mich.	119	32	.269
Mezquitlán	Gro.	851	46	.054
Olinala	Gro.	4,468	1,064	.238
Ometepec	Gro.	1,693	938	.551
Oxtutla	Gro.	458	58	.129
Pantla	Gro.	212	48	.226
Papalutla	Gro.	924	73	.079
Petatlán	Gro.	31	9	.290
Pochotitlán	Gro.	254	117	.461
Pustlán	Gro.	133	10	.075
Tecomatlán	Gro.	121	31	.256
Tecpan	Gro.	644	248	.385
Temalhuacán	Gro.	102	17	.167
Tiaupan	Mich.	528	68	.129
Tlacozautitlán	Gro.	4,264	1,256	.295
Tlapa, Atliztac, Caltican, Atlamajalcingo	Gro.	8,572	6,581	.768
Topetina	Gro.	106	25	.236
Ximaltoca	Gro.	100	29	.290
Xochixtlahuaca	Gro.	568	296	.521
Xocutla	Gro.	282	182	.645
Zihuatlán	Gro.	86	17	.198
Zihuatlán	Mich.	144	2	.014
Zoyatlán	Mich.	166	29	.175
Total		58,403	20,036	0.343
Number of cases	51			

TABLE 1.1, REGION VII, PART B

*Towns on the 1646 list for which there is no corresponding figure
for 1568, or which should be omitted from Part A, for various reasons.*

Name	Loc.	Population in 1646	Comment
Aguacayuca	Gro.	48	Not in 1568 list
Anacuilco	Gro.	61	"
Asuchitlán	Gro.	5	"
Mexcaltepec	Gro.	325	"
Pochotitlán	Gro.	31	"
Total		470	
Number of cases	5		

TABLE 1.1, REGION VII, PART C

*Towns on the 1568 list for which a population is given but
which are not found on the 1646 list. Towns on the 1568 list
for which no separate population is given are omitted.*

Name	Loc.	Population in 1568
Acaguapisca	Gro.	46
Acalpica	Gro.	13
Acamalutla	Gro.	771
Acayaco	Gro.	108
Atlán	Gro.	90
Atlán	Mich.	79
Autepec	Gro.	90
Ayutla	Gro.	169
Azoyú	Gro.	693
Cacalotepec	Gro.	189
Cacatipa	Gro.	341
Camutla	Gro.	88
Capulalcolulco	Mich.	502
Cintla	Gro.	121
Ciquila	Gro.	282
Coatepec	Gro.	33
Cocoalco	Gro.	604
Cocula	Gro.	1,696

TABLE 1.1, REGION VII, PART C (Cont.)

Name	Loc.	Population in 1568
Colutla	Gro.	287
Copalillo	Gro.	891
Coyuca	Gro.	45
Coyuquilla	Gro.	564
Cuacuatlán	Mich.	42
Cuachapa	Gro.	310
Cuezala	Gro.	23
Cuitlapa	Gro.	2,078
Cuscacuautlán	Mich.	19
Chacala	Mich.	87
Chachalacametla	Gro.	87
Chiepetlán	Gro.	584
Chipila	Gro.	66
Echancaleca	Gro.	21
Guaytlaco	Gro.	26
Guimixtlán	Gro.	787
Hinhitlán	Gro.	45
Huamuxtitlán	Gro.	5,660
Huetlaco	Gro.	26
Huitlalotla	Gro.	390
Huiztlán	Gro.	168
Ixhuatlán	Gro.	375
Ixtapa	Gro.	138
Ixtapancingo	Gro.	70
Japutica	Gro.	56
Juluchuga	Gro.	32
Maucuila	Mich.	126
Metlalpan	Mich.	43
Mexcaloacán	Mich.	25
Mila	Gro.	705
Miquitla	Gro.	256
Mitepec	Gro.	155
Mitancingo	Gro.	178
Mizquitlán	Gro.	621
Mochitlán	Gro.	1,525
Nexpa	Gro.	317
Nexpa	Gro.	62
Nexuca	Gro.	256

TABLE 1.1, REGION VII, PART C (Cont.)

Name	Loc.	Population in 1568
Nuxco	Gro.	69
Oapan	Gro.	2,201
Ocuyuo	Gro.	282
Omitla	Gro.	113
Ostopila	Mich.	106
Pamutla	Gro.	34
Paxalo	Gro.	211
Pechique	Gro.	28
Petlacala	Oax.	416
Piquitla	Mich.	75
Quiotepec	Gro.	26
Suchitepec	Gro.	26
Suchitonalá	Gro.	330
Tamaloacán	Gro.	127
Tamazula	Gro.	310
Tecamalacazingo	Gro.	730
Tenancingo	Gro.	638
Tenango-Tepexi	Gro.	522
Tequepa	Gro.	982
Teutla	Gro.	116
Tlacolula	Gro.	122
Tlachinola	Gro.	15,025
Tlapistla	Mich.	57
Tolimán	Gro.	224
Tonatla	Gro.	1,370
Totomixtlahuacán	Gro.	984
Tulimán	Gro.	321
Tututepec	Gro.	564
Xaputegua	Gro.	539
Xihuacán	Gro.	160
Xocutla	Gro.	465
Xochitepec	Gro.	42
Xuchitepec	Gro.	85
Zacalutla	Gro.	71
Zacualpán	Mich.	128
Zacualpán	Gro.	590
Zahuatlán	Gro.	77
Zapotitlán	Gro.	62

TABLE 1.1, REGION VII, PART C (Cont.)

Name	Loc.	Population in 1568
Zigua	Gro.	24
Zihuatanejo	Gro.	33
Zintla	Gro.	79
Ziutla	Gro.	53
Zolcoacoa	Gro.	108
Zoytlán	Gro.	677
Zumpango	Gro.	113
Total		52,376
Number of cases	101	

We calculate the probable true population of Region VII in 1620–1625 by using proportions and assuming that the ratio between the two sets of data was the same for all towns alike (in totals). This would mean that 110,779 × 0.343 = 37,997. The difference between this value and that of the actual list (20,506) is considerable. It should be noted that Region VII contains a group of fairly large interior towns, such as Tlapa, Chilapa, and Iguala, all of which continued to exist, but that it also had many small places in Zacatula, most of which had disappeared by 1646. These two components should give quite different results, but the difference is obscured by their fusion into a single region.

Our verification by use of 1595 data is in Table 1.1, Region VII, parts D and E. According to part D, we have values for 14 places in both the 1568 and 1595 data; almost all of them are relatively large towns. In 1568 the population of these 14 places is 34,400; in 1595 it is 24,761. The ratio 1595/1568 is 0.720. By proportion, the entire Indian population of Region VII in 1595 would be 110,779 × 0.720 = 79,761. Part E shows similar data for 1595 and 1646, with 8 places. Here the totals are respectively 18,078 and 9,006, and the ratio 1646/1595 is 0.498. The entire Indian population of Region VII, calculated from the total in 1646 (20,506 ÷ 0.498), would be 41,177. The two results are widely different, and may be referable to the extinction of the coastal strip of Zacatula.

TABLE 1.1, REGION VII, PART D

Towns Found in Both 1568 and 1595 Lists

Name	Loc.	Population in 1568	Population in 1595	Ratio 1595 / 1568
Acaguapisca	Gro.	46	28	.609
Ayutla	Gro.	591	1,054	1.783
Cacahuatepec	Gro.	1,042	180	.173
Chilapa	Gro.	12,111	7,880	.650
Huamuxtitlán	Gro.	5,660	2,430	.429
Huitziltepec	Gro.	341	302	.886
Huiztlán	Gro.	168	127	.756
Mochitlán	Gro.	1,525	1,241	.814
Oapan	Gro.	2,201	2,180	.992
Ometepec	Gro.	1,693	2,183	1.290
Tixtla	Gro.	3,729	3,160	.848
Tlacozautitlán	Cro.	4,264	2,444	.573
Xocutla	Gro.	465	677	1.456
Xochistlahuaca	Gro.	564	875	1.551
Total		34,400	24,761	0.720
Number of cases	14			

TABLE 1.1, REGION VII, PART E

Towns Found in Both 1595 and 1646 Lists

Name	Loc.	Population in 1595	Population in 1646	Ratio 1646 / 1595
Ayutla	Gro.	1,054	394	.374
Cacahuatepec	Gro.	180	143	.794
Chilapa	Gro.	7,880	3,817	.485
Huitziltepec	Gro.	302	62	.205
Ometepec	Gro.	2,183	938	.429
Tixtla	Gro.	3,160	2,100	.665
Tlacozautitlán	Gro.	2,444	1,256	.514
Xochistlahuaca	Gro.	875	296	.338
Total		18,078	9,006	0.498
Number of cases	8			

Region VIII. Michoacán. This region is Tarascan Michoacán, except for the area south and west of the Tepalcatepec River. The region is true plateau, but in aboriginal times was separate from the core of the Central Plateau because of the clear independence of the Tarascan state from the Triple Alliance and the cultural divergence of the inhabitants from the Nahua linguistic groups. Even today it has regional individuality.

Our data are in Table 1.1, Region VIII, parts A-E. Part A shows 35 places which occur in both the 1568 and 1646 lists. In 1568 the population of these 35 plaees is 138,364; in 1646 it is 34,310. The ratio 1646/1568 is 0.248. According to part B, the 1646 report contains the names of 3 places not found in the 1568 list. The population of these 3 places is 1,033, making the total for the 1646 list 35,343. Conversely, part C shows 20 places which occur in the 1568 list but are not found in the 1646 report. The total 1568 population of these 20 places is 60,596. The aggregate for 1568 would be 138,364 plus 60,596, or 198,960, of which the towns missing in the 1646 list would account for 30.5%.

TABLE 1.1, REGION VIII, PART A

Towns Found in Both 1568 and 1646 Lists

Name	Loc.	Population in 1568	Population in 1646	Ratio 1646/1568
Acámbaro	Gto.	7,897	5,140	.651
Capula	Mich.	2,280	167	.073
Chilchota	Mich.	1,914	597	.312
Chucándiro, Cupándaro	Mich.	1,409	68	.098
Comanja	Mich.	3,102	361	.116
Cuitzeo	Mich.	5,735	1,302	.227
Cutzco	Mich.	2,162	1,405	.650
Huacana	Mich.	1,043	112	.107
Huango	Mich.	1,960	156	.080
Huaniqueo	Mich.	1,330	190	.143
Indaparapeo	Mich.	944	240	.254
Jacona	Mich.	15,329	906	.059
Jaso, Teremendo	Mich.	1,281	313	.244
Jiquilpan	Mich.	1,129	1,119	.992
Jirosto	Mich.	6,489	2,322	.358
Maravatío	Mich.	3,142	544	.173

TABLE 1.1, REGION VIII, PART A (Cont.)

Name	Loc.	Population in 1568	Population in 1646	Ratio $\frac{1646}{1568}$
Necotlán	Mich.	604	298	.494
Sevina, Pomucuarán	Mich.	6,050	3,188	.527
Taimeo	Mich.	1,205	648	.538
Tancítaro	Mich.	2,129	1,549	.728
Tarécuato	Mich.	1,690	910	.539
Tarímbaro	Mich.	3,934	471	.120
Tepalcatepec	Mich.	930	673	.724
Tigüindín	Mich.	1,716	510	.297
Tiripitío	Mich.	3,509	340	.097
Tlazazalca	Mich.	1,950	541	.278
Turicato	Mich.	2,247	536	.229
Ucareo	Mich.	3,775	430	.114
Uchichila, Tzintzuntzan, Santa Clara	Mich.	35,759	5,296	.148
Uruapan	Mich.	4,752	1,495	.315
Yuriria, Celaya	Gto.	4,488	945	.210
Zacapu	Mich.	2,820	476	.169
Zinagua	Mich.	726	284	.391
Zinapécuaro	Mich.	2,105	308	.146
Zirándaro, Guayameo	Mich.	829	471	.569
Total		138,364	34,310	0.248
Number of cases	35			

TABLE 1.1, REGION VIII, PART B

Towns on the 1646 list for which there is no corresponding figure for 1568, or which should be omitted from Part A, for various reasons.

Name	Loc.	Population in 1646	Comment
Huanajo	Mich.	474	Not in 1568 list
San Francisco del Rincón	Gto.	241	Not in 1568 list (new town)
Tacámbaro	Mich.	318	Not in 1568 list
Total		1,033	
Number of cases	3		

TABLE 1.1, REGION VIII, PART C

Towns on the 1568 list for which a population is given but
which are not found on the 1646 list. Towns on the 1568 list
for which no separate population is given are omitted.

Name	Loc.	Population in 1568
Ario	Mich.	2,123
Bacaneo	Mich.	800
Coeneo	Mich.	3,515
Chiquimitío	Mich.	1,082
Erongarícuaro	Mich.	2,592
Guayangareo	Mich.	310
Iztaro	Mich.	706
Jerécuaro	Mich.	122
Matalcingo	Mich.	1,835
Mutzantla	Mich.	980
Pajacuarán	Mich.	14,120 (from 1580 list)
Pátzcuaro	Mich.	13,200
Peribán	Mich.	3,944
Pómaro	Mich.	2,492
Puruándiro	Mich.	1,690
Suchi	Mich.	267
Tanátaro	Mich.	1,062
Taximaroa	Mich.	8,455
Undameo	Mich.	1,037
Xichú	Gto.	264
Total		60,596
Number of cases	20	

We calculate the probable true population of Region VIII in
1620-1625 by using proportions and assuming that the ratio
between the two sets of data was the same for all towns alike
(in totals). This would mean that 198,960 × 0.248 = 49,342.
The difference between this value and that of the actual list
(35,343) is moderate and probably can be accounted for mainly
by the omission on the 1646 list of fairly large towns, such as
Pajacuarán and Pátzcuaro, which continued to exist throughout
the colonial period.

Our resort to 1595 data for verification is in parts D and E. Part D shows the population of 17 places which are in both the 1568 and 1595 reporting. The total of the former is 63,188 and of the latter 38,182. The ratio 1595/1568 is 0.604. By proportion, the entire Indian population of Region VIII in 1595 would be 198,960 × 0.604 = 120,172. Part E shows similar data for 1595 and 1646, with 14 places. Here the totals are respectively 30,586 and 18,330, and the ratio 1646/1595 is 0.599. The entire Indian population of Region VIII, calculated from the total in the 1646 data (35,343 ÷ 0.599), would be 59,003. This is very different from the value obtained from the 1568 data.

TABLE 1.1, REGION VIII, PART D

Towns Found in Both 1568 and 1595 Lists

Name	Loc.	Population in 1568	Population in 1595	Ratio 1595/1568
Acámbaro	Gto.	7,897	3,480	.441
Comanja	Mich.	3,102	1,391	.448
Cuitzeo	Mich.	5,735	2,086	.364
Huacana	Mich.	1,043	344	.330
Indaparapeo	Mich.	944	525	.556
Jirosto	Mich.	6,489	4,428	.682
Peribán	Mich.	3,944	2,482	.630
Pomucuarán, Sevina	Mich.	6,050	6,110	1.010
Puruándiro	Mich.	1,690	795	.470
Suchi	Mich.	267	993	3.715
Tancítaro	Mich.	2,129	2,014	.947
Tarécuato	Mich.	1,690	994	.588
Tarímbaro	Mich.	3,934	1,082	.275
Taximaroa	Mich.	8,455	4,310	.510
Turicato	Mich.	2,247	2,093	.933
Uruapan	Mich.	4,752	3,184	.670
Zacapu	Mich.	2,820	1,871	.664
Total		63,188	38,182	0.604
Number of cases	17			

TABLE 1.1, REGION VIII, PART E

Towns Found in Both 1595 and 1646 Lists

Name	Loc.	Population in 1595	Population in 1646	Ratio 1646/1595
Acámbaro	Gto.	3,480	5,140	1.478
Comanja	Mich.	1,391	361	.259
Cuitzeo	Mich.	2,086	1,302	.625
Huacana	Mich.	344	112	.325
Indaparapeo	Mich.	525	240	.457
Jirosto	Mich.	4,428	2,322	.524
Sevina, Pomucuarán	Mich.	6,110	3,188	.522
Tacámbaro	Mich.	984	318	.323
Tancítaro	Mich.	2,014	1,459	.769
Tarícuato	Mich.	994	910	.915
Tarímbaro	Mich.	1,082	471	.435
Turicato	Mich.	2,093	536	.256
Uruapan	Mich.	3,184	1,495	.469
Zacapu	Mich.	1,871	476	.254
Total		30,586	18,330	0.599
Number of cases	14			

Region IX. Eastern Jalisco–Zacatecas. This region is in the high cold country of west-central Mexico. It includes the Avalos towns and the Guadalajara plain as far west as, but not including, the volcano of Colima and the low-lying valleys of Autlán and Milpa. To the north, the region extends to the great canyon of the Santiago River and the southern valleys of Zacatecas. To the east, it extends to Tarascan Michoacán and the Chichimec frontier. Part of the western boundary lies in what in the sixteenth and seventeenth century was the deeply dissected, inaccessible country of eastern Nayarit and the Bolaños area of Jalisco. A very large part of our Region IX lay in the Audiencia of Nueva Galicia and was governed from Guadalajara. Accordingly, its Indian towns paid tribute to the royal treasury in Guadalajara. Only the Avalos towns in southwestern Jalisco were in the Audiencia of Mexico, or New Spain.

Table 1.1, Region IX, part A shows 16 places which occur in both the 1568 and 1646 lists. These 16 places are all within that part of Jalisco that was under the jurisdiction of New Spain, and were located either on the plateau or in the zone intermediate between the plateau and the coast. In 1568 the population of these 16 places is 26,878; in 1646 it is 10,347. The ratio 1646/1568 is 0.385. Part B shows 1 place found on the 1646 list which is not in the 1568 reporting. The population of this place is 1,081, making the total for the 1646 list 11,428. Part C shows 10 places which are in the 1568 list but not in the 1646 report. These 10 places are all located in New Spain. All others which could be identified as being located in Nueva Galicia were omitted. The total 1568 population of these 10 places is 5,354. The aggregate for 1568 of that part of Region IX lying within New Spain would be 26,878 plus 5,354, or 32,232, of which the towns not found in the 1646 reporting would account for 16.6%.

TABLE 1.1, REGION IX, PART A

Towns Found in Both 1568 and 1646 Lists

Name	Loc.	Population in 1568	Population in 1646	Ratio 1646 / 1568
Amacuoca	Jal.	2,090	648	.310
Ameca	Jal.	779	134	.172
Ajijic	Jal.	835	398	.477
Atoyac	Jal.	2,346	486	.207
Chapala	Jal.	614	656	1.068
Cocula	Jal.	1,838	610	.332
Etzatlán	Jal.	2,291	626	.273
Jilotlán	Jal.	849	94	.111
Jocotepec	Jal.	386	332	.861
Sayula	Jal.	2,630	1,826	.695
Tamazula	Jal.	1,393	457	.328
Techalutla	Jal.	2,083	219	.105
Teocuitatlán	Jal.	1,073	272	.254
Tuxpan	Jal.	2,581	1,035	.401
Zacoalco	Jal.	2,855	1,583	.554
Zapotlán	Jal.	1,135	971	.856
Total		26,878	10,347	0.385
Number of cases	16			

TABLE 1.1, REGION IX, PART B

*Towns on the 1646 list for which there is no corresponding
figure for 1568, or which should be omitted from Part A, for
various reasons. Starred populations are omitted from the total.*

Name	Loc.	Population in 1646	Comment
Atoyac	Jal.	1,081	Not in 1568 list
Milpa, Matlán	Jal.	102*	Should be in Region X
Total		1,081	
Number of cases	1		

TABLE 1.1, REGION IX, PART C

*Towns on the 1568 list for which a population is given but
which are not found on the 1646 list. Towns on the 1568 list
for which no separate population is given are omitted.*

Name	Loc.	Population in 1568

Part I. Towns in southwestern Jalisco. To be equated with the
1646 list in *Nueva España*.

Name	Loc.	Population in 1568
Ahualulco	Jal.	351
Atemajac	Jal.	845
Atotonilco	Jal.	339
Copala	Jal.	204
Huachinango	Jal.	1,128
Ixtlán	Jal.	282
Jocotlán	Jal.	1,269
Tala	Jal.	208
Tequila	Jal.	282
Tesixtán	Jal.	446
Total		5,354
Number of cases	10	

Part II. Towns in northeastern Jalisco and adjacent Zacatecas.
All towns to the north and east of the Avalos province
and Lake Chapala were in *Nueva Galicia*, not New Spain.
The 1646 list includes only towns in New Spain. Therefore the towns in Nueva Galicia must be omitted when
the 1646 list is being compared with the 1568 list.

We calculate the probable true population of Region IX in 1620–1625 for that portion lying within New Spain by using proportions and assuming that the ratio between the two dates was the same for all towns alike (in totals). This would mean that 32,232 × 0.385 = 12,409. The difference between this value and that of the actual list (11,428) is very small.

Our resort to 1595 data for verification is in parts D and E. Part D shows the population of 9 places, all in the province of Avalos, in 1568 and 1595. In 1568 the population of these 9 places is 14,404; in 1595 it is 18,760. The ratio is 1.303. By proportion, the entire Indian population of this portion of Region IX in 1595 would be 32,232 × 1.303 = 41,998. Part E gives similar data for 1595 and 1646, with the same 9 places. Here the totals are respectively 18,760 and 6,544, and the ratio 1646/1595 is 0.349. The entire Indian population of this portion of Region IX, calculated from the total in 1646 (11,428 ÷ 0.349), would be 32,745. This result is not widely different from the value obtained from the 1568 data.

TABLE 1.1, REGION IX, PART D

Towns found in both 1568 and 1595 lists.
Note that this table covers only Avalos towns.

Name	Loc.	Population in 1568	Population in 1595	Ratio 1595/1568
Ajijic	Jal.	835	868	1.040
Amacuaca and Tepec	Jal.	2,090	1,846	.884
Chapala	Jal.	614	1,089	1.770
Cocula	Jal.	1,838	3,554	1.936
Jocotepec	Jal.	386	784	2.031
Sayula	Jal.	2,630	5,085	1.932
Techalutla	Jal.	2,083	1,496	.718
Teocuitatlán	Jal.	1,073	812	.757
Zacoalco	Jal.	2,855	3,226	1.130
Total		14,404	18,760	1.303
Number of cases	9			

TABLE 1.1, REGION IX, PART E

Towns found in both 1595 and 1646 lists.
Note that this table covers only Avalos towns.

Name	Loc.	Population in 1595	Population in 1646	Ratio 1646/1595
Ajijic	Jal.	868	398	.458
Amacueca, Tepec	Jal.	1,846	648	.351
Chapala	Jal.	1,089	656	.603
Cocula	Jal.	3,554	610	.172
Jocotepec	Jal.	784	332	.423
Sayula	Jal.	5,085	1,826	.359
Techalutla	Jal.	1,496	219	.146
Teocuitatlán	Jal.	812	272	.335
Zacoalco	Jal.	3,226	1,583	.490
Total		18,760	6,544	0.349
Number of cases	9			

Region X. Colima–Nayarit. Actually this region includes Colima, a small part of Michoacán, western Jalisco, and Nayarit. It is large but relatively homogeneous ecologically. The topography and climate vary widely, ranging from temperate valleys, at altitudes of 1000 to 1200 meters, to hot coastal plain. Region X lay partly in the Audiencia of Nueva Galicia and partly in the Audiencia of Mexico, and we have to treat the data as we did for Region IX. Table 1.1, Region X, parts A–E lists the data for the towns in the Audiencia of Mexico. Part A lists 51 places which occur in both the 1568 and 1646 reporting. They include the Autlán–Tuscacuesco area of Jalisco, the entire state of Colima, and the Motines area of western Michoacán. They do not include coastal Jalisco, Nayarit, or Sinaloa. In 1568 the population of these 51 places is 15,892; in 1646 it is 5,692. The ratio 1646/1568 is 0.358. Part B shows 7 places found in the 1646 report but not in the 1568 list. The population of these 7 places is 317, making the total for the 1646 list 6,009. Conversely, part C lists towns in the 1568 reporting but not in that for 1646; there are 57 such places, all within New Spain. (The remainder of the towns, which were in Nueva Galicia, have been omitted.) The total 1568 population of these

57 places is 10,528. The aggregate for 1568 would be 15,892 plus 10,528, or 26,420, of which the towns omitted from the 1646 report would account for 39.8%.

TABLE 1.1, REGION X, PART A

Towns Found in Both 1568 and 1646 Lists

Name	Loc.	Population in 1568	Population in 1646	Ratio $\frac{1646}{1568}$
Acatlán	Col.	124	82	.661
Ahuacatitlán	Col.	168	19	.113
Alcozahue	Col.	127	46	.363
Almoloya	Col.	53	36	.680
Atenguillo	Jal.	1,690	167	.099
Atengo	Jal.	685	65	.095
Atliacapan	Col.	144	26	.181
Ayuquilla	Jal.	119	48	.403
Ayutitlán	Jal.	246	65	.264
Ayutla	Jal.	557	192	.345
Chiametla	Col.	198	44	.222
Chipiltitlán	Jal.	157	70	.446
Coatlán	Col.	78	27	.346
Comala	Col.	257	150	.584
Cuzalapa	Jal.	244	287	1.177
Ixtlahuacán	Col.	243	145	.595
Juluapan, Zumpamanique	Col.	363	148	.408
Malacatlán	Col.	56	44	.786
Milpa and Matlán	Jal.	970	102	.105
Nahuala	Col.	225	150	.667
Ocotlán	Col.	622	27	.043
Petlatlán	Col.	113	24	.212
Popoyutla	Col.	56	25	.447
Quezalapa	Col.	114	102	.895
Salagua	Col.	130	37	.285
Tamala	Col.	72	63	.875
Tecociapa	Col.	141	53	.376
Tecocitlán	Col.	247	226	.915
Tecolapa and Cajitlán	Col.	241	65	.270
Tecolotlán	Jal.	263	131	.498

TABLE 1.1, REGION X, PART A (Cont.)

Name	Loc.	Population in 1568	Population in 1646	Ratio 1646/1568
Tecomán	Col.	154	56	.364
Tecuxuacan	Col.	418	49	.117
Tenamaxtlán	Jal.	123	136	1.105
Tepetitango	Col.	347	29	.084
Tequepa	Col.	154	34	.221
Teutitlán	Jal.	198	29	.147
Tlacaloastla	Col.	86	20	.233
Tlaquaban	Col.	50	48	.960
Tototlán	Col.	55	56	1.018
Totolmoloya	Col.	40	34	.850
Tuxcacuesco	Jal.	558	352	.631
Xicotlán	Col.	165	24	.145
Xiloteupan	Col.	97	17	.175
Zacapala	Jal.	87	54	.621
Zapotitlán, Amula	Jal.	1,226	836	.682
Zihuatlan	Col.	88	41	.466
Zoquimatlán	Col.	85	133	1.565
Motines: Col. and Mich. Aquila		287	77	.268
Coalcomán		884	258	.292
Maquili		371	148	.399
Zinacamitlán, et al.		1,716	595	.347
Total		15,892	5,692	0.358
Number of cases	51			

TABLE 1.1, REGION X, PART B

Towns on the 1646 list for which there is no corresponding figure for 1568, or which should be omitted from Part A, for various reasons.

Name	Loc.	Population in 1646	Comment
Cueyatlán	Col.	20	Not in 1568 list
Ixtlahuacán	Col.	153	Not in 1568 list
Izatlán	Jal.	19	In 1568 included other towns

TABLE 1.1, REGION X, PART B (Cont.)

Name	Loc.	Population in 1646	Comment
Tecocitlán	Col.	34	Not in 1568 list
Tepetlica	Col.	22	Not in 1568 list
Zacualpan	Col.	46	Not in 1568 list
Zapotlanejo	Col.	23	Not in 1568 list
Total		317	
Number of cases	7		

TABLE 1.1, REGION X, PART C

Towns on the 1568 list for which a population is given but which are not found on the 1646 list. Towns on the 1568 list for which no separate population is given are omitted.

Name	Loc.	Population in 1568

Part I. Towns in southwestern Jalisco, Colima, and southwestern Michoacan. To be equated with the 1646 list in *Nueva España*.

Name	Loc.	Pop.
Acatlán	Col.	124
Ahuacapan, Mixtlán Tecomantlán	Jal.	622
Ahuacatlán	Jal.	648
Ahuacatitlán	Col.	44
Ahuatitlán	Col.	155
Alima	Col.	108
Ameca	Col.	58
Apamila	Jal.	44
Apatlán	Col.	282
Autlán	Jal.	1,670
Cacalutla	Col.	58
Cayamaca	Col.	101
Chalatipan	Col.	144
Chiapan	Col.	101
Coatlán	Col.	374
Contlán	Col.	31
Copala	Jal.	224

TABLE 1.1, REGION X, PART C (Cont.)

Name	Loc.	Population in 1568
Coxiutlán	Col.	79
Coyutlán	Jal.	40
Coyutlán	Col.	110
Cuzcatlán	Col.	366
Ecatlán	Col.	149
Espuchiapa	Col.	19
Estapa	Col.	58
Estapa	Col.	73
Gualoxa	Mich.	84
Huepantitlán	Col.	42
Ixcatlán	Col.	19
Mahuala	Col.	115
Maloastla	Col.	55
Mascota	Jal.	225
Mixtanejo	Col.	26
Moxuma	Col.	863
Naopala	Col.	52
Petlazoneca	Col.	150
Pomayagua	Col.	71
Puchutitlán	Col.	432
Tapazoneca	Col.	79
Tecociapa	Col.	141
Temacatipan	Col.	110
Tepehuacán	Col.	60
Tepitango	Col.	103
Tezontlán	Col.	235
Tezuacán	Col.	32
Tezuatlán	Mich.	92
Tlacalnagua	Col.	28
Tlacavanas	Mich.	85
Tlapuma	Jal.	74
Tlila	Col.	32
Tototlán	Col.	46
Xaltepozotlán	Col.	66
Xocotlán	Col.	147
Zaliguacan	Col.	662

TABLE 1.1, REGION X, PART C (Cont.)

Name	Loc.	Population in 1568
Zautlán	Col.	43
Zayula	Col.	129
Zecamachantla	Col.	139
Zoyatlán	Col.	409
Total		10,528
Number of cases	57	

Part II. Towns in coastal Jalisco, Nayarit, and Sinaloa.
All towns in coastal Jalisco (Banderas, Purifi-
cación), and the states of Nayarit and Sinaloa
were in *Nueva Galicia* and hence must be omitted
from consideration, since none of them were reported in the 1646 list.

We calculate the probable true population of Region X (i.e., that portion lying within New Spain) by using proportions and assuming that the ratio between the two sets of data was the same for all towns alike (in totals). This would mean that $26,420 \times 0.358 = 9,458$. The difference between this value and that of the actual list (6,009) is relatively moderate.

Our use of 1595 data is in parts D and E. Part D shows the population of 17 places which occur in both the 1568 and 1595 reporting. The total of the former is 5,338 and of the latter 4,193, most of the difference being referable to Autlán alone. The ratio is 0.786. By proportion, the entire Indian population of this portion of Region X in 1595 would be $26,420 \times 0.786 = 20,766$. Part E shows similar data for 1595 and 1646, with 13 places. Here the totals are respectively 3,441 and 1,242, and the ratio 1646/1595 is 0.361. The entire Indian population in 1595 of this portion of Region X, calculated from the 1646 data ($6,009 \div 0.361$), would be 16,645. This result differs moderately from that obtained from the 1568 data.

TABLE 1.1, REGION X, PART D

Towns Found in Both 1568 and 1595 Lists

Name	Loc.	Population in 1568	Population in 1595	Ratio 1595/1568
Ahuacatitlán	Col.	168	85	.506
Alcozahue	Col.	127	203	1.598
Atengo	Jal.	685	693	1.011
Autlán	Jal.	1,670	310	.186
Ayuquila	Jal.	119	40	.336
Ayutitlán	Jal.	246	356	1.448
Ayutla	Jal.	557	377	.677
Comala	Col.	257	382	1.488
Chiapan	Col.	101	126	1.247
Chipiltitlán	Jal.	157	65	.414
Ixtlahuacán	Col.	243	632	2.600
Popoyutla	Col.	56	42	.750
Tecocitlán	Col.	247	240	.972
Tenamaxtlán	Jal.	123	225	1.830
Tlacoloaxtla	Col.	86	141	1.640
Zacapila	Jal.	87	45	.517
Zoyatlán	Col.	409	231	.565
Total		5,338	4,193	0.786
Number of cases	17			

TABLE 1.1, REGION X, PART E

Towns Found in Both 1595 and 1646 Lists

Name	Loc.	Population in 1595	Population in 1646	Ratio 1646/1595
Alcozahue	Col.	203	46	.227
Atengo	Jal.	693	65	.094
Ayuquila	Jal.	40	48	1.200
Ayutitlán	Jal.	356	65	.106
Ayutla	Jal.	377	192	.510
Chipiltitlán	Jal.	65	70	1.077
Comala	Col.	382	150	.392

TABLE 1.1, REGION X, PART E (Cont.)

Name	Loc.	Population in 1595	Population in 1646	Ratio 1646/1595
Ixtlahuacán	Col.	632	145	.229
Popoyutla	Col.	42	25	.595
Tecocitlán	Col.	240	226	.942
Tenamaxtlán	Jal.	225	136	.605
Tlacaloastla	Col.	141	20	.142
Zacapila	Jal.	45	54	1.200
Total		3,441	1,242	0.361
Number of cases	13			

Central Mexico as a Whole: We are now ready to reach totals for the Indian population of the royal treasury district of Mexico City—that is, the Audiencia of Mexico—and for the larger area of central Mexico as we have defined it in previous studies. Our regional tabulations have necessarily been lengthy, and the important point perhaps deeply buried. We summarize regional totals and give overall totals in Table 1.2, parts A-D. Table 1.2, part A summarizes all parts A of Table 1.1, which contained the comparison of values for towns and entities whose names appeared on both the 1568 and 1646 lists. The proportion of change in the paired values gives us our proportion of change between 1568 and the data of 1646 (which must still be adjusted to an average date). For further comparison, we have segregated the regions into the two categories of plateau and coast. Table 1.2, part B is a test of the significance of difference between the values for plateau and coast. Table 1.2, part C summarizes aggregate population for the regions, again segregated into plateau and coast. We here compare aggregate populations for 1568 with aggregate populations for the same regions arrived at by totaling values for towns in the 1646 list. We then calculate the probable true aggregate populations of the regions by correcting for the deficiency revealed in the total for each region in the 1646 data, through our previous examination region by region. Table 1.2, part D summarizes the earlier series of parts D and E of Table 1.1—that is, our comparison with 1595 data for verification.

TABLE 1.2, PART A

Comparison of population totals in the regions shown in Table 6, page 48 of Ibero-Americana #44. The values for the 1646 lists are as adjusted in the detailed summaries of regions. The values for 1568 are the corresponding ones taken from the appendix to Ibero-Americana #44.

Region	Population in 1568	Population in 1646 list	Ratio 1646 / 1568	Number of cases
PLATEAU:				
I.	1,321,329	303,717	.230	206
IIA.	22,394	10,065	.449	25
IV.	183,601	60,785	.331	87
VIII.	138,364	34,310	.248	35
IX.	26,878	10,347	.385	16
Total	1,692,566	419,224		369
Ratio of totals			.248	
Mean ratio of regions			.329	
COAST:				
II.	35,316	8,559	.242	28
III.	20,751	5,183	.250	33
V.	37,142	22,774	.613	72
VI.	50,316	30,106	.600	45
VII.	58,403	20,036	.343	51
X.	15,892	5,692	.358	51
Total	217,820	92,350		280
Ratio of totals			.424	
Mean ratio of regions			.401	
ALL REGIONS:	1,910,386	511,574		
Ratio of totals			.268	

TABLE 1.2, PART B

*Test for significance between values of plateau and those
of the coast for ratio between population in 1568 and
1646 lists. In order to minimize wide variations at the
extremes the logarithms of the individual ratios were used.*

Plateau		Coast	
Sum of the logarithms of the individual ratios after the latter were multiplied by 10		Sum of the logarithms of the individual ratios after the latter were multiplied by 10	
500.425		445.822	
Number of cases	368	Number of cases	280
Mean logarithm	1.360	Mean logarithm	1.598
Antilogarithm	0.229	Antilogarithm	0.396

Value of t (critical ratio of the mean logarithm)

with 646 degrees of freedom: 7.46

Significant far beyond the 1 percent level.

TABLE 1.2, PART C

*Total count of population, according to region, 1568 and 1646 lists. The
latter is determined in two ways: 1) the actual sum shown in the document itself, 2) the sum calculated by applying the ratios shown in Part A
to the figures obtained for 1568. The final column gives the deficiency
found in the document. This is expressed as a percent by subtracting the
population found in the document from that obtained by calculation from
the ratios, and dividing by the calculated population.*

Region	Aggregate Population in 1568	Aggregate population by 1646 document	Aggregate population of 1646 list by calculation from ratio	Percent deficiency in 1646 document
PLATEAU				
I.	1,717,635	313,379	395,056	20.6
IIA.	32,700	11,749	14,682	20.0
IV.	223,333	62,074	73,923	16.0
VIII.	198,960	35,343	49,342	28.4
IX.	32,232	11,428	12,409	7.9
Total	2,204,860	433,973	545,412	
Mean percent deficiency				18.6

TABLE 1.2, PART C (Cont.)

Region	Aggregate Population in 1568	Aggregate population by 1646 document	Aggregate population of 1646 list by calculation from ratio	Percent deficiency in 1646 document
COASTS				
II.	73,134	8,912	17,698	49.6
III.	47,679	6,646	11,920	44.2
V.	69,569	27,051	42,646	36.5
VI.	62,996	30,128	37,798	20.3
VII.	110,779	20,506	37,997	36.6
X.	26,420	6,009	9,458	34.7
Total	390,577	99,252	157,517	

Mean percent deficiency   37.0

Value of t for the mean percent deficiency of the two regions:

3.50 - Highly significant

ALL REGIONS	2,595,437	533,225	702,929	

Percent deficiency of total   24.1

TABLE 1.2, PART D

The population of New Spain in 1595. The population is calculated for the usual regions in two ways. The first is by determining the ratio 1568/1595 for those towns for which a population is given at both dates, and then applying the mean ratio to the entire population in 1568. The second is by using the same method with the 1646 list. It is noted that the 1646 data consistently give lower populations for 1595. Hence we include the percent deficiency in 1595 population as calculated from the data of the 1646 list.

Region	Population in 1595, calculated from 1568	Population in 1595, calculated from 1646
PLATEAU		
I.	849,767	773,775
IIA.	19,522	10,909
IV.	119,930	121,002
VIII.	120,172	59,003
IX.	41,998	32,745
Total	1,151,389	997,434

Percent deficiency in value calculated from 1646 data:

13.4

TABLE 1.2, PART D (Cont.)

Region	Population in 1595, calculated from 1568	Population in 1595, calculated from 1646
COAST		
II.	64,358	24,894
III.	28,750	10,754
V.	44,455	25,837
VI.	52,728	42,846
VII.	79,761	41,177
X.	20,766	16,645
Total	290,881	162,153

Percent deficiency in value calculated from 1646 data:
44.3

ALL REGIONS	1,442,270	1,159,587

Percent deficiency in value calculated from 1646 data:
19.6

TABLE 1.2, PART E

Towns on the 1646 List That Could Not Be Identified

Name	Population
Coatejo	316
Huchutlan	676
Tequiliac, San Mateo	691

Let us now examine this material in a somewhat different way, less bound to the exact format of these tables. We have already determined that the lag in recounts and reassessments of Indian tributes in the first decades of the seventeenth century indicates that data in the 1646 list really refer to an average date between 1620 and 1625. Accordingly, our references to data in the 1646 list should be given this placement in time. We have also discussed the problem of deficiency in the data of the 1646 list, both in terms of coverage of number of towns and coverage of aggregate population. We anticipated our finding, based upon regional examination, summarized in Table 1.2, part

C, that the data cover 75.9% of the aggregate population and constitute a very substantial sample.

Our reconstructed aggregate Indian population for the district of the royal treasury of Mexico City on the basis of data in the 1646 list is 702,929. This is an estimate and hardly exact to the last digit or even the last thousand. It should be compared to a value of 2,595,437 for the same area in 1568 and one of 1,442,270 in 1595. These values for 1568 and 1595 differ slightly from those we arrived at previously for a number of reasons: (1) The selection of data for comparison involves small differences which would result in insignificant variation in totals. One result here is that the total for 1595 is somewhat higher than our earlier one and may suggest a minor adjustment upward of that value in terms of the comparison with data from the 1646 list. (2) Perhaps the more important reason for difference is that our totals here do not cover territories in the Audiencia of Nueva Galicia which were parts of our Regions IX and X, including southern Sinaloa up to and just beyond the Culiacán Valley. To bring our 1620–1625 value to full comparability with our earlier estimate for 1568, we should adjust our total by adding 22,000 as a compromise value between 1620 and 1630 for Nueva Galicia exclusive of southern Sinaloa.[20]) An adjustment for southern Sinaloa is much more difficult, since we have virtually no information on Indian population there for the seventeenth century. It functioned as an autonomous fiscal entity which reported merely totals to Guadalajara. We may guess from the data in the *Suma de Visitas* and the general course of Indian population in the Audiencia of Nueva Galicia that the Indian population of southern Sinaloa in the early decades of the seventeenth century fell below 10,000 and perhaps below 5,000. If we add 27,000 as an adjustment for all territories in Nueva Galicia, to bring our corrected aggregate total for Indian population in the Audiencia of Mexico in 1620–1625 to coverage of central Mexico, we cannot be far off the mark. The Indian population of central Mexico in 1620–1625, then, would be approximately 730,000. This value should be compared with our earlier values of 25.2 million for the same area in 1518, 2.65 million in 1568, and 1.375 million 1595. The decline was distinctly greater than we had previously thought.

20. From our study of the population of west-central Mexico in Cook and Borah, *Essays*, I, chap. 5, esp. p. 310.

There was, of course, great regional variation in the extent of loss of population. Our segregation of regions by plateau and coasts gives evidence on climatic influence. We had previously determined that loss of population proceeded much more rapidly in coastal regions, that here population reached its nadir earlier than on the plateau, and that some measure of recovery started earlier.[21] Our comparison of data from the 1568 and 1646 lists confirms these determinations. (See Table 1.2, parts A-C.) Although the deficiency in reporting in the 1646 data is greater for the coasts than for the plateau, the large sample in the list indicates that the loss of population in coastal regions was less than in those on the plateau. Our test for significance of the difference gives a value of t that is far beyond the 1% level of probability; that is, the chance that the difference arises from mere random variation of the data is much less than 1%.

One further point remains to be discussed here. Does the average date 1620–1625 come close to the low point of Indian population in central Mexico? Most scholars, except for the increasingly fewer ones who insist in the teeth of all evidence that there was no decline, have found the turning point somewhere between 1610 and 1650. In the first decade of the seventeenth century, population loss was still going on. Shortly after the midcentury, the Spanish authorities began to recount Indian towns and found population increase. Obviously, the low point and beginnings of increase of population must have taken place at different times and perhaps in somewhat different circumstances in various regions. In addition, the years between the birth of more Indians and their reaching tributary status, plus the normal lag in royal fiscal awareness of the change and consequent move to reassessment of tributes, would mean some lapse of time before fiscal material would reflect the new state of affairs. Our study of the Mixteca Alta suggested that the turning point came about 1620. In terms of the evidence now available to us, we cannot be sure that 1620–1625 should be taken as the exact low point of all Indian population in the Audiencia of Mexico, but in the present state of our knowledge, it is close enough to the low point to serve—i.e., again a

21. Cook and Borah, *The Indian Population of Central Mexico, 1531–1610,* pp. 49–56; Cook and Borah, "Quelle fut la stratification sociale au centre du Mexique durante la premiere moitié du XVIe siècle?," pp. 238–241; Cook and Borah, "On the Credibility of Contemporary Testimony on the Population of Mexico in the Sixteenth Century," pp. 235–237; Cook and Borah, *Essays,* I, pp. 79–118.

reasonable compromise date in what must have been considerable regional variation involving a small span of years in either direction. We conclude, then, that the Indian population of central Mexico, under the impact of factors unleashed by the coming of the Europeans, fell by 1620-1625 to a low of approximately 3% of its size at the time that the Europeans first landed on the shore of Veracruz.

3. THE ROYAL REVENUES

When we turn from Indian population to royal revenues, the information in the report of 1646 deals directly with that year or a short term of years immediately preceding 1646. The report is one of a long series of similar documents, prepared at irregular intervals during the three centuries of the colonial administration, to give an idea of the yield of the royal revenues. It is a *tanteo*, a trial balance or estimate, in this instance a mixture of information on theoretical yield of some taxes, such as the bulls of the Holy Crusade, and of actual yield for others, especially those which in part or in whole were leased out to cities or farmed to private collectors and so called for fixed yield. It is striking testimony of the disorder in the royal treasury at the time, that the visitador-general should be unable quickly to get exact information on the nature and yield of taxes from the central fiscal agencies in Mexico City.

Let us start not with yield but with the system of Indian tributes: obligation to pay, assessments, kind of payment, and cession of the royal right to receive tribute to Spaniards through encomiendas. From the middle of the sixteenth century, there was a steady move toward extinction of encomiendas as such grants passed through a third life and reverted to the Crown. By the time of the encomenderos' petition to the Crown in 1597-98, approximately two-thirds of the towns in the Audiencia of Mexico were in the Crown, either through original retention or reversion.[22] By 1646 almost all of the original

22. In the famous petition of encomenderos of 1597-98 and the legal proceedings carried out in support of it, the encomenderos declared that the proportion of privately held encomiendas still in existence at that time was less than one-quarter. A count of the certified statement of towns still in encomienda gives approximately 463 towns and fractions of towns, or approximately one-third. Francisco del Paso y Troncoso, comp., *Epistolario de Nueva España, 1505-1818*, XIII, pp. 3-165, *passim*.

grants for three lives should have run out, since it would require three long-lived males with unusually wide spacing between generations to have held an encomienda for more than a century. On the other hand, a few of the grants, such as the very substantial one to the Cortés family, would not lapse, since they were in perpetuity. Furthermore, the Crown did make further grants, despite a general policy of letting encomiendas lapse, although the later grants were most often pension arrangements secured upon the tributes of specific towns. Some of the new grants were for one or more lives; some were in perpetuity.[23] The report of 1646 shows the interaction of these counterbalancing tendencies. It lists, after elimination of duplicate entries, approximately 871 entities. (We deal here with the listings of 1646, which in many instances divide entities as they existed in 1568. We have had to recombine them for our earlier section on Indian population.) There were 202 towns still held by encomenderos in their entirety, and 32 whose tributes were divided between the Crown and an encomendero. Encomienda then affected 234 entities listed in the report, that is, 26.8%. If the towns omitted from the report were entirely in the Crown, adjustment for omission at maximum would require reducing this value to perhaps 18% as the proportion of towns and other entities still paying tribute to encomenderos through old or new grants. Attrition since 1597 then had reduced the former proportion of one-third by nearly half.[24]

The tribute reform of the middle of the sixteenth century, implemented town by town in a steady series of reassessments, removed exemptions from obligation to pay and imposed a standard definition of tributary and half-tributary. There is no reason to think that these changes, which were fully implemented, changed in any significant way until the middle of the eighteenth century, when unmarried and widowed women were freed from payment of half-tribute. The mid-sixteenth-century reform also began to move assessments toward a standard quota, one silver peso of eight reales and half a fanega of maize as the ordinary tribute. It was supplemented by the half peso of

23. These matters are treated at considerable length in Lesley Byrd Simpson, *The Encomienda in New Spain*, chaps. 11 and 12, and Silvio A. Zavala, *La encomienda indiana, passim*.

24. A comparison of the number of towns in encomienda in 1646 with that of 1597 yields the same proportion.

real servicio instituted in the 1590's, payable by all Indian tributaries whether in royal towns or encomienda.[25] We have ignored the real servicio in this discussion, because it was collected uniformly with perhaps two exceptions.[26]

Movement toward a standard quota per tributary was hampered by the fact that not all Indian towns were able to pay in money and maize and that the commodities in which they could pay were not as yet easily convertible to money by them. Accordingly, many towns continued to be assessed in local products, usually cloth, clothing, and cacao, occasionally more unusual products such as salt or wheat. As access to Spanish markets and the money economy increased, payment in all kinds of products also increasingly became commuted to coin, usually at the average the tribute had sold at in the preceding three or five years.[27] That change introduced new elements of variation, for over the years the rise in prices affected different commodities at varying rates, and the towns which earlier had managed to commute their commodity payments to coin found themselves at an advantage compared to those which did so later. In the years from 1627 to 1631, the royal treasury finally set commutation rates for the two major tribute commodities at 9 reales the fanega for maize and 9 reales the pierna for cloth. That remained the rate despite later fluctuations of prices.[28] Most towns listed in the 1646 report as delivering maize probably paid in coin, for the report indicates that all maize was converted to money at the commutation rate. However, towns which had commuted their maize at an earlier date and lower rate, if the assessment had been changed to coin, continued to pay at the lower rate. Even at the end of the eighteenth century, differences in commutation rates continued to keep tributes, by then almost all paid in coin, from being uniform.[29] Towns assessed in textiles continued to deliver products after 1631 despite the permission to commute, for the report of 1646 explicitly declares that no estimate of yield could be made, since tribute cloth and clothing were sold at public auction for varying prices.

25. Cook and Borah, *Essays*, I, pp. 19–22.

26. See below.

27. See the discussion for the sixteenth century in Borah and Cook, *Price Trends of Some Basic Commodities in Central Mexico, 1531–1570*, pp. 5–7 and 18–22.

28. Cook and Borah, *Essays*, I, p. 20; Fabian de Fonseca and Carlos de Urrutia, *Historia general de real hacienda*, I, p. 422.

29. Fonseca and Urrutia, I, table between pp. 450–451.

The extent to which tribute quotas had moved toward the standard assessment by the 1640's may be gauged from the 1646 report. Of 669 entities held in whole or in part by the Crown, 269, or 40.2%, varied from the standard of one silver peso and a half fanega of maize, or the money equivalent of 1/2/6. Accordingly, approximately 60% were at the standard. Our data cover only Crown towns or fractions thereof and do not touch towns entirely in encomienda. Neither can they give information on the very substantial number of towns omitted from the report. Clearly the movement toward a standard quota went somewhat more slowly than studies to date have supposed, and by the end of the sixteenth century came to a halt. It was resumed in the later seventeenth century, but the vagaries of commutation prevented adoption of a uniform tribute in money.

In Table 1.3 we list by region all of the royal towns, or fractions of towns, in the 1646 report that varied from the standard quota per tributary, either one peso and a half fanega of maize or the equivalent in money at the 1627–1631 commutation rate of 9 reales the fanega. The lowest quotas, and the greatest departures from the standard, involved Tlaxcala, Analco, and the two frontier towns. The province of Tlaxcala paid only one-half fanega of maize per tributary as a special royal favor for its services to Cortés and the Spaniards in the Conquest. Analco (Region V) paid only real servicio:

La prouinçia de çapotecas que cuyo sugeto es el pu[ebl]o de analco esta reseruado de la paga del tributo y deue por El Seruy[ci]o R[ea]l veynte y dos pessos y quatro tom[ine]s por quarenta y çinco tributarios.
(The province of Zapotecas, of which the town of Analco is a dependency, is exempt from tribute and owes for real servicio 22/4 for 45 tributaries.)

Since the other towns of the Zapotecas all paid tribute, this statement and arrangement are both puzzling. The exemption was probably a remnant of a once much wider one which through negligence or difficulty in bringing the town to pay had been allowed to continue.

The two frontier towns, Tancajual and Tanleón in the Huaxteca (Region II), paid respectively totals of 20/ and 15/ because they were on the Chichimec frontier. Those sums included whatever was given on account of real servicio as well.

Much of the variation revealed in Table 1.3 can be ascribed to small adjustments made as compensation for sterility or unusu-

ally favorable fertility of land. Thus a number of towns paid at
the rate of one peso per tributary without maize, or paid a
lower quota in money but more maize, the latter kind of
adjustment being particularly prominent in the Chalco district,
one of the granaries of Mexico City, where the local quota was
0/6 and one fanega of maize. The Indian suburbs of Mexico
City represent another kind of adjustment, since they paid only
1/0 on the ground that they were held to provide special
services in the city.[30] It is also true that they raised relatively
little maize. Still other towns with quotas ranging from 1/1 to
1/2 without maize probably represent towns that took early
advantage of the possibility of commuting commodity payment
to coin, that is, they did so when the commutation value of
maize was lower. In the instance of Tehuantepec (Region VI),
where the commutation of maize took place at different times
for two separate fractions of the town, commutation at different rates meant different quotas per tributary within the same
town. The heaviest impact of commutation upon tributary
quota came in Huapanapa (Region IV), where an original quota
of 0/2 and a pound of cochineal became 1/7/4 upon commutation of the cochineal. Tribute quotas calling for delivery of
wheat, still not commuted in 1646, were likely to follow a
similar course.[31]

30. See the assessment of Santiago Tlaltelolco, 7 September 1565, in Mexico,
AGN, *El libro de las tasaciones,* pp. 515–516.
31. Borah and Cook, *Price Trends,* p. 18.

TABLE 1.3

Towns with Tribute Quotas Departing from the Standard
REGION I

Town	Loc.	Assessment per t (less servicio real)	
Ajuchitlán	Gro.	1/0 + 10 alm m	
Amecameca	Mex.	0/6 + 1 fm	Chalco dis.
Atlatlahuacán	Mor.	1/0 + 2 p de huipil	
Atlatlahuca	Mex.	0/4 + 1 fm	
Atzala	Pue.	0/6	
Ayotzingo	Mex.	0/6 + 1 fm	Chalco dis.
Chiautla	Pue.	1/2	

TABLE 1.3, REGION I (Cont.)

Town	Loc.	Assessment per t (less servicio real)
Chimalhuacán	Mex.	0/6 + 1 fm - near Chalco dis.
Chinantla	Pue.	2,500 cacao beans
Cuautzotzongo	Mex.	0/6 + 1 fm Chalco dis.
Cuilucan	Pue.	0/1
Huatlatlauca	Pue.	1/2
Huayacocotla, Zontecomatlán[a]	Ver.	6 v cotton cloth
Tlachichilco, Ixcuincuitlapilco	Hid.	1/2
Ixmiquilpan[b]	Hid.	0/5/2¾ + 5 7/10 alm w
Ixtapan de la Sal	Mex.	1/0 + 1 pilón salt
Ixtepec	Pue.	0/2 + 1½ p de m
Ixtlahuaca	Mex.	0/6 + ½ fm
Jalatlaco	Mex.	0/1
Jilotepec de Abasolo[c]	Mex.	
Jonotla	Pue.	0/2 + 1 p de m (= 5 v)
Malila	Hid.	1¾ p de m (1 p de m = 4 1/3 or 4 3/8 v)
Mexicalcingo	D.F.	1/2
México, Parcialidad of San Juan	D.F.	1/0
Molango	Hid.	1¾ p de m (1 p de m = 4 1/3 or 4 3/8 v)
Puebla, Barrios of	Pue.	1/2
Tenango and Ayapango	Mex.	0/6 + 1 fm Chalco dis.
Teotenango[d]	Mex.	0/6 + 1 fm
Teotlalpa	Hid.	1¾ p de m
Tepeji de la Seda	Pue.	1/0
Tlalmanalco and Chalco Atengo	Mex.	0/6 + 1 fm Chalco dis.
Tlatelolco, Santiago	D.F.	1/0
Tlatzintla[e]	Hid.	0/6/8 1/5 + 2 5/8 alm w
Tlaxcala, province	Tlax.	½ fm
Tlayacapan	Mor.	1/0 + 2 p de huipil
Totolapa	Mor.	1/0 + 2 p de huipil
Xochiaca	Mex.	0/4 + 1 fm
Xochicuautla	Mor.	1¾ p de m (6¾ v)
Yahualica	Hid.	1 1/3 p de m
Zumpango	Gro.	0/6 + ½ fm

TABLE 1.3, REGION II

Town	Loc.	Assessment per t (less servicio real)	
Alcececa	Ver.	1/0	
Atlán	Ver.	2 p de m	
Chalchitlán	Ver.	1 p de m	
Huejutla	Hid.	3/4 p de m	
Maguayos	Ver.	1 fm	New
Mecatlán	Ver.	1 p de m	
Metateyuca	Ver.	1 p de m	
Nexpa	Hid.	0/6	
Tamohi (Tamuín)	SLP	0/6	
Tampamolón	SLP	0/6	
Tanboate	SLP	1 fm	frontier
Tancalicoche	SLP ?	1 fm	frontier
Tancajual^f	SLP		
Tanchinamol	Ver.	1 p de m (5 v)	
Tancuayalab	SLP	0/6	
Tancuiname	Ver.	1 fm	
Tanleón^f	SLP		
Tempoal	Ver.	0/6	
Tesontlal	Ver. ?	1 p de m (5 v)	
Tezapotitlán	Ver.	2 p de m	
Tlacolula de los Maguayos	Ver.	0/6	
Tlacuilola de Busto	Ver.	0/6	
Tlalchicuautla	Ver.	1 p de m	
Tlamintla en las Loxas	Ver.	0/6	
Zozocolco and Tonatico	Ver.	0/3 + 1 fm	

TABLE 1.3, REGION IIA

Actopan	Ver.	1/2
Almolonga	Ver.	1/0
Chicocentepec	Ver.	1/2
Chiconquiauco and Miahuatlán	Ver.	1/2
Chiltoyac	Ver.	1/0
Jalapa, province^g	Ver.	1/0 + 4 1/3 alm m
Papalote	Ver.	1/0
Tlacotepec, San Martín	Ver.	1/2

TABLE 1.3, REGION IIA (Cont.)

Town	Loc.	Assessment per t (less servicio real)
Tlateca	Ver.	1/2
Zempoala	Ver.	1/2

TABLE 1.3, REGION III

Acalapa	Ver.	1,600 cacao beans + ½ fm
Acayucan	Ver.	1,600 cacao beans + ½ fm
Agualulco	Tab.	1,600 cacao beans + ½ fm
Amatlán[h]	Ver.	0/2/7 + 7/8 p de m
Atecolotepeque	Oax. ?	0/6 + ½ fm
Atoco	Tab.	1,450 cacao beans
Ayautla	Oax.	0/1
Chicoacán	Tab.	1,600 cacao beans + 1 fm
Chiltepec	Oax.	0/6 + ½ fm
Cihuatlán[i]	Ver.	1,689 cacao beans + ½ fm
Chilapa	Ver.	1,600 cacao beans + ½ fm
Chinameca	Ver.	1,600 cacao beans + ½ fm
Cosamaloapan	Ver.	1/0
Cuitlatlán	Ver. ?	1,600 cacao beans + ½ fm
Goatzoyulapa (Guazuilapa)	Ver.	1,600 cacao beans + ½ fm
Huatzpaltepec	Oax.	1,000 cacao beans
Hueilutla	Ver.	1,375 cacao beans + ½ fm
Hueytlán	Ver.	1,600 cacao beans + ½ fm
Jotlapa	Ver.	1,600 cacao beans + ½ fm
Macayapa	Ver.	1,600 cacao beans + ½ fm
Mecatepec	Ver.	1,600 cacao beans + ½ fm
Miezapa, San Francisco	Ver.	1,600 cacao beans + ½ fm
Michoacán	Tab. ?	1,600 cacao beans + ½ fm
Minzapa, Santiago	Ver.	1,600 cacao beans + ½ fm
Moloacán	Ver.	1,600 cacao beans + ½ fm
Ocoapa	Ver.	1,600 cacao beans + ½ fm
Ojitlán	Oax.	1/2
Oteapa	Ver.	1,600 cacao beans + ½ fm
Ostotitlán	Tab.	1,600 cacao beans + ½ fm
Otiliacac	Tab.	1,600 cacao beans + ½ fm
Ozolotepec	Ver.	1,600 cacao beans + ½ fm

TABLE 1.3, REGION III (Cont.)

Town	Loc.	*Assessment per t (less servicio real)*
Puctla (Acula)	Ver.	3 p de nagua (4 p to 1 nagua) + 3/4 fm
Putlancingo	Oax.	1/2
Tapalan	Ver.	1,600 cacao beans + ½ fm
Tenango	Oax.	1/2
Tenantitlán	Ver.	1,600 cacao beans + ½ fm
Teotalco	Ver.	1,600 cacao beans + ½ fm
Teotalco	Ver.	1/2
Tepeapa	Oax.	1/2
Tequipac	Tab. ?	1,600 cacao beans + ½ fm
Tequistepec	Ver.	1,600 cacao beans + ½ fm
Teutalco	Tab. ?	1,600 cacao beans + ½ fm
Tuxtepec	Oax.	0/6 + ½ fm
Uliacán	Ver.	1,600 cacao beans + ½ fm
Zayultepec	Ver.	1,600 cacao beans + ½ fm

TABLE 1.3, REGION IV

Amatlán	Oax.	1/1
Amoltepec	Oax.	1/0
Coyotepec	Oax.	1/1
Cuautitlán	Oax.	1/2/2½
Elotepec	Oax.	1/1
Estetla	Oax.	1/1
Huajolotitlán (Peñoles)	Oax.	1/1
Huautla	Oax.	1/0
Huapanapa	Oax.	0/2 + 1 lb. cochineal,
Ixcuintepec	Oax.	1/1
Ixtepec	Oax.	1/2
Malinaltepec	Oax.	1/0 + ¼ fm
Mitlantongo, Stgo. and Sta. Cruz	Oax.	1/2
Suchitepec	Oax.	1/2
Tenatepec	Oax.	1/0
Tepeucila	Oax.	1/0
Tequecistepec	Oax.	1/2
Tequixtepec	Oax.	1/2

TABLE 1.3, REGION IV (Cont.)

Town	Loc.	Assessment per t (less servicio real)
Tilantongo	Oax.	1/2
Totomachapa	Oax.	0/6 + 1 fm
Tuchitlapilco	Oax.	1/1/8 4/5
Tutla	Oax.	1/2
Tututepetongo	Oax.	1/0
Zoyatepec	Oax.	1/0

TABLE 1.3, REGION V

Town	Loc.	Assessment per t (less servicio real)
Amaltepec	Oax.	5 v cotton cloth + ½ fm
Analco	Oax.	Only servicio real but RC
Ayacastepec	Oax.	5 v cotton cloth + ½ fm
Cacalotepec	Oax.	5 v cotton cloth + ½ fm
Camotlán	Oax.	5 v cotton cloth + ½ fm
Camotlán	Oax.	5 v cotton cloth + ½ fm
Chimaltepec	Oax.	5 v cotton cloth + ½ fm
Choapan	Oax.	5 v cotton cloth + ½ fm
Coatlán	Oax.	5 v cotton cloth + ½ fm
Comaltepec	Oax.	5 v cotton cloth + ½ fm
Huayatepec	Oax.	5 v cotton cloth + ½ fm
Huazcomaltepec	Oax.	5 v cotton cloth + ½ fm
Huitepec	Oax.	5 v ropa + ½ fm
Huixtepec	Oax.	0/6 + ½ fm
Ixcuintepec	Oax.	5 v cotton cloth + ½ fm
Jaltepec	Oax.	5 v cotton cloth + ½ fm
Lahoya	Oax.	5 v cotton cloth + ½ fm
Lalana	Oax.	5 v cotton cloth + ½ fm
Lalopa	Oax.	5 v cotton cloth + ½ fm
Lobani	Oax.	2½ v cotton cloth + ¼ fm
Macihuixi	Oax.	5 v cotton cloth + ½ fm
Malacatepec	Oax.	5 v cotton cloth + ½ fm
Malinaltepec	Oax.	5 v cotton cloth + ½ fm
Metepec	Oax.	5 v cotton cloth + ½ fm
Mixitlán	Oax.	5 v cotton cloth + ½ fm
Manacatepec	Oax.	5 v cotton cloth + ½ fm
Pazoltepec	Oax.	5 v cotton cloth + ½ fm

TABLE 1.3, REGION V (Cont.)

Town	Loc.	Assessment per t (less servicio real)
Petlalcatepec	Oax.	0/6 + ½ fm
Petlapa	Oax.	2½ v cotton cloth + ¼ fm
Quezalapa	Oax.	1/0 + 2 petates
Quiauecuça	Oax.	5 v cotton cloth + ½ fm
Quilacohe	Oax.	5 v cotton cloth + ½ fm
Suchitepec	Oax.	5 v cotton cloth + ½ fm
Tagui and Lazagaya	Oax.	5 v cotton cloth + ½ fm
Tagui	Oax.	5 v cotton cloth + ½ fm
Tava	Oax.	5 v cotton cloth + ½ fm
Teococuilco	Oax.	0/6
Teotalcingo	Oax.	5 v cotton cloth + ½ fm
Tepetotutla	Oax.	1 p de m
Teotlaxco	Oax.	5 v cotton cloth + ½ fm
Tetepetongo	Oax.	5 v cotton cloth + ½ fm
Tianguillo Achate	Oax.	5 v cotton cloth + ½ fm
Tiçatepec	Oax.	5 v cotton cloth + ½ fm
Tiltepec	Oax.	2½ v cotton cloth + ½ fm
Tlacatepec	Oax.	1/0
Tlacoatzintepec	Oax.	1/0 + 2 petates
Tonacayotepec (S. Bartolomé Yautepec)	Oax.	1/0
Tonaguía	Oax.	5 v cotton cloth + ½ fm
Totontepec	Oax.	5 v cotton cloth + ½ fm
Usila	Oax.	1/2
Xareta	Oax.	5 v cotton cloth + ½ fm
Xossa	Oax.	5 v cotton cloth + ½ fm
Yacoche	Oax.	5 v cotton cloth + ½ fm
Yagalaci	Oax.	5 v cotton cloth + ½ fm
Yagavila	Oax.	5 v cotton cloth + ½ fm
Yagayo	Oax.	5 v cotton cloth + ½ fm
Yatao	Oax.	5 v cotton cloth + ½ fm
Yatobe	Oax.	5 v cotton cloth + ½ fm
Yatzilan	Oax.	2½ v cotton cloth + ¼ fm
Yavago	Oax.	5 v cotton cloth + ½ fm
Yaxila	Oax.	5 v cotton cloth + ½ fm
Zapotequilla	Oax.	5 v cotton cloth + ½ fm

TABLE 1.3, REGION VI

Town	Loc.	Assessment per t (less servicio real)
Ayutla	Oax.	1/0
Huamelula	Oax.	1/0
Huatulco	Oax.	1/0
Jicayán	Oax.	970 cacao beans
Pinotepa (Nacional)[g]	Oax.	811 cacao beans
Pochutla	Oax.	1/0
Potutla	Oax.	1/0
Tecpa (Teipa)	Oax.	0/6
Tehuantepec[h]	Oax.	(1/3/6 (1/2
Tetepec	Oax.	0/6 + ½ fm
Tlacolula	Oax.	0/6
Totoltepec	Oax.	1/0
Xilotepequillo	Oax.	0/6
Yautepec	Oax.	1/0

TABLE 1.3, REGION VII

Town	Loc.	Assessment per t (less servicio real)
Acamalutla	Gro.	2,600 cacao beans
Acapulco	Gro.	2,800 cacao beans
Anacuilco	Gro.	1/2
Arimao	Mich.	1/2
Ayacapal	Gro.	2,600 cacao beans
Citlala	Gro.	2,600 cacao beans
Copalitas	Gro.	1/0
Coyuca (de Benítez)	Gro.	2,600 cacao beans
Coyucan, Huatlalutla, Coahualutla, Pustlan	Gro.	1 p de m + ½ fm
Cuitlatenamic	Gro.	1/2
Lacoaba	Mich.	1 p de m + ½ fm
Pochotitlán	Gro.	1,600 cacao beans
Pustlán	Gro.	1 p de m + ½ fm
Tixtlançingo and Sotlavista	Gro.	2,600 cacao beans
Xaltianguis	Gro.	2,600 cacao beans
Xocutla	Gro.	1,600 cacao beans
Zitlaltomagua	Gro.	1,600 cacao beans

TABLE 1.3, REGION VIII

Town	Loc.	Assessment per t (less servicio real)
Zinagua	Mich.	1/2

TABLE 1.3, REGION IX

Etzatlán	Jal.	0/6 + 1 fm
Jilotlán	Jal.	1 p de m + ½ fm

TABLE 1.3, REGION X

Acatlán	Col.	3 p de m + ½ fm [sic]
Ahuacatitlán	Col.	3 v cotton cloth + ½ fm
Aquila	Mich.	3 v cotton cloth + ½ fm
Atliacapan	Col.	3 v cotton cloth + ½ fm
Chiametla	Col.	3 v cotton cloth + ½ fm
Chiamila	Col.	3 v cotton cloth + ½ fm
Cinacamitlán	Col.	3 v cotton cloth + ½ fm
Coatlán	Col.	2 v cotton cloth + ½ fm
Cuzalapa	Jal.	1 p de m + ½ fm
Ixtlahuacán	Col.	2 v cotton cloth + ½ fm
Juluapan	Col.	0/6/1½ + ½ fm
Malacatlán	Col.	3 v cotton cloth + ½ fm
Maquili	Mich.	1,200 cacao beans + ½ fm
Motín	Mich.	3 v cotton cloth + ½ fm
Nahuala (Nagualapa)	Col.	3 v cotton cloth + ½ fm
Papatlán	Col.	3 v cotton cloth + ½ fm
Quezalapa	Col.	1 v cotton cloth + ½ fm [sic]
Salagua	Col.	3 v cotton cloth + ½ fm
Tecociapa	Col.	3 v cotton cloth + ½ fm
Tecolapa and Caxitlán	Col.	1,200 cacao beans + ½ fm
Tepetitango	Col.	3 v cotton cloth + ½ fm
Tepetlica	Col.	3 v. cotton cloth + ½ fm
Tlaquaban	Col.	3 v cotton cloth + ½ fm
Totolmoya	Col.	3 v cotton cloth + ½ fm
Tototlán	Col.	3 v cotton cloth + ½ fm
Xiloteupa	Col.	2 v cotton cloth + ½ fm
Zapotlanejo	Col.	2 v cotton cloth + ½ fm

TABLE 1.3, REGION X (Cont.)

Town	Loc.	Assessment per t (less servicio real)
Zoquimatlán	Col.	3 v cotton cloth + ½ fm
Zumpamanique	Col.	0/6 + ½ fm

NOTES TO TABLE 1.3

a Huayacocotla, etc.: The text and accompanying table of the list do not agree. The text states 10 cargas of mantas, 503 piernas, 2 varas (manta is 4 p of 5 v) for 719 1/2 t. That works out to 9.058 v per t. The table gives 4,317 v, which works out to exactly 6 v per t.

b Ixmiquilpan: 694 t pay 455/ o. c. and 330 f w. The quotas shown here are as close as one can come since the global figure does not work out to an exact quota per t, within usual units and fractions of units.

c Jilotepec de Abasolo: 1,456 t, divided between the Crown and an encomendero, yield the royal treasury 1,009/1/4 o. c., 420 f 3 alm m, and 728/ real servicio. The best explanation is that the encomendero had 615 1/2 t, and the rate of assessment was 0/7 + 1/2 f m. The fit in silver is slightly off.

d Teotenango: The quota in the report is 0/3 + 1/2 f m but this is actually the royal share since the town was half in the Crown and half in encomienda. Gerhard, p. 271.

e Tlatzintla: 74 1/2 t pay 62/6 + 16 f 3 alm w. The global figures do not work out to an exact quota per t in normal units and fractions.

f Tancajual and Tanleón: Tancajual pays a total of 20/; Tanleón, 15/. The list states that there are no formal assessments, for both are "*frontera de chichimecas.*"

g Jalapa, province: The total for the province works out to this average per t. On the other hand, statements for individual towns show a standard quota. Since the sum for the towns reported is less than the total for the province, the most likely explanation is a smaller quota of maize or none at all for one or more towns not reported individually but included in the total for the province.

h Amatlán: 54 t pay 17/3/4 o. c. + 17 mantas 2 p 1 1/3 v (4 p to 1 manta). These figures cannot be brought to an exact fit.

i Cihuatlán: 9 t pay 15,200 cacao beans + 4 1/2 f m. The fit for the cacao is not exact since 1 t pays 1,688.89 cacao beans.

j Pinotepa: 90 t pay 3 cargas 1,000 cacao beans (73,000). This works out to 811.11 cacao beans per t.

k Tehuantepec: 1,843 1/2 t pay 1/3/6; 274 1/2 t pay 1/2. The difference is in the rate of commutation of maize.

Abbreviations and symbols:

alm	almud
f	fanega
m	maize
o. c.	oro común
p	pierna
p de m	pierna de manta
t	tributary
v	vara
w	wheat

Inspection of Table 1.3 suggests that implementation of the standard quota was linked rather directly to altitude and its concomitant climate, that is, towns on the plateau were most likely to have been brought to or close to the proposed norm, whereas towns at lower elevations on the coasts or intermediate zone were more likely to be assessed in cotton cloth of various kinds, cotton clothing, and in cacao. Thus Regions III, V, VII, and X had both the highest proportion of variation from the standard quota as well as the highest proportion of quotas in cloth or cacao. Region V, the Zapotecas, was the most prominent in these respects. There tended to be variations in the quotas in cloth and cacao, largely by district and probably based upon quality, capacity to produce, and perhaps accessibility. In Region V the unusually inaccessible area of the Huatenicamanes had a tributary quota of 2½ varas of cloth and ¼ fanegas of maize, in general half that of the other towns of the region. Since a pierna of cotton cloth, that is, a strip woven on a backstrap loom, most often of 5 varas, was worth 9 reales under the commutation circular of 1631, many of the quotas in cloth came close to the value of the standard assessment.

Variations in quality alone probably will not explain differences in the quotas of cacao, although cacao did come in different grades. In Regions VI and VII, the range of variation in quota was from 2800 beans per tributary through 2600, 1600, and down to 970 and 811. The last, the quota for Pinotepa del Rey, now Pinotepa Nacional, is not exact, since the total tribute divided by the number of tributaries does not come to an exact number of cacao beans. The assessment must have been by global amount. At the standard sixteenth-century long-term wholesale price for cacao, 20/ the carga of 24,000 beans, a quota for 1600 beans had a money value of 1/3 in Mexico City.

Let us turn now to the yield to the royal treasury, and examine the curious mixture of theoretical amount and actual collection in the report of 1646. We have tabulated the sums and amounts given in the report in Tables 1.4A and 1.4B, adjusting the way amounts are listed to reflect somewhat more orderly categories than were customary in seventeenth-century fiscal accounts. One difficulty that there is no way of handling without detailed knowledge of the accounts lies in the reporting of some royal revenue by subtreasury, those of San Luis Potosí and Veracruz, with specification only of what taxes were not covered. Presumably all others for those districts are grouped under the global amounts, but probably the sums represent primarily one tax. Thus, the total for the subtreasury of Veracruz is largely or entirely almojarifazgo (customs revenue), and that for the subtreasury of San Luis Potosí the royal taxes on mined silver and other specie.

We have organized our presentation to show by column the gross revenue, the amount entering the general revenues of the Crown, and the amount earmarked for special application. The important special applications were the diversion of money and maize from tributes for the stipends of doctrineros and the application of new taxes and parts of old to maintain the *Armada de Barlovento,* a permanent fleet created to deal with the menace of corsairs, pirates, and foreign forces in the Caribbean. The last columns in the table are there because of the fortunate circumstance that when Fonseca and Urrutia prepared a history of the royal treasury for Viceroy Revillagigedo II in 1790-91, they attempted to calculate the average yield of many taxes in the past from the records in the viceregal treasury. In each case they calculated decennial collections and the average for the ten-year period, their decades coinciding with the standard ones of the calendar. Accordingly, we have a means of verifying for some of the revenues the actual average annual collections, as far as Fonseca and Urrutia were able to locate records.

Indian tributes, because of the more intricate nature of the sums and items entering the *ramo,* are further analyzed in Table 1.4B. The clerks who prepared the report of 1646 counted 160,948 ½ t, and listed a total yield in coin of 190,522/4/6. In that sum were the payments in coin for the ordinary tribute, the amounts realized from maize and items commuted to coin, and the real servicio. We should note further that already deducted from the maize before calculating its money value at the standard commutation rate were the tithe, a proper charge before calculating treasury yield, and the stipend in maize delivered to the doctrineros, some 9,737 fanegas 10 almudes, worth 10,954/7/8. The clerks did not convert to money value nor estimate the yield in coin of the very substantial quantities of cloth received as tribute nor such relatively minor items as clothing, cacao, wheat, and salt. Their explanation was that

TABLE 1.4A

Royal Revenues in the Audiencia of Mexico, 1646 (in silver pesos)

Tax or Royal Monopoly	Total	Royal Share	Special Application		Fonseca & Urrutia Calculation	Reference
Alcabala (Sales Tax) 6%						
Mexico City - farm to city to end of 1646	254,800	194,800	60,000	Armada de Barlovento		
Puebla - farm to city to end of 1646; includes Amozoc	53,300	39,150	14,150	Armada de Barlovento		
Veracruz - farm	21,500	14,333/2/8	7,166/5/4	Armada de Barlovento		
San Luis Potosí - farm	8,500	5,666/5/4	2,833/2/8	Armada de Barlovento		
Carrión, Valley of Atlixco, Tuchimilco - farm	7,700	5,133/2/8	2,566/5/4	Armada de Barlovento		
Jacona and Zamora - farm	270	180	90	Armada de Barlovento		
Remainder of Audiencia collected by alcaldes mayores	ca. 60,000	40,000	20,000	Armada de Barlovento		
Subtotal	406,070	299,263/2/8	106,806/5/4	Armada de Barlovento	266,039	2:93
Zacatecas[a] (19-20,000)	[19,500]	19,500]				
Guadalajara[a]	[4,800]	4,800]				
Total Alcabala	[430,370	323,563/2/8]				

118

TABLE 1.4A (Cont.)

Tax or Royal Monopoly	Total	Royal Share	Special Application	Fonseca & Urrutia Calculation	Reference
Salt Deposits of Peñol Blanco (28,000 f sold at 0/4)	14,000		14,000 Armada de Barlovento		
Playing Cards - farm[b]	88,400	88,400			
Gunpowder - farm[c]	12,200	12,200			
Censos in favor of the Royal Treasury	1,400		1,400 Repair of *Casas Reales*		
Pension paid by alguacil mayor of Mexico City	1,102/7/6		1,102/7/6 Desagüe and Armada		
Indian Tributes[d]	190,522/4/6	170,301/4/2	20,221/0/4 Missionary Stipends	269,224	1:450
Tributes of Free Negroes and Mulattoes	2,600	2,600			
Customs (Almojarifazgo) and Quinto on Silver - Caja de México	85,000	85,000			
Taxes on Gold	1,000	1,000			
Seigniorage	44,000	44,000			
Bulls of the Crusade	150,000	150,000			
Rental of the *Casas Reales*	740	740			

TABLE 1.4A (Cont.)

Tax or Royal Monopoly	Total	Royal Share	Special Application	Fonseca & Urrutia Calculation	Reference
Mesadas	1,300	1,300			
Royal *Dos Novenos* of Tithes	31,000	31,000			
Monopoly of *Solimán* (Mercury Chloride)	1,100	1,100			
Monopoly of Alum	600	600			
Tithes of Pánuco	4,000	4,000			
Customs and Taxes on Freights and Avería of Ships in Philippine Trade	60,000	60,000			
Customs of Huatulco	600	600			
Media Anata	60,000	60,000			
Monopoly of Mercury[e]	120,000	120,000		70,258	2:512
Tax of 25/ per Pipe of Wine	85,000		85,000 Armada de Barlovento		
Caja of Veracruz, less Alcabala and 25/ per Pipe of Wine	89,000	89,000			

TABLE 1.4A (Cont.)

Tax or Royal Monopoly	Total	Royal Share	Special Application	Fonseca & Urrutia Calculation	Reference
Caja of San Luis Potosí, less Alcabala	120,000	120,000			
Subtotal	1,569,635/4	1,341,104/6/10	228,530/5/2		
Yield of Indian Tribute in Commodities	85,837/6	85,837/6			
Total	1,655,473/2	1,426,942/4/10			

121

TABLE 1.4B

Indian Tributes

	Indian Tribute Products	Rate of Commutation	Money
160,948 1/2 t paid:			
Basic tribute in coin			79,120/2/7
Real Servicio			80,474/2
Maize^f	41,108:5 1/4 f	0/9 f	30,667/1/9
Cotton Cloth^g	917 car. 1 p 1-1/2 v	?	
Huipiles^h	1,003	?	
Naguas^i	51	?	
Cacao^j	81 car. 11,125 beans	?	
Wheat^j	346:3 f	?	
Petates	507	0/1	63/3
Salt^j	85 pilones	?	
Cohineal - yield			197/3/2
Total yield in money			190,522/4/6

Possible Yield of Commodities on Auction

Cloth		0/9 p	82,531/2/8
Huipiles		0/6 ea	752/2
Naguas		0/6 ea	38/2
Cacao		20/ car	1,629/2/4
Wheat		2/4 f	865/5
Salt		0/2 pilón	21/2
Total additional yield			85,837/6

NOTES TO TABLE 1.4

^{a} In the Audiencia of Guadalajara, but administered by the viceroy. Since the list indicates no distribution or earmarking of part of this revenue for the Armada de Barlovento, the table carries the whole as going to the Crown without special application. However, it is almost certain that some part of the receipts went to the Armada de Barlovento, probably the third of outlying districts rather than the smaller fraction from Mexico City and Puebla.

^{b} Monopoly was rented for 90,000/ but the tax farmer got 1,600/ a year.

^{c} The monopoly was rented for 200 quintales of gunpowder and 3,000/. At 0/4 a pound the gunpowder brought 10,000/, which, with the money payment by the tax farmer, should be 13,000/, but the contract specified a net yield to the Crown of 12,200/.

^{d} See *Part B*.

NOTES TO TABLE 1.4 (Cont.)

e No real yield to the Crown since as much was spent on this as the amount
collected.

f Maize:

Total tribute		41,108:5 1/4 f
Tithe	4,110:10 1/4 f	
Allowance to parish priests according to moderation by Gelves	9,737:10 f	13,848:8 1/4 f
Net maize of Crown		27,259:9 f
At commutation of 0/9 f		30,667/1/9

g Each carga was 20 mantas of 4 p of 5 v each, or 400 varas to the carga.
Since there was as yet, according to the report, no commutation for
these items, they were sold at auction. Prices varied greatly since
quality varied widely. So the report cites merely the commodity. However, Fonseca and Urrutia (I,422) cite a circular of 1631 setting commutation at 0/9 the pierna.

h Each huipil is stated to have been 3 p even though at least one of the
tribute schedules called for huipiles of 4 p. These were also sold at
auction and reported in kind for the reasons set forth above.

i No statement of number of piernas; probably as in note h.

j Reported as a commodity with no indication of yield in money on auction.

these items were sold at public auction and varied so much in
quality and in the prices bid from year to year that no exact
figure could be given. Nevertheless, if we are to glean some idea
of the state of the royal revenues, we must arrive at an idea of
approximate value. So little is still known about prices in
seventeenth-century Mexico that we are forced to guesses. We
have used the standard conversion rate of 0/9 the pierna of
cotton cloth set by treasury circular in 1631 as the best rate for
the cloth. For clothing we have used 0/6 per item, on the
theory that quotas per tributary attempted to come close to a
standard of 1/2 or 1/2/6. Cacao we have valued at the later
sixteenth-century long-term legal maximum of 20/ the carga of
24,000 beans. Wheat we have valued at 2/4 the fanega, on the
basis of the trend line in our previous calculation of movement
of tribute commodity prices.[32] That would mean a ratio of
20:9 between wheat and maize, so that we are probably low.
Lastly, salt has been valued at 0/2 the cone on the same theory
as clothing. On the basis of these estimates, the tribute commodities listed without calculation of yield in coin would have

32. Ibid.

been worth approximately 85,837/6, a considerable addition to the other tribute and the servicio real together. Since Fonseca and Urrutia found that collections in these years averaged 269,224/ annually for tributes of all kinds, our estimate may be near the mark.

The factors that have to be taken into account in examining yield from tributes are somewhat intricate: (1) The report of 1646 lists the tribute assessments, on which its calculations are based. (2) The proportion of omission in the report should be applied to arrive at the actual value of total assessments of Indian tribute at the time; that is, the totals of the report should be increased by perhaps a third. (3) The report does not take into account the substantial amount of arrears in payment of tribute. The statement in Fonseca and Urrutia relates to actual collections. Failure to pay in full was especially prominent in this period and may have led to global arrearages of nearly a third. Accordingly, it is possible to find a rough agreement among all of this testimony and calculation.

Fonseca and Urrutia included in their estimate of yield for tributes those of free people of color, the *negros y mulatos libres*. For this item the report of 1646 gives an estimate based on actual collections, 2600/. The yearly quota for this group of tributaries was set by Viceroy Enríquez in 1579, when the levy was instituted, at 2/ a married couple and 1/ for each unmarried or widowed adult male or female, effectively a quota of 1/ a year per adult.[33] In 1646 the population of color in the Audiencia of Mexico must have comprised approximately 50,000 persons.[34] We have no means of determining at this time the proportion of slaves, but it cannot have been much more than half. Of the free people of color, less than half at maximum would have been exempt from tribute as too young or too old. So there would be left at a minimum perhaps 12,500 adults subject to a quota of 1/ a year. The royal treasury collected from approximately a fifth of these. Two factors were operating: a proportion of exemption for militia service on the coasts, even at this early date, and, most important of all, very substantial evasion. In the degree of evasion from tribute, the Audiencia of Mexico shared the experience of other jurisdic-

33. Fonseca and Urrutia, I, p. 418.
34. See Cook and Borah, *Essays*, II, chap. 2, esp. table 2.1b.

tions as fiscal agents attempted to enforce collection upon the free people of color.[35]

Simple inspection of Table 1.4A indicates that the tax yielding the most revenue was the alcabala. The estimate in the report is based upon actual yield, since most·of the tax was leased to cities. Within the district of the Caja de México, the ordinary alcabala yielded 299,263/ and the extraordinary levy for the Armada de Barlovento another 106,806/. The calculations by Fonseca and Urrutia of average yield in the 1640's, probably to be equated with the ordinary tax, come only to 266,039/, a discrepancy of about 11%. The next largest yields were those of the taxes on silver and customs (almojarifazgo), which in the report of 1646 are somewhat difficult to disentangle since for the collections directly in the Caja de México the two items are lumped as a single amount and the subcajas are listed as to total yield without a breakdown. The total of the two sets of taxes comes to 399,600/. If we allocate all of the yield of San Luis Potosí to imposts on mining, all of that of Veracruz to customs, and divide the mixed item for the Caja de México equally, taxes on mining would come to perhaps 207,500/ and customs to 192,100/. The yield of both fell below that of tributes from Indians and pardos. Fifth in order of yield came the Bulls of the Crusade, which theoretically were worth 150,000/ a year to the royal treasury. The remaining items each fell below 100,000/ annually, ranging from the 88,400/ a year theoretically due from the monopoly of playing cards, farmed out to a private holder, to the small sums derived from rental of the royal houses in Mexico City (actually the rental of the ground floor for shops) and the royal monopolies of mercury chloride (*solimán*) and alum. The royal monopoly of mercury, carried in the report as worth 120,000/, involved an equal amount of expenditure for the royal treasury, since the Crown had to buy the mercury, transport it to Mexico, and then to the mines.

A substantial part of the royal revenue was specifically earmarked for the Armada de Barlovento, which constituted the overwhelming destination of earmarked revenue.[36] An addi-

35. Cook and Borah, *Essays*, I, pp. 33–34; Borah, "Los tributos y su recaudación," p. 39.

36. On the armada, see Fonseca and Urrutia, II, pp. 12–16 and 304–305; Palafox y Mendoza, Instrucción reservada, Bancroft Library, Mexican MS 162, ff. 16v–22v.

tional quota of 2%, added to the standard sales tax, and an additional impost of 25/ on each pipe of wine landed at Veracruz, yielded a theoretical 205,806/5/4 for the fleet plus its share of any surplus in the pension paid by the alguacil mayor of Mexico City that was not absorbed by the drainage of the Valley of Mexico.

The actual facts of collection and yield were somewhat different from the estimates in the report of 1646. The Fonseca and Urrutia calculations indicate that the collection of the ordinary alcabala ran perhaps 11% below the theoretical yield, although we cannot tell exactly where the discrepancy lay; tributes including yield from auctions were in reasonable agreement as to yield if one allows for arrears; and the yield of the third tax for which Fonseca and Urrutia give a calculation, the media anata (half of the first year's income of a new appointment), came to more than the estimate in the report of 1646. The worst discrepancies show up through the *relación de mando* prepared by Palafox. According to that report, the revenues earmarked for the Armada de Barlovento fell far short of raising the funds needed to maintain the fleet. When the armada was established, it had been estimated that an additional 2% of alcabala and 2 reales per pack of playing cards would raise 200,000/. The province of Yucatán was to contribute 40,000/ a year through a new levy of a *tostón* or half-peso per tributary, and the Audiencia of Guatemala was to raise 40,000/. The rise in alcabala indeed provided the sum envisaged, but it had never been possible to persuade the concessionnaire of the royal monopoly on playing cards to accept the new burden, and he was 500,000/ behind on the existing contract. The tax of a tostón in Yucatán had had to be abandoned; the Audiencia of Guatemala was able to contribute only 12,000/. At the time Palafox prepared his *relación de mando,* the sum of 200,000/ was urgently needed for the Armada de Barlovento merely to keep it in operation.[37]

Palafox reported great arrears and negligence everywhere in the collection and administration of the royal revenues. The administration of the Bulls of the Holy Crusade was 300,000/ behind; the miners of Zacatecas, which lay outside the district

37. Palafox y Mendoza, ff. 16v–22v.

of the Caja de México, owed the royal treasury 600,000/, probably a mixture of arrears of payments for mercury and slowness in paying the tax on mined silver.[38] So the royal treasury in its sales of mercury was actually advancing credit to the miners through deliveries of mercury which the Crown had paid for. We know from other sources that the assessment and collection of Indian tributes was under an especially negligent and corrupt administration.

It is true that some ramos undoubtedly existing in the royal treasury at that time are not included in the report of 1646. A major one, stamped paper, recently instituted, was expressly excluded because it had not been in existence for three full years preceding the preparation of the report. *Quitas y Nuevas Leyes,* essentially the yield of encomiendas forfeit under the New Laws, was earmarked for the support of descendants of conquerors. It yielded small sums that may have been subsumed under tribute yield in the report of 1646. *Penas de Cámara y Gastos de Justicia,* the yield of fines and assessments for costs, probably had no surplus after charges, for from it were paid many costs of the courts and special grants. There should have been yield from other ramos such as *Oficios Vendibles y Renunciables,* the sale and transfer of office; licenses for slaughter of cattle and other livestock; goods confiscated as contraband; and the fees for *Ventas, Composiciones y Confirmaciones de Tierras y Aguas,* that is, the sums paid the Crown for grants of land and water or for issuing clear title to land and water in cases of clouded title or none at all. In addition, there were the payments for *composiciones* of all other kinds, the payments to the Crown for overlooking irregularities in status or violation of ordinances and laws. So there was royal revenue of varying but probably not substantial amounts that does not show up in the report of 1646.[39]

Nevertheless, there can be no doubt of the basic truth of Palafox's judgment. It may well be that the yield of the royal revenues did not meet the costs of royal government. Even less did it provide a surplus to be sent to Spain for a Crown perennially short of revenue and embroiled in the quagmire of

38. *Ibid.,* ff. 40f–44f.

39. These are ramos antedating 1646 but not listed in the report of 1646. See Fonseca and Urrutia, I–VI, *passim.*

European wars. It was not until the administration of Mancera
(1664–1673) that a steady deficit in the treasury of the Audiencia of Mexico was brought to surplus.[40] The fiscal confusion of
the mid-seventeenth century was so bad that there was substantial reform and overhaul in advance of the far-reaching changes
of the eighteenth century.

40. "Instrucción que de órden del Rey dió el virey de Méjico (D. Antonio
Sebastian de Toledo, marqués de Mancéra) á su sucesor (el Excmo. Señor D. Pedro
Nuño Colón, duque de Veraguas), 22 October 1673," in *Colección de documentos
inéditos para la historia de España*, XXI, pp. 523–552.

Chapter II

Indian Food Production and Consumption in Central Mexico Before and After the Conquest (1500-1650)

1.

That the Spanish conquest of central Mexico meant sweeping and cataclysmic change for the natives has been self-evident for centuries. That such sweeping change occurred in native production of food and in diet during the first century and a quarter after the Conquest is far from self-evident. In the 1930's and early 1940's the topic of food production and consumption before and after the Conquest attracted a good deal of attention, perhaps the most distinguished study forming part of the long series of inquiries on the Valley of El Mezquital by Miguel Othón de Mendizábal, published posthumously in 1947.[1] Since the Second World War the topic has attracted relatively less attention, as inquiry has tended to focus upon current food production and levels of nutrition. The many community studies usually contain inquiries of this kind. This change in emphasis in part undoubtedly reflected the growing concentration of the government and of anthropologists within and without the country upon contemporary problems and upon improvement in existing standards of living. In part, however, it also may have reflected an opinion that in terms of materials

1. Miguel Othón de Mendizábal, "Evolución económica y social del valle del Mezquital," in *Obras completas*, VI, pp. 7–195. See also Nathaniel Whetten, *Rural Mexico*, pp. 304–316.

and the knowledge available, inquiry into food production and diet immediately before and after the Conquest had approached a limit in yield of further insight.

Yet since the 1930's considerably more historical sources have become available, and new understanding from scientific inquiry has continued to accumulate. Mendizábal had available the greater part of the Relaciones Geográficas known to be extant, as well as a considerable body of other materials. Since his death many of the remaining extant Relaciones Geográficas have been published, and access to those in manuscript has become much easier through use of microfilm.[2] Perhaps more important, a very substantial body of new material has come to light in the tribute assessments of Indian towns, and continuing inquiry has taught us much more about the nature and meaning of the sources.[3] We have also learned a great deal more about changes in land use in central Mexico.[4] At the same time that the body of historical material available to us has increased, our general knowledge of human nutritional needs has also expanded, especially as regards situations of undernourishment and actual famine. The first scientific study of the effects of famine was a product of the First World War and its aftermath. The Second World War stimulated inquiries that have vastly extended that initial study.[5] In addition, historical inquiries on food production and nutrition in other areas during past epochs have continued to contribute new information that, fragmentary though it remains, nevertheless begins to permit us a basis for comparative judgment.[6] Accordingly we now may inquire,

2. For a bibliography of published and manuscript Relaciones Geográficas, see the essays by Howard F. Cline, "A Census of the Relaciones Geográficas of New Spain, 1579–1612" and "The Relaciones Geográficas of Spain, New Spain, and the Spanish Indies: An Annotated Bibliography," in *HMAI*, XII, pp. 324–369 and 370–395.

3. Here perhaps the key publications have been Mexico, AGN, *El libro de las tasaciones de pueblos de la Nueva España, Siglo XVI*, and José Miranda, *El tributo indígena en la Nueva España durante el siglo XVI*. See also the discussion in Cook and Borah, *Essays*, I, chap. 1.

4. Perhaps most notably Lesley Byrd Simpson, *Exploitation of Land in Central Mexico in the Sixteenth Century*, but also two of the studies of Sherburne F. Cook, *The Historical Demography and Ecology of the Teotlalpan* and *Soil Erosion and Population in Central Mexico*. Charles Gibson's *The Aztecs Under Spanish Rule* has brought to light and systematized a vast amount of information about the Valley of Mexico.

5. See the discussion later in this chapter.

6. Among the more notable of such studies are Nicolas Sanchez-Albornoz,

with the hope of gaining new insight, into questions deemed largely exhausted.

At the outset we require certain definitions and understandings of limitation. Food production obviously includes agriculture, but also all other activity that brings materials for human ingestion to availability through gathering, hunting, and fishing. Even warfare must be considered if the contending groups either eat each other, whatever the formal justification, or redistribute the results of each other's efforts at amassing foodstuffs. Similarly, one must take into account the distributive mechanisms inherent in political, social, religious, and economic structures that move foodstuffs, without warfare although frequently the result of previous warfare, from one stratum in the population to another or from one region to another. Tribute may loom large here. Consumption we must equate with nutrition, that is, the measurement of adequacy and kinds of intake in per capita terms. The best measure is probably in the kilocalories of physiologists, equal to the Calories of nutritionists, and in the further assessment of adequacy of intake of proteins, fats, carbohydrates, vitamins, amino acids, trace elements, and so on. In short, we must look at total intake in terms of adequacy of caloric intake, and further in terms of adequacy of elements necessary to sustain life and labor.

The century and a half covered by this study was a period of cataclysmic change in the religious, social, political, and economic life of central Mexico. We shall therefore examine patterns of food production and consumption as they existed just before the coming of the Europeans brought far more rapid and fundamental elements of change than were previously in operation. We shall also compare those patterns with what the opera-

---

Gastos y alimentación de un ejército en el siglo XVI según un presupuesto de la época, and the long series of studies published in *Annales: Economies, sociétés, civilisations,* frequently under the heading "Vie matérielle et comportements biologiques." See, for example, the articles in the bibliography by Frank Spooner, Frederick C. Lane, Jean-Jacques Hémardinquer, Michel Morineau, J.-P. Filippini, and B. Bennassar and J. Goy, eds. See also José Gentil Da Silva, *Desarrollo ecónomico, subsistencia y decadencia en España,* pp. 17⁻63; and Fernand Braudel, *Civilisation matérielle et capitalisme (XVᵉ–XVIIIᵉ siecles),* esp. pp. 97 *et seq.* Most of these studies are based on the records of formal provision for soldiers, sailors, people in charitable institutions, and wealthy families. The mass of the population, and especially the lower levels, had far less available. Braudel suggests 2,000 kilocalories a day as a fair estimate for the mass of the European population.

tion of those elements of change wrought in the decades down to the middle of the seventeenth century.

Our area, central Mexico, unfortunately must be treated as a whole. It is approximately 514,000 square kilometers (about the size of Spain or of California), comprising regions of widely different topography and climate as well as peoples of considerable differences in technology and culture. The Spanish Conquest destroyed or reorganized many of the native states but did not erase the differences, which have since lessened under the erosion of time and operation of new cultural influences, but in many instances are still perceptible. Ideally, treatment should be by discrete regions, but with the possible exceptions of the Valley of Mexico and that of El Mezquital, we still do not have enough information for such treatment. Yet, thanks to the efforts of scholars, we have considerably more than we did three or four decades ago. Our essay, therefore, as all essays on this topic must be at this time, is an assessment of highly tentative nature.

2.

On the eve of the Conquest, central Mexico had a very large population. We have estimated it at 25,000,000, the midpoint of a range of from 18,000,000 to 30,000,000. The rural population was probably denser at that time than in any period since. Even today, when the total of population stands higher and is rising, a far greater proportion of it is concentrated in large cities. We have further estimated the average density of aboriginal population at 49 persons to the square kilometer, or 125 to the square mile.[7]

The agriculture upon which this population depended for its existence rested technologically upon the digging stick in its various forms as the basic instrument for cultivation. This implement made possible exploitation of land and slopes that could not be cultivated with the European plow introduced in the sixteenth century, and even less with present-day machinery. The basic systems of cultivation were various. On the coasts and intermediate slopes, the Indians cleared land by

7. See Borah and Cook, *The Aboriginal Population of Central Mexico on the Eve of the Spanish Conquest*, pp. 88–90; Mexico, Dirección General de Estadística, *Anuario estadístico de los Estados Unidos Mexicanos, 1970–1971*, p. 30, table 2.3.

felling or girdling and then burning off bush or forest, planted crops (usually two a year) for a period of two to five years, and let the land revert to wild growth in order to recover its fertility and eliminate weeds. Angel Palerm calls this the system of *roza*, but it is as frequently known as the slash-burn or swidden technique. It corresponds to Ester Boserup's forest fallow, with its practice of relatively long periods between cultivation. At higher altitudes or in dryer areas, where woody growth develops more slowly and the natural growth could not recover rapidly on land left fallow, a similar system of milpa is called *barbecho* by Palerm. The intervals of fallow are markedly shorter; the land tends to be cropped only once a year, except in unusually favorable conditions. This type of land use corresponds clearly to Ester Boserup's bush fallow. Although the systems of roza and barbecho appear to be almost alike, the difference in climate dictates very different conditions and the intervals of fallow are markedly different. The barbecho system permits a denser occupation of land.[8]

What in Boserup's conceptions would be called permanent cultivation—that is, without long periods of reversion to natural growth—was also practiced by the Indians of central Mexico in a variety of forms. Where soil and climate favored the practice, the land was cropped annually or more often on the basis of rain and retained moisture. Land of considerable slope might be terraced to improve conservation of soil and moisture and yield. Perhaps the most notable instance of extensive terracing was in the area around Chalco, famous as a pre-Conquest producer of maize. An even more favorable development appeared where there was a supply of water available by conduction through canal or channel, or by raising it from wells or lakes. The Indians used the water for irrigation to insure steady yield, and in the lower-lying areas especially, two crops or even more a year. A special variant was and is the *chinampa*, often described

8. A good description may be found in Gordon R. Willey, Gordon F. Ekholm, and René F. Millon, "The Patterns of Farming Life and Civilization," in *HMAI*, I, pp. 446–498; and in Angel Palerm, "Agricultural Systems and Food Patterns," in *HMAI*, VI, pp. 26–52—which, although a description of present-day practice, is easily adjusted to pre-Conquest times. See also Palerm's essay, "La base agrícola de la civilisación urbana prehispánica en Mesoamérica," in Angel Palerm and Eric Wolf, *Agricultura y civilización en Mesoamerica*, pp. 65–108; and Ester Boserup, *The Conditions of Agricultural Growth: The Economics of Agrarian Change Under Population Pressure, passim*.

as a floating garden but actually a manmade plot of brush and mud in a marshy area or shallow part of a lake, that can be watered from the lake or marsh and is capable of steady, prolific yield. The chinampa is really a further development of a widespread Indian practice of raising mounds or ridged fields for cultivation in marshy soil or on lands subject to flooding. Wherever found, their presence indicates pressure of population upon the supply of cultivable land.[9] As yet there has been little inquiry to detect the possible presence of the more widespread form of raised mounds or ridged fields in central Mexico.

In general, land on the plateau yielded one crop a year, the yield varying with fertility of soil and rainfall or irrigation, whereas land at the lower altitudes more normally yielded two crops. Irrigation and the chinampas made possible multiple crops, the chinampas coming close to the garden cultivation of the Mediterranean or the Far East. In the Valley of Mexico the chinampas benefited from a remarkable system of control of water that is only now being studied with any care. Its functions were to control water levels and to prevent the saline waters of Lake Texcoco from contaminating other lakes and the chinampas in them.[10]

The crops that were raised under these varying systems[11] were maize, regarded as the staple, an unusually productive crop, more so than wheat; beans, perhaps best described as *frijoles* to avoid the ambiguities in the English term; squash; chiles of many kinds; chía; and huautli. These last two were often gathered from plants growing wild rather than cultivated. Huautli is thought by Eusebio Dávalos Hurtado and Jonathan Sauer to have been utilized especially for ritual purposes. In addition, the more arid areas supported stands of cactus (*no-*

9. See references in note 8; additionally, Kent V. Flannery et al., "Farming Systems and Political Growth in Ancient Oaxaca"; Robert C. West and Pedro Armillas, "Las chinampas de México: Poesía y realidad de los 'Jardines Flotantes' "; and Armillas, "Gardens on Swamps."

10. Palerm, references given in note 8 plus *Obras hidráulicas prehispánicas en el sistema lacustre del valle de México, passim.*

11. The following paragraphs are based upon: Eusebio Dávalos Hurtado, "La alimentación entre los mexicas"; Enrique Beltrán, "Plantas usadas en la alimentación por los antiguos mexicanos"; the answers in the Relaciones Geográficas 1577–1585, published and manuscript; Bernardino de Sahagún, *Historia general de las cosas de Nueva España, passim,* but esp. II, pp. 65–70, 134–159, and 317–492; Francisco Hernández, *Historia natural de Nueva España, passim;* and Jonathan D. Sauer, "The "The Grain Amaranths," pp. 564–582.

pal), which yielded cactus apples (*tunas*), and stands of agave (*maguey*), again a versatile plant from which the Indians extracted juice for pulque and used the blades and heart for food. Use of wild stands shaded into cultivation for both nopal and maguey, the latter perhaps being more often cultivated. It was also an important source of fiber, used widely in the uplands for clothing as well as other purposes, but always inferior to the lowland cotton. There were root crops, but they were of lesser significance. The sweet potatoe (*camote*), raised in the lowlands, was perhaps the most important. For central Mexico as a whole, Spanish reporting emphasized that the staple was maize, which was ground to dough for tortillas, to mush for tamales or atole, or was eaten in a wide variety of ways.

These products of field cultivation were supplemented by a wide variety of fruits and vegetables, some deliberately planted, some growing wild. The lists and references in the Relaciones Geográficas, in Sahagún, in Francisco Hernández, and in the accounts of many other writers, are long and embrace almost every edible fruit and plant, with the exception in most regions of the acorn.

The pre-Conquest Indians of central Mexico secured food of animal origin more from wild than domesticated animals. Honey they obtained from the stingless American bee; meat from Muscovy ducks, dogs raised and fattened for food, and turkeys.[12] The list of domesticated animals is short, but the large expanses of water, forest, bush, and fallow land supported game and fish, as well as offering wild fruits and plants. Thus the products of agriculture could be supplemented by extensive hunting, fishing, and gathering. This pursuit, which was carried on at a very sophisticated level, yielded mammals, birds, fish, reptiles, amphibians, crustaceans, insects, worms—in fact anything that could be eaten, to the disgust of Spaniards. As Francisco López de Gómara commented, "they eat any living thing, even their own lice. . . ."[13]

12. There has been much doubt that the Mesoamerican Indians really had domesticated the turkey, but the declaration of the city council of Veracruz in its letter to Charles V, 10 July 1519, should be conclusive: " . . . y crían muchas gallinas como las de Tierra Firme, que son tan grandes como pavos." (Hernán Cortes, *Cartas y documentos*, p. 23.) See also M. de Cárcer Disdier, "Los pavos."

13. Francisco López de Gómara, *Historia general de las Indias*, II, p. 400. See also the description of the foods offered in the marketplace of Tenochtitlán-Tlatelolco, *ibid.*, pp. 147–148.

Two sources of food have always been the cause of considerable comment. One was derived from the lakes in the Valley of
Mexico, in which there was a strong development of algae. The
Indians gathered these plants by scraping the scum off the rocks
or collecting it from the water in nets, dried it and compressed
it into cakes, which became an article of trade and food.
However unappetizing and even revolting to Europeans, the
blue-green cells furnished an excellent source of vitamins and
carbohydrates. A similar use of algae is now being suggested as
one solution to the increasing need for food, as the human
population of the earth presses more severely upon known
sources of nutrition. We should note that algae or "bloom"
appear in lakes which are polluted by fertilizer and sewage, that
is, by unusually large supplies of nitrates and phosphates. If the
lakes, and especially Lake Texcoco, received heavy amounts of
raw sewage from Tenochtitlán and other urban aggregations,
one would expect the very heavy growth of algae, that in fact
occurred. The Indians, with their skill in using any possible
source of food, then ate the algae. The incidence of intestinal
diseases from the polluted lakes must have been enormous.[14]

The other source of food was cannibalism, an activity ritual
or otherwise which has been much debated. From a strictly
dietary point of view, it is undoubtedly true that for most of
the population the ceremonial portions consumed of the sacrifi-
cial victims were so small that their addition to the annual food
intake was completely negligible. On the other hand, for the
upper classes, who benefited most from this type of nutrition,
the addition of human flesh to an otherwise low-meat diet may
have been of consequence. Indignant denials by some apologists
are meaningless, because a nutritional craving is not necessarily
apparent to the consciousness and could easily be masked by a
highly developed ceremonial motivation.

The one potential source of food which seems to have been
underutilized is the acorn, a surprising item in the long list of

14. Hernández, *Historia natural*, II, pp. 408–409; Gibson, *The Aztecs Under
Spanish Rule*, p. 141; Sahagún, II, p. 372; Toribio de B. Motolinía, *Memoriales*, pp.
327–328; Bernal Díaz del Castillo, *Historia Verdadera de la Conquista de la Nueva
España*, I, p. 279; Gómara, II, p. 147; W. V. Farrar, "Tecuitlatl: A Glimpse of Aztec
Food Technology"; and Edward S. Deevey, Jr., "Limnologic Studies in Middle
America," pp. 226–228. Farrar identifies tecuitlatl as a member of Cyanophyta, or
blue-green algae, probably now extinct. On algae, see further F. E. Round, *The
Biology of the Algae*, pp. 72–73, 147–156, 211, 217, 219–225.

efficient use of available resources. Mexico is a major center of development of oaks, with more species than any other similar area. Oaks, black and white, deciduous and evergreen, grow throughout the country except in the regions of tropical rain forest or high aridity; all bear acorns varying from very small to quite large. In suitable areas, of which there are many, the production of acorns is certainly as prolific as in California.[15] Yet in California the Indians before the appearance of Europeans made use of the acorns as a major source of food. The acorns were gathered, shelled, most often pounded to meal, the tannin then leached from the meal by pouring hot water through it, and the purified, sweetened meal made into mush or thin cakes, just like the Mexican atole, tamales, or tortillas. In other uses, the acorns shelled or unshelled were placed in river sand or mud so that the action of cold water could remove the tannin more slowly. The acorns were then shelled if necessary and roasted.[16] This use of acorns extended into the Southwest, large parts of the rest of the United States,[17] and into Mexico in times before the immediate pre-Conquest.[18] It is therefore surprising to find that the Spaniards, who themselves were familiar with the use of acorns as human food,[19] mention the presence of oaks and that the large supply of acorns would make excellent fodder for pigs, but do not mention their use by the Indians.[20] The Relaciones Geográficas similarly mention the

15. See the section on quercus in Paul C. Standley, *Trees and Shrubs of Mexico,* pp. 171−198. This section is actually by William Trelease and, although out-of-date as to classification of varieties, is nevertheless valid for our purposes. Trelease, citing V. Havard, "Food Plants of the North American Indians," asserts that acorns were widely used by the Mexican Indians. Havard (p. 118) actually refers to the Indians of the United States and adjacent parts of northern Mexico.

16. Alfred L. Kroeber, *Handbook of the Indians of California,* pp. 87−88 *et passim.*

17. Havard, "Food Plants," pp. 118−119.

18. See Richard H. Brooks et al., "Plant Material from a Cave on the Rio Zape, Durango, Mexico," pp. 360−362 and 367. The studies in the Valley of Tehuacán have turned up very little sign of use of acorns, but the region is too arid for much development of oaks. Douglas Byers and Richard S. MacNeish, eds., *The Prehistory of the Tehuacan Valley,* I, table between pp. 232−233, shows the scanty finds of acorns.

19. See Gonzalo F. de Oviedo y Valdés, *Historia general y natural de las Indias,* I, p. 298, and his *Sumario de la natural historia de las Indias,* p. 213, both of which mention finding oaks bearing acorns in Panamá and Nicaragua, and the Spaniards' eating them.

20. Sahagún, II, pp. 397−398 and all of 396−407. See also below.

presence of oaks and the supply of acorns, but almost never their use by the Indians.[21]

It is true that the mention often is that the acorns, being small and bitter, were suitable only for pigs.[22] On the other hand, the California Indians and others preferred the bitter acorns as having more character,[23] and removal of a noxious or lethal element by leaching or other ways is a widespread American Indian cultural trait that extends from the cleansing of acorn meal to the preparation of farinha from the highly poisonous bitter manioc. The argument that cultivation of maize yielded a grain deemed far more satisfactory will not hold, since anything else that could be hunted, fished, or gathered was put to use in human nutrition. It is possible that the central Mexican Indians did indeed make use of acorns in the decades immediately preceding the Conquest, but that the rising and easier availability of other foods as population shrank led to abandonment of a more time-consuming alternate supply. Even that possibility seems unlikely, since the Relaciones Geográficas were prepared approximately sixty years after the landing of the Spaniards on the coast of central Veracruz, a rather short interval for the loss of all memory. In the end, we are forced to leave this matter with a question mark: we do not know.

Even with the omission of the acorn, the list of foods adds up to an easy basis for a rich and varied diet, fully supplied with human requirements in protein, fat, vitamins, and minerals, provided that the total caloric intake available to all the population was adequate and provided further that all parts of the population had access to the scarcer items, particularly those secured through hunting and fishing. Here regional differences

21. The Relación de las minas de Temazcaltepec, 1 December 1579–1 January 1580, has a clear statement of the use of acorns, in the description of Texcaltitlán: "22. Los arboles que tiene *Tescaltitlan* en sus montes son enzinas, que algunas dan bellotas que las comen los naturales, y moliendolas hazen dellas *tamales* ques çierto genero de pan entre ellos. . . ." (Francisco del Paso y Troncoso, *PNE,* VII, p. 23.) On the other hand, see the report for towns around Jalapa in the Relación de Jalapa de la Veracruz, 10 October 1580, where the statement is: "Ay en este pueblo ençinas con bellotas y no se aprouechan de ellas . . ." (*ibid.,* V, p. 107) and variations on it (pp. 110 and 111–123). The reports on the occurrence of oaks and acorns may be traced through the answers to question 22.

22. See, for example, the Relación de Tepeaca y su partido, 4–20 February 1580, *ibid.,* V, p. 35.

23. Oral communication of field observation by Professor Martin Baumhoff, Department of Anthropology, University of California, Davis.

must have loomed large, since climate, fertility of soil, and the availability of resources for hunting and fishing varied greatly. The range would have been from the rich central Veracruz coast and Valley of Mexico to the arid Valley of the Mezquital. In this last, too, the role of maize as staple diminished greatly, to be replaced by the remarkably versatile maguey.[24]

With respect to equable distribution of those food resources at the disposal of the total population, there is abundant evidence in reports of the sixteenth century that there were very substantial differences between the diet available to the nobility and in lesser degree to the merchants, artisans, and other favored groups at one extreme, and to the peasantry at the other. The nobility ate abundantly and well of all foods. In their diet, the products of hunting, fishing, and gathering made up for the scarcity of domesticated animals, and there was available an unusually varied choice of plants, grains, and fruits. The Relaciones Geográficas in reports from a number of towns stress the fact that the choicer products of cultivation and the more desirable results of hunting, fishing, and gathering were reserved to the upper classes.[25] Within the upper classes there were obviously significant differences in supplies of food, based not merely upon status within the local society but also upon regional power relationships. The redistributive mechanism of the local political and class structure was modified further by the operation of tribute within the larger structures established by conquest, which moved substantial quantities of foodstuffs as well as nonedible commodities to the centers of imperial power. The most striking instance was the huge tribute levied by the Triple Alliance upon subject towns, to the enrichment especially of Tenochtitlán, but also of Texcoco and Tlacopan. In effect, the Valley of Mexico enlarged its supply of foodstuffs, particularly for its upper classes, by levy upon perhaps half of central Mexico. The Tarascan state in Michoacán must

24. Mendizábal, "Evolución económica y social," *Obras completas*, VI, pp. 54–59 *et passim*, emphasizes the importance of the maguey and the impossibility of supporting the population in the Mezquital by raising maize.

25. Sahagún, II, pp. 65–70 and 134–159; Oviedo y Valdés, *Historia general*, IV, pp. 248–250. Some examples of such declarations are: Relación de Mitlantongo, 12 November 1579; Relación de Mitla, 12 November 1581; Relación de Atlatlauca y Malinaltepec, 8 September 1580; Relación de Cuicatlán, 15 September 1580; Relacion de Teutitlán del Camino—in *PNE*, IV, pp. 79, 149–150, 171, 186, and 211 respectively; and Relación de Texcoco, 5 March 1582, in Joaquin García Icazbalceta, *Nueva colección*, III, pp. 40 and 49.

have had a similar distribution in favor of its upper class centered in Pátzcuaro. So long as imperial tribute did not strip towns too far, the local nobility were able to shift to their peasantry the loss through regional redistribution.[26]

The peasants, who constituted the overwhelming bulk of the population, ate a much leaner diet of maize, beans, chile, and agave, but these staples too were supplemented by a wide variety of other foods. Fruits were abundant, and there were available such products of hunting, fishing, and gathering as were not reserved for the upper classes. There was a great variety of wild fruits, vegetables, nuts, berries, greens, roots, and the like, which could be gathered over the countryside. The peasants could obtain animal protein from smaller mammals and birds, together with the lower forms of the animal kingdom such as iguanas, snakes, lizards, amphibians, worms, and grubs. As we have already mentioned, even the algae in the lakes were utilized. A number of the Relaciones Geográficas state emphatically that just about everything edible was eaten.[27]

This diversity is one key to the survival of a huge population. If we forget the esthetic aspects of the matter, we see that the Indians as a whole were exploiting in an amazingly efficient manner the total biomass of the environment, and that in terms of essential elements, vitamins, and protein they probably had enough, except in years of complete crop failure. Even then the deficiency was quantitative, not qualitative. Our own tendency to emphasize agricultural technology and to neglect natural productivity has led too often to an underestimate of the carrying capacity of a region. All that is needed is a population with the experience and the resourcefulness to utilize the reservoir which is there. A very simple technology is all that is required.

3.

The matter of per capita caloric intake of the peasantry is more difficult, even in terms of countrywide generalizations. We have

26. See the discussion in Borah and Cook, *The Aboriginal Population of Central Mexico on the Eve of the Spanish Conquest,* pp. 6–21, 60–71, *et passim.*
27. For example, Relación de Nexapa, 12 September 1579; Relación de Piaztla, 2 January 1581; Relación de Atitalaquia y su partido, 22 February 1580–in *PNE,* IV, p. 42; V, p. 79; VI, p. 207. See the very explicit statement in Gómara, II, pp. 400 and 147.

no firm basis for estimating overall production and dividing it by the probable number of people. However, certain aspects of the problem can yield insight under discussion. One of these relates to the energy requirement of the Aztecs and kindred tribes in the conditions of their existence. A present-day European or American man of average size, doing moderate work, is thought to require 3,000 kilocalories a day. Women and children need correspondingly less, such that the mean may be near 2,500 kilocalories. It is very doubtful whether the aboriginal peoples of central Mexico got anywhere near this amount. There is, indeed, an increasing body of evidence suggesting that, except in unusually favorable circumstances, few people even in Europe enjoyed average daily caloric intakes that would correspond to present-day standards of nutrition.[28]

In order to pursue further our examination of the dietary and metabolic status of the central Mexican Indians prior to the coming of the Europeans, we must first determine certain anatomical and physiological constants. These may be obtained with relative ease for a living population, but can be secured only by indirection and difficulty for a long-extinct people. The first of these magnitudes is simple body size, in its most elementary terms defined as height and weight. From these factors we may derive the probable basal metabolic rate and the caloric ration necessary to support it. Additional data are available concerning physical effort and expendable labor.

Estimates of body size for the pre-Conquest inhabitants of central Mexico must be drawn from three sources. The first is contemporary statements, which are surprisingly scanty. The earliest mention, the report of the city council of Veracruz to Charles V, describes the natives as of medium stature with well proportioned bodies.[29] Gómara, presumably summarizing the testimony he gathered from Hernán Cortés and other conquerors in Spain after central Mexico was under Spanish control, makes almost the same statement: "of medium stature, but robust."[30] The Anonymous Conqueror's statement is also close: "well-shaped, rather tall than short."[31] The implications are

28. Braudel, *Civilisation matérielle et capitalisme*, pp. 97–99; Ashtor, "Essai sur l'alimentation des diverses classes sociales dans l'Orient médiéval," pp. 1043–1053.

29. Veracruz, 10 July 1519, in Cortés, *Cartas y documentos*, p. 23.

30. Gómara, II, 398.

31. [Anonymous Conqueror], *Relación de algunas cosas de la Nueva España . . .*, p. 41.

that relative to the Spaniards of the time, the Indians were of average size and weight. Since by our standards the Spaniards of that time were small men, with an average height of perhaps 160 centimeters (5 feet 3 inches) and an average weight of perhaps 60 kilos (132 lbs.), the Indians can have been no taller and no heavier.

The second source of information on body size is the measurement of skeletons of the fifteenth and sixteenth centuries found in excavations in central Mexico. Here too our information is surprisingly scanty, but what there is of it yields reconstructed statures for males ranging from 1.59 to 1.64 meters.[32]

A third method of estimate is by comparison with present-day conditions. It is possible that some change has occurred in the more than four centuries since the Conquest, particularly through nutritional betterment. However, in rural areas, among the Indians, dietary conditions are much the same as they were in the sixteenth century. Moreover, except in the North of Mexico (which lies outside our area of study) and among the mestizos, no increase in size has been noted, and certainly no decrease. We are therefore justified in thinking that body size among the rural indigenous population has not altered significantly since the time of Cortés.

There have been literally scores of investigations which have included measurements of the height and weight of groups of people all over the earth. It is manifestly impossible and also unnecessary to cite most of these. However, it is worthwhile to mention some of the data which concern the aboriginal inhabitants of both North and South America, with the emphasis upon Mexico. These figures have been compiled and are presented in condensed form in Table 2.1.

For height, the eighteen averages of adult males in Indian groups living north of central Mexico have a range of 161.1 to 174.9 and a mean of 166.5 centimeters. These values are as good as can be obtained with present-day anthropometric methods. The samples are adequate and the techniques satisfactory. For the set of twenty averages obtained for Indians in central Mexico, the analogous mean is 158.5 and the range from 154.2 to 163.4 centimeters. If the individual averages for each area, central Mexico and north of central Mexico, are compared

32. Genovés T., "Anthropometry of Late Prehistoric Remains," in *HMAI*, IX, table 3 between pp. 40–41.

TABLE 2.1

Average Height and Weight of Indian Tribes from Various Sources

(Adult Males)

Sample	Number of Cases	Average Height in Centimeters	Average Weight in Kilos	Source
United States and Canada				
Southern Oregon	17	162.3		Boas, 1891, p. 27
Central Oregon	9	165.3		Boas, 1891, p. 27
Northern Oregon	7	165.1		Boas, 1891, p. 27
Columbians	8	169.9		Boas, 1891, p. 27
Washington	6	164.7		Boas, 1891, p. 27
Harrison Lake	9	161.1		Boas, 1891, p. 27
Vancouver Island	7	163.5		Boas, 1891, p. 27
Bilqula	23	165.9		Boas, 1891, p. 27
Pueblo	447	164.3		Hrdlička, 1935, p. 267
Hopi	105	164.5		Hrdlička, 1935, p. 269
Maricopa	40	174.9		Hrdlička, 1935, p. 269
Seneca	507	173.3	72.8	Gould, 1869, in Newman, 1960, pp. 289-291
Choctaw	26	171.4	66.1	Collins, 1925, in Newman
Papago	219	168.8	71.4	Gabel, 1949, p. 17
Navajo	125	169.6	62.7	Gabel, 1949, p. 17
Navajo	166	169.8	68.7	Darby, et al., 1956, in Newman, 1960, p.290

TABLE 2.1 (Cont.)

Sample	Number of Cases	Average Height in Centimeters	Average Weight in Kilos	Source
United States and Canada (cont.)				
Hopi	276	161.1	60.8	Gabel, 1949, p. 17
Zuñi	348	161.4	56.3	Gabel, 1949, p. 17
Mean		166.5		
Range		161.1 - 174.9		
Northern Mexico				
Tarahumara	50	163.0	60.0	Basauri, 1929, in Newman, 1960, p. 290
Yaqui	100	166.7	62.0	Seltzer, 1936, in Newman, 1960, p. 290
Mean		165.5	60.0	
Range		163.0 - 166.7		
Central and Southern Mexico				
Tarascan – Janitzio	116	160.0	58.1	Gómez Robledo, 1943, in Newman, 1960, pp. 290-291
Tarascan – Paracho	47	161.4	56.1	Gómez Robledo, 1943, in Newman, 1960, pp. 290-291
Tarascan – Paracho	92	162.4		Lasker, 1953, p. 56
Otomí – El Zapote	100	157.0	52.6	Faulhaber, 1950-6, in Newman, 1960, pp. 290-291
Otomí – Ixmiquilpan	105	157.6	53.2	Schreicher, 1954, in Newman

144

TABLE 2.1 (Cont.)

Sample	Number of Cases	Average Height in Centimeters	Average Weight in Kilos	Source
Central and Southern Mexico (cont.)				
Totonac – Papantla	100	158.0	52.0	Faulhaber, 1950–6, in Newman
Tepehuán – Pisaflores	100	157.7	52.8	Faulhaber, 1950–6, in Newman
Huastec – Tantoyuca	100	157.2	50.4	Faulhaber, 1950–6, in Newman
Chinantec	45	157.6	52.8	D'Aloja, 1939, in Newman
Mixtec – Tilantongo	148	155.9	54.0	Romero, n.d., in Newman
Mixtec – Oaxaca	78	154.2	50.2	Leche, 1936b, in Newman
Zapotec – Oaxaca	50	155.4	50.3	Leche, 1936a, in Newman
Trique – San Andrés	101	156.5	50.8	Comas, 1944, in Newman
Nahua – Huatusco	99	158.6	54.7	Faulhaber, 1950–6, in Newman
Nahua – Pajapan	100	161.9	56.4	Faulhaber, 1950–6, in Newman
Nahua – Zongolica	100	154.8	49.5	Faulhaber, 1950–6, in Newman
Nahua – Chiconamel	99	157.0	50.3	Faulhaber, 1950–6, in Newman
Nahua – Tepoztlán	159	163.1	56.4	Field, 1954, in Newman
Nahua – Gabriel Mariaca	36	163.4	56.6	Field, 1954, in Newman
Nahua – Tlahuica	50	160.0	52.0	Basauri, n.d., in Newman
Mean		158.5	53.6	
Range		154.2 – 163.4		

145

TABLE 2.1 (Cont.)

Sample	Number of Cases	Average Height in Centimeters	Average Weight in Kilos	Source
Yucatan – Maya				
Yucatan	120	155.4	54.2	Steggerda, 1941, in Newman, 1960, pp. 290–291
Yucatan	69	155.1	53.5	Steggerda, 1932, in Newman, 1960, pp. 290–291
Tzeltal	50	153.6	53.9	Leche et al., 1944, in Newman
Tzeltal	50	158.2	56.0	Leche et al., 1944, in Newman
Tzeltal	47	155.6	51.4	Leche et al., 1944, in Newman
Yucatan	163	154.7	52.9	Williams, 1931, in Newman
Tzotzil	100	155.7	53.3	Leche et al., 1944, in Newman
Tzotzil	25	158.4	54.7	Leche et al., 1944, in Newman
Chol	100	158.6	57.4	Gould, 1946, in Newman
Tojolabales	100	158.6	56.6	Basauri, 1931, in Newman
Kanhobal	74	154.8	52.6	Stewart, n.d., in Newman
Quiché	63	154.2	51.1	Stewart, n.d., in Newman
Quiché	30	159.3	57.6	Crile and Quiring, 1939b, in Newman
Cakchiquel	72	155.3	51.4	Stewart, n.d., in Newman
Cakchiquel	82	154.8	50.8	Stewart, n.d., in Newman
Cakchiquel	42	156.8	54.2	Méndez and Behrhorst, 1963, p. 460
Mean		156.2	53.8	
Range		153.6 – 159.3		

146

TABLE 2.1 (Cont.)

Sample	Number of Cases	Average Height in Centimeters	Average Weight in Kilos	Source
South America				
Araucanian- Mapuche	31	163.3	66.8	Pi-Suñer, 1933, in Newman, 1960, p. 292
Tucano – Decana	10	154.2	55.8	Bastos d'Avila, 1950, in Newman, 1960
Oajana	15	155.0	55.1	Droogleever-Fortuyn, 1946, in Newman
Trumai	11	158.8	58.4	Ranke, 1910, in Newman
Wai Wai	20	158.6	56.6	Newman and Jones, n.d., in Newman
Quechua – Morococha	478	159.0	55.4	Hurtado, 1932, in Newman
Quechua – Vicos	180	154.6	51.5	Newman, *et al*., n.d., in Newman
Cashinahua (Peru)	38	154.7	61.3	Johnston, *et al*., 1971, p. 411
Quicha (Peru)		158.3		Ferris, 1916, in Harris, 1926, p. 42
Mean		157.4	57.1	
Range		154.2 – 163.3		
United States and Canada	18	166.5		
			t = 6.39	
Central and Southern Mexico	20	158.5		
			t = 2.83	
Yucatan – Maya	16	156.0		F = 1.30
South America	9	157.4		

147

TABLE 2.2

Height of Males and Females in Various Indian Tribes, and Other Ethnic Groups

Sample	Mean Cm.: Male	Mean Cm.: Female	Ratio: Female/Male	Source
San Blas, North	149.9	140.4	93.7	Harris, 1926, p. 42
Quechua, Peru	158.3	142.6	90.1	Ferris, 1916, in Harris, 1926, p. 42
Chiriguán	163.4	151.1	92.5	Lehmann – Nitsche, in Harris
Hopi	163.8	150.7	92.1	Hrdlička, in Harris
Maricopa	174.9	160.4	91.8	Hrdlička, in Harris
Cashinahua, Peru	154.7	145.1	93.7	Johnston, et al., 1971
Paracho – Tarascan	162.4	151.2	93.2	Lasker, 1953, p. 56
Pueblo	164.3	151.9	92.5	Hrdlička, 1935
Mean			92.5	
Labrador Eskimo	157.5	148.0	94.0	Boas, 1891, in Harris, 1926, p. 42
Japanese	159.3	147.2	92.4	Miwa, in Harris, 1926, p. 42
Mexicans, mean of adult ages			92.5	Goldstein, 1943, in Lasker, 1953, p. 57
Americans, mostly white	174.0	161.5	92.7	Stewart, et al., 1960, Table 1, p. 334

numerically, the value of t is 6.39. A very significant difference in height between the Indians of the two areas is therefore indicated.

There are in Table 2.1 sixteen averages for Maya groups in Yucatán and Guatemala. For them the mean is 156.0 centimeters. If t is calculated for the Maya against the central Mexican samples, it is found to be 2.83, a figure just at the 1% level of probability and hence definitely significant statistically. However, the Mesoamerican and South American samples may be compared by making an analysis of variance for the three aggregates, representing central Mexico, Yucatán, and South America. The value of F equals 1.30, a totally nonsignificant figure. Therefore, these reports as a whole show heights within a very narrow range, probably within the margin of error of sampling and measurement.

For the central Mexican group, in which we are particularly interested, the mean is 158.5 centimeters, but the variation is considerable. The Tarascans and some of the Nahuas are taller than the Otomí and the Oaxaca Indians. Nevertheless, the mean of the entire twenty samples must represent substantially the true condition. This mean may be taken as 159 centimeters, especially in view of the fact that the Nahua average is 159.8 for seven samples. In English units, 159 centimeters equals 5 feet 2½ inches. The Nahuas would average one-half inch taller than the general mean.

With one exception, the averages for body weight of Mexican Indians shown in Table 2.1 are taken from the compilation by Marshall Newman.[33] Those for central Mexico give a mean of 53.6 kilos, and those for the Maya 53.8 kilos. In order to check the consistency of this mean, Newman's formula may be employed: the ratio of the stature to the cube root of the weight equals a value which lies between 38.0 and 43.0. There are other formulas, but none are perfect, and Newman's is close enough for ordinary purposes. For central Mexico plus Yucatán, we get 42.1, a value which lies well within the prescribed range. Our final values for central Mexico are: height 159 centimeters, weight 53.6 kilograms.

These values relate to adult males. The other half of the adult population, the female, is universally smaller. The male/female

33. Marshall T. Newman, "Adaptations in the Physique of American Aborigines to Nutritional Factors."

ratio of size can be approximated from some of the data given by various investigators, such as are presented in Table 2.2 for height alone. Clearly there is variation because of both sampling error and differences in body build. However, the average female/male ratio is very close to 92.5 (the female/male ratio is more convenient for use than its reciprocal). A very large sample of white Americans shows 92.7;[34] Goldstein's series of Mexicans in several age groups over nineteen years averages 92.5.[35] In view of the uniformity found in the published accounts, the pre-Conquest Mexicans can be regarded as differing little in this respect from those of the present day. Then, if the ratio is 92.5, the height of pre-Conquest females was 159 × .925, or 147 centimeters. The approximate average weight may be obtained by taking 92.5 percent of the average male weight: 53.6 × .925, or 49.6 kilograms.

In order to estimate the basal metabolism and hence the caloric requirements of a person having the dimensions just specified, we should know the surface area and the number of calories required per square meter of surface. It is true that much present-day research stresses the importance of body composition and utilizes fat-free body weight as readily as it does surface area. However, when we are dealing with an extinct population, and since we know absolutely nothing about the body composition of the pre-Conquest Indians, surface area provides a better criterion. We shall try both methods.

Without considering surface area, it is possible to calculate the probable basal metabolism directly from weight if one follows the prescription of Max Kleiber. Kleiber asserts that the interspecific mean intrinsic metabolic rate is 70 kilocalories per day per weight in kilograms to the three-quarters power.[36] If this formula is applied to the average Aztec or Mixtec, as may be, the result is $70 \times (53.6)^{3/4}$, or 1,387 kilocalories per day, or 57.8 kilocalories per hour.

The original formulation of the relation between surface area and height and weight was worked out many years ago by Dubois and is shown graphically in numerous standard texts of physiology and biochemistry. It represents a broad average for

34. Howard W. Stoudt et al., "Heights and Weights of White Americans."

35. Reproduced in Gabriel Ward Lasker, "The Age Factor in Bodily Measurements of Adult Male and Female Mexicans," p. 57, table 2.

36. Max Kleiber, "Body Size and Metabolic Rate," p. 512.

most of humanity, and its validity for man has never been seriously attacked. Therefore we may use the relationship thus set forth with reasonable confidence that it applied to pre-historic as well as to living populations. A chart after Dubois is shown by Ruch and Patton[37] and by Philip Bard.[38] The closest it can be read for 159 centimeters and 53.6 kilos is 1.54 square meters, plus or minus 0.02 square meter. Since this error is less than 1% it may be ignored.

A tabulation by Bard, based on data from Benedict and from Rubner, indicates that 41 men with an average weight of 53.4 kilos produce 914 kilocalories per square meter of body surface in 24 hours; the total heat would be 1,408 kilocalories per day.[39] Another formulation shows, according to the Aub and Dubois standards, that a man between 18 and 30 years of age produces about 40 kilocalories per square meter of body surface per hour.[40] Hence 40 × 24 × 1.54 = 1,478 kilocalories per day. Since these data have never been controverted in principle, we may conclude that if the pre-Conquest Mexican Indian adult men of 14 to 40 years averaged 159 centimeters and 53.6 kilos, then their mean basal metabolic rate was approximately 1,425 kilocalories per day (1,425 is the mean of 1,387, 1,408, and 1,478).

It should be emphasized that the values just given relate only to the average adult man under basal conditions. If we are concerned with populations, we must know the comparable figures for other components, specifically women and children. For adult women our estimate of body size indicates a height of 147 centimeters and a weight of 49.6 kilos. The closest reading of the Dubois graph gives a surface area of 1.41 square meters. Thus the metabolic rate of women is close to 36.5 kilocalories per square meter per hour, and the daily rate is 1,235 kilo-calories.

The basal metabolism of children collectively is much more difficult to assess, for several reasons. First, the number of children varies in different populations; second, the intrinsic metabolic rate varies with age, i.e., the heat production per unit

37. Theodore C. Ruch and Harry D. Patton, *Physiology and Biophysics,* p. 1045, fig. 12.
38. Philip Bard, ed., *Medical Physiology,* p. 482, fig. 171.
39. *Ibid.,* p. 480, table 37.
40. *Ibid.,* p. 478, table 31.

weight decreases after late infancy; third, the total metabolism increases with increase in size.

With respect to the proportion of children in the population, we do not, of course, have any direct information concerning the situation prior to the Conquest. However, there is a considerable body of evidence for the colonial period, particularly the late eighteenth century. Furthermore, we know that the demographic status of the central Mexican population was much the same in both the fifteenth and the eighteenth centuries. Both must have been characterized by high birth and death rates. Both were under strong pressure toward increase. Hence the proportion of children in both must have been more or less similar. In a previous essay, our examination of data for the late eighteenth century made it clear that, in spite of numerous ethnic and geographical differences, the number of children in Mexico under the age of sixteen years approached 45% of the total population.[41] In the absence of any contrary evidence, the same proportion reasonably may be assumed for the population in, let us say, 1518.

Since body size and metabolism both vary enormously with age, and since we have little refined data pertaining to the distribution of these magnitudes in the youthful population, some type of short-cut is mandatory. The simplest procedure is to take the features characteristic of the median age in the range 0–16 years, and let them stand as an average, although a very crude one, of all children. In a primitive population of this sort, if children, metabolically speaking, are all those under 16 years of age, the median can be estimated from the late-eighteenth-century data.[42] The value lies somewhere near the age of 6 years.

The size and the intrinsic metabolic rate of 6-year-old children can be calculated only by the use of data derived from present-day American or European sources. When applied to pre-Conquest Mexican Indian children, the result is likely to contain a relatively large error. Hence we can arrive at only a crude approximation, although even an approximation is preferable to nothing. According to Wohl and Goodhart, 6-year-olds of the smallest size, both boys and girls, are 42.8 inches tall and have an average weight of 38.75 pounds. We select the smallest

41. Cook and Borah, *Essays*, I, pp. 201–299, esp. p. 255 *et seq.*
42. *Ibid.*, pp. 257–259.

size (5th centile) in order to approach as closely as possible the probable size of Mexican children.[43] Then, converting units to the metric system, we have 108 centimeters in height and 17.6 kilos in weight.

We employ next the Dubois graph, with extrapolation where necessary, to estimate the body surface at 0.7 square meter. Closer estimate is not feasible. Finally, the metabolic rate is found by reference to the table in Ruch and Patton, according to which for 6-year-old boys and girls a mean of 51.7 kilocalories is produced per square meter per hour.[44] Then the metabolic rate per child becomes 869 kilocalories per day, say 870 kilocalories. An error of plus or minus 10–20% will have to be allowed, but a working mean of 870 kilocalories per day is reasonable.

We are now in a position to make an approximate estimate of the metabolism of the population. An adult male produces per day 1,425, an adult female 1,235, and a child 870 kilocalories. According to our data already cited, there are 55% adults (27.5% adult males and the same percentage of females) and 45% children. Therefore, 1,000 people produce 275 × 1,425 plus 275 × 1,235 plus 450 × 870 kilocalories. The total is 1,123,000 kilocalories per day, or 1,123 per person. This would be the basal value, the minimal amount needed to maintain organic integrity, with no excess even for the easiest kind of physical activity or for the digestion of normal food.

In order to evaluate the caloric requirement in daily life of the pre-Conquest central Mexican Indians, we have to know something about the level of their physical effort. In turn, it is necessary to equate this activity with the increase caused thereby in the metabolic rate over the basal value. We shall examine the second phase of the problem first, and do so by considering data derived from study of present-day populations.

There have been a great many investigations of the effect of various types of physical exertion upon the energy flow through the human organism. These studies have one aspect in common: they all pertain to present-day subjects who are of European-American physique and who subsist according to what are considered nutritionally adequate standards. For the central

43. Michael G. Wohl and Robert S. Goodhart, eds., *Modern Nutrition in Health and Disease: Dietotherapy*, p. 10, tables 1.6 and 1.7.
44. Ruch and Patton, p. 1045, table 3.

Mexican Indians we can make some adjustments for body size, but the nutritional aspect remains a separate problem.

We select a few of the most accessible and at the same time representative figures. The activity data refer to moderately large, well-conditioned North Americans or Europeans. The basis of at least some estimates is a 70-kilo man who is approximately 170 centimeters tall (154 pounds and 5 feet 7 inches). Such an individual has a surface area of 1.8 square meters. His basal metabolism would be $40 \times 1.8 \times 24 = 1,728$ kilocalories a day, or in a round figure 1,730. If we use the hourly rate, we have a basal value of 72 kilocalories.

We now present two simple lists. Each shows the extra energy expended, presumably by a 70-kilo man, in performing certain tasks. The values per square meter have been converted to those for the whole person by using the multiplication factor 1.8. The units shown are kilocalories per hour. The lists are modified from the sources indicated, the figures in parentheses representing a further modification to arrive at values for an average central Mexican Indian adult male.

A. Sherman[45]

Sitting upright at rest	28	(23)
Walking slowly (2.6 miles per hour)	128	(106)
Walking fast (3.75 miles per hour)	228	(188)
Running	570	(470)

B. From Ruch and Patton[46]

Sitting upright at rest	18	(15)
Standing	81	(67)
Washing—Dressing	108	(89)
Housework	180	(148)
Walking (3 miles per hour)	180	(148)
Bicycling	378	(312)
Running	528	(435)

Sherman also shows a balance sheet in which is set forth a hypothetical 24-hour day, divided into portions according to activity.[47] The basal metabolism is included in these figures:

45. Henry C. Sherman, *Chemistry of Food and Nutrition*, p. 189, table 23.
46. Ruch and Patton, p. 1045, table 2.
47. Sherman, p. 190.

8 hours sleep	520	(429)
2 hours light exercise	340	(280)
8 hours carpenter work	1,920	(1,582)
6 hours sitting at rest	600	(494)
Total	3,380	(2,785)

The activity load of the pre-Conquest central Mexican Indians is difficult to estimate. Initially, however, there must be established a reduction factor. A group which averages small size is sure to expend less energy than one of large dimensions. While we may know the comparative sizes, we are not sure of the exact relationship between the two groups in energy expenditure. On the other hand, some sensible assumption is required, and the simplest is that of direct proportionality. Therefore, if the mean basal rates in the two populations are in the proportion of 1,780 to 1,425, the values for the activity levels given above should be reduced to 82.4 percent. In the lists, the values thus adjusted for the central Mexican Indians are placed in parentheses. For example, the kilocalories used per day are reduced from 3,380 to 2,785.

The labor schedule of the overwhelming majority of pre-Conquest Mexican Indians was based upon farming, an activity conducted without aid from domesticated animals, by means of the digging stick as the principal implement. The work must be regarded as moderate, although numerous individual tasks were performed which might be classed as heavy. Relatively little work was done as strenuous as our really intensive manual labor displayed in both agriculture and industry. The women, of course, assumed all domestic duties, and their level of labor would have resembled what Ruch and Patton had in mind when they mentioned housework. Labor at home and in public service for the men, associated with occupations such as farming or building, would have been more onerous, but hardly could have surpassed the demands of steady bicycling for an equal amount of time. If so, the extra energy cost above the basal level would not have exceeded 155-160 kilocalories per hour. The same approximate value can be put on the energy cost of carrying loads, both domestically and over long distances, for the human *cargador* performed the function of the beast of burden used in the Old World. These cargadores carried a load of 50 pounds each and traveled approximately one league an hour, or 2.5 to 3.0 miles depending upon the terrain. This activity, disregarding the loads, corresponds quite closely to Sherman's slow walk, which consumes an extra 106 kilocalories an hour. With the load, the value would certainly rise to 155–160 kilocalories.

Thus we formulate a workload estimate of 155–160 kilocalories per hour per man (for the sake of convenience, we shall use the value 156.7), and 70 kilocalories per day per woman. For children the value would be much smaller, but even the youngest children did a little work beyond their normal activity in helping their parents support the domestic establishment. On the other hand, it is extremely difficult to segregate work from play, so that it is preferable to reconsider children after a discussion of some other matters.

Another factor of importance is the allocation and distribution of time. In the instance of cargadores, we have the explicit testimony of Bernal Díaz, reporting on the situation in 1519 before the Europeans had had a chance to alter it, that a day's march was five leagues, or five hours' travel under load.[48] The workday for the bearers must have included the time needed to make and break camp and to mount and dismantle the loads, perhaps an additional hour in all. The working day, then, was six hours. This is just about what the present-day Mexican farmer puts in, if one counts sustained work. Indeed, the six-hour day is prevalent throughout Latin America. It is a response to dietary limitations and also an adaptation to the climate. The serious working day extends from 6:00 or 7:00 a.m. to 12:00 or 1:00 p.m., at which time the heat in the tropical areas becomes unbearable. In many instances, although not always, a little more work may be done in the late afternoon, but approaching darkness precludes any extended effort. The rest of the time is spent eating, sleeping, and relaxing. This regimen is of very ancient origin and conforms to the exigencies of the region.[49]

Let us now reconstruct a hypothetical day for an Aztec

48. See the explicit statements of Bernal Díaz del Castillo (I, pp. 146 and 177): "... indios de carga, que en aquellas partes llaman *tamemes,* que llevan dos arrobas de peso a cuestas y caminan con ellas cinco leguas." The league was one hour's walk, the distance traveled varying with the difficulty of the terrain.

49. If one allows for coffee breaks, visits to the toilet, and other interruptions in sustained work, the regime may not be much different from that in industrialized societies.

macehual, farmer, or cargador. He gets about eight hours sleep at night and one hour at noon. He works reasonably hard for six hours. He divides the remaining nine hours such that he indulges in light exercise for three hours and sits quietly the other six hours. Alternately, we may say that during these nine hours he engages in light activity. In either case, we may allow him an average extra expenditure of 37 kilocalories per hour. Then his formula is as follows:

9 hours sleep @ 53.6 Kcal per hour total metabolism	482
15 hours waking:	
basal rate @ 59.4 Kcal per hour	890
cost of digestion	140
6 hours work @ 156.7 Kcal per hour	940
9 hours light activity @ 37 Kcal per hour	333
Total	2,785

Further adjustments are in order, the chief one of which relates to the number of days annually during which a full workload was carried. Throughout the year a proportion of days would be devoted to rest from all types of labor possible; that they came in our frequency of one in seven (now two in seven) seems unlikely; rather, they undoubtedly came in a relation to the Mesoamerican calendar with its 20-day units. Further, the accounts of Sahagún and those of other writers, native and Spanish, make it clear that the pre-Conquest Mexican Indians enjoyed a great many religious celebrations and festivals throughout the year.[50] Some of these were confined to the ruling classes, priests, and nobility, but the common people participated in many of them. Merely as an estimate, let us say that days of rest and days of celebration and festival for the peasants gave them about 75 work-free days. If the work is deleted from the schedule shown above for 75 days in the year, and light activity is substituted, the value 940 is changed to 222 for the 75 days. Hence on these days the energy output was 2,067 kilocalories instead of 2,785. The annual output was reduced from 2,785 × 365 = 1,016,525 kilocalories to 75 × 2,067 + 290 × 2,785 = 962,675 kilocalories per year. This is equivalent to 2,637 kilocalories per day, say 2,635.

Let us turn now to the women. We know that they assisted

50. See Sahagún, I, pp. 93–281; Motolinía, *Historia,* pp. 35–71.

to a significant extent in the farm work in addition to their work in the home. The extent of this extra labor cannot be precisely ascertained. However, we know that it could not have equaled that of the men, because so much time had to be spent in housekeeping, child care, and other necessary duties. On the other hand, the amount of farm labor must have been appreciable. It will be a moderate supposition to allocate to the adult female two hours of the six hours of labor on 290 days of the year. In kilocalories, the female balance sheet for a working day therefore looks as follows, where the cost of all types of work and activity is taken as having the same values as for men:

9 hours sleep @ 49 Kcal per hour	440
15 hours waking:	
basal rate @ 52 Kcal per hour	780
cost of digestion	140
2 hours work @ 156.7 Kcal per hour	314
13 hours light activity @ 37 Kcal per hour	481
Total	2,155

If we allow the same 75 days of rest and fiesta as for the men, we get per year for a female adult $2,155 \times 290 + 1,915 \times 75 = 768,575$ kilocalories. This means 2,106 kilocalories per day, say 2,105.

We may now revert to the problem of the children. These young individuals cannot be said to have undergone labor in the strict sense. They performed many tasks, some of them onerous, but on the whole their activity must be classed as light. On the other hand, particularly with very young children, the hours of sleep must have been extended. In order to take these variables into account to some degree, although strict accuracy is impossible, we shall consider that the children slept ten hours (including a siesta) and spent their waking hours in light activity.

The basal metabolism of a child at the median age of 6 years was estimated to be 870 kilocalories per day, or 36.3 per hour. The sleeping metabolism is roughly 10% below the basal, or close to 33 kilocalories per hour and 330 per day. The basal value for 14 hours of waking is 508 kilocalories, rounded off to 510. The cost of digestion, because of the smaller size, may be reduced to 80 kilocalories. The extra energy cost for 14 hours light activity in a child may be considered as lying between one-half and three-quarters of the value for an adult, or approximately 25 kilocalories per hour. This is admittedly a very crude estimate, but in view of the great range in age and size must represent an approach to the actual value. Thus we add to the other items 14 X 25 kilocalories per day, or 350, making a total energy output of 1,270 kilocalories per day. Since childhood activities will continue on nearly the same level, regardless of social events, no deduction need be made for days of rest or fiesta.

We now have a general average of 2,635 kilocalories for men, 2,105 for women, and 1,270 for children. If we apply the same proportions of these three components in the population as previously (27.5, 27.5, and 45.0% respectively) the average energy production per person per day becomes 1,875 kilocalories, a value we round off to 1,900 kilocalories. This value takes into account body size, age, and physical activity. It also assumes a diet adequate to supply the necessary calories. It does not take into account protein, accessory substances, or other factors which may affect the energy yield of the food eaten. Perhaps the most important point for our discussion is that it does not take into account circumstances that might reduce the caloric allowance available to the population, which might live not at a level of adequate nutrition but rather at one of semistarvation. This matter of possible semistarvation requires further exploration in our discussion.

The data concerning metabolism we have discussed up to now are based upon contemporary European and American dietary standards. They assume, unless otherwise indicated, that what is today considered an adequate diet was available to all persons, including Mexican and South American inhabitants, and that both the basal and the activity rates were determined only by such factors as age and body size. There is room, and indeed evidence, for doubting that this assumption is valid and warranted.

The level of nutrition today among the various groups in the Mexican population, both urban and rural, is the subject of acrimonious comment by many medical authorities and sociologists. They contend that a large segment of the population suffers from chronic undernutrition.[51] If this is true at present, and there is considerable evidence for the view, then it has been true throughout the history of the region. Consequently, the estimates offered here for mean energy production are too high and do not correspond to a human aggregate which was underfed. At this point we are interested primarily in the effect of inadequate caloric intake upon the mean output. By inadequate, we have in mind any level between that which is agreed upon as appropriate to maintain a population at full working efficiency and that which produces severe, manifest clinical symptoms such as are associated with outright chronic starvation.

The classical study involving undernutrition in great masses of people was carried out by Alexis Ivanovsky in Russia and made available to the western world in 1923.[52] Ivanovsky followed the condition of over 2,000 adults for three years during a rigorous famine, and found an average reduction in height of 4.7 centimeters in males and 3.5 centimeters in females. The weight diminished to a varying degree, but the range was approximately from 20 to 60% of the initial value. He also found that among those who were exposed to inanition for long periods, the loss in size took place in the first year. Thereafter there was relatively little change.

A more rigidly controlled experiment was that of Ancel Keys and his colleagues at the University of Minnesota in the late 1940's, after the experiences of the Second World War had stimulated interest in the matter.[53] In the Minnesota studies, a rapid initial loss of weight was observed; it was followed by a slower reduction until equilibrium was reached. The basal metabolism of the subjects also fell to a new low level. The changes are described by Keys and Francisco Grande:

Equally important is the fact that, given time, the body weight tends to

51. See, for example, Richmond K. Anderson et al., "A Study of the Nutritional Status and Food Habits of Otomí Indians in the Mezquital Valley of Mexico"; Mendizábal, "Evolución económica y social," *Obras Completas*, VI, tables on food consumption between pp. 192–193; Salvador Zubirán and Adolfo Chávez V., "Algunos datos sobre la situación nutricional en México"; Carlos Pérez Hidalgo et al., "Recopilación sobre el consumo de nutritivos en diferentes zonas de México"; Ana María Flores, *La magnitud del hambre en México, passim,* esp. pp. 9–25; and Whetten, *Rural Mexico,* pp. 304–316.

52. Alexis Ivanovsky, "Physical Modifications of the Population of Russia Under Famine."

53. Ancel Keys and his colleagues have given a full report in the two volumes of *The Biology of Human Starvation.*

reach a steady state and calorie expenditure tends to balance calorie intake, no matter what the level of the latter may be. When we changed the diet of young men from 3,500 to 1,500 Calories daily, the weight loss was rapid at first and decreased exponentially with time until calorie equilibrium was achieved with the body weight being 25% less than it had been.[54]

A similar result had been obtained in the well-known experiment of Benedict, Miles, Roth, and Smith (1919). These investigators kept a squad of young men on a low-calorie diet, an average of 1,930 kilocalories per day per man, after they had become accustomed to a diet consisting of 3,000 kilocalories per day. During the last three days of the restricted ration, the average net kilocalories produced per day was 2,245 and there was marked reduction in both the basal rate and the rate during moderate exercise. The subjects, however, felt no ill effects and were able to perform their tasks with facility. Sherman described the state of all these subjects as follows:

When conditions are otherwise favorable, healthy young men can adjust themselves to lowered energy intakes through reduced body weight and lowered BMR so that they can get along with 1/3 less food calories and still feel and act normal.[55]

It is thus generally conceded that the food intake can be diminished from the high level associated with what are considered adequate diets with no permanent ill effects. There will be reduced weight, even reduced height, and at the same time lowered energy costs for all phases of life. If the reduction of intake is not too severe, the individual goes into and remains in what has been called the compensated phase of undernutrition. No clinical changes are observed except those mentioned; the person can continue a quite normal daily life.[56]

We suggest that such a condition was present in the population of central Mexico on the eve of the Conquest, the cause being a low caloric intake. Such testimony as has come down to us all points in this one direction. The Relaciones Geográficas in many instances emphasize the frugality of diet for commoners

54. Ancel Keys and Francisco Grande, "Body Weight, Body Composition, and Calorie Status," in Wohl and Goodhart, p. 24.
55. Sherman, *Chemistry of Food and Nutrition,* p. 195.
56. In addition to works already cited, see Francisco Gomez Mont, "Undernutrition," in Wohl and Goodhart, pp. 984–995, esp. p. 988.

before the coming of the Spaniards. In the report for Cuilapan, written by Fray Agustín de Salazar, the comment is especially striking:

> El comer de ellos es grima y espanto porque con unas tortillas de maíz y poco de agí y otras cosillas se contentan. . . .
> (Their food is a matter of disgust and horror, for with a few maize tortillas, a little chile, and other trifles, they are satisfied. . . .)[57]

Fray Agustín de Salazar was writing about his own time in 1581, but the Indian diet he described was that of the pre-Conquest as well. In Cuilapan it had not changed, much less improved.

In the history of Gonzalo Fernández de Oviedo y Valdés, who was never himself in central Mexico but questioned Spaniards who had been, including men of Cortés' army, is a summary of early testimony. According to Oviedo, the Indians of New Spain were the poorest of the many peoples who up to his time had been encountered in the New World. Their diet for the most part was maize and vegetables flavored with chile. The quantity was little, as he explains carefully, "not because they would not eat more if they had the food," but because the upper classes carefully assessed harvests and left them the bare minimum to sustain life and work until the next harvest.[58] Oviedo's description of poverty is corroborated by Motolinía, who spent many years in New Spain:

> Estos Indios cuasi no tienen estorbo que les impida para ganar el cielo . . . porque su vida se contenta con muy poco, y tan poco, que apenas tienen con qué se vestir y alimentar. Su comida es muy paupérrima, y lo mismo es el vestido. . . .
> (These Indians have almost no hindrance that might keep them from earning entrance to Heaven . . . for in life they are satisfied with very little, so little that they scarcely have the wherewithal to clothe and feed themselves. They eat most poorly indeed and clothe themselves in equal poverty. . . .)[59]

The Anonymous Conqueror summed up the matter tersely and elegantly:

> . . . es gente que se mantiene con poco alimento. (They live on little food.)[60]

---

57. In *Tlalocan*, II, p. 25.
58. Oviedo y Valdés, *Historia general*, IV, pp. 248–250. See also [Anonymous Conqueror], *Relación*, p. 50.
59. Motolinía, *Historia*, p. 85.
60. [Anonymous Conqueror], pp. 41 and 50.

There is no certainty, however, that the level of food intake fell much below the compensated phase of undernutrition, for, irrespective of areas of seriously deficient diet today, no one has adduced evidence to show widespread clinical manifestations of starvation among the natives before Cortés. If the farmers and laborers, who constituted the overwhelming bulk of the population, were just below or even definitely below the present-day standard of adequate nutrition, then the mean daily rate of energy production fell below the 1,900 kilocalories we have calculated above. How far cannot be determined with any exactness. Sherman's level of a one-third reduction, which would mean here a reduction to 1,265 kilocalories, seems extreme. We shall be safer if we estimate the level as lying between 1,400 and 1,800 kilocalories. Clearly the marginal diet of the commoners would support a considerable amount of physical effort, but distinctly less than that possible to the better-fed and larger European or American laborer of today. The subliminal energy intake could be compensated by reducing physical effort. That there was malnutrition as against undernutrition seems unlikely, because the wide diversity of foodstuffs that were eaten would supply needed elements. The requirement for protein and amino acids would be met largely from maize, beans, and other plant components in the diet. Any requirement for protein of animal origin would be small, on the order of perhaps 15 to 30 grams daily for an adult male, and was easily met by eating insects, grubs, snakes, amphibians, birds, small mammals, and indeed "any living thing."[61]

Our discussion has now arrived at the point at which we may make some examination of the probable amount of maize

61. Anthony A. Albanese and Louise A. Orto, "The Proteins and Amino Acids," in Wohl and Goodhart, pp. 95–155, esp. pp. 97, 108, and 113–116; National Academy of Sciences–National Research Council, *Evaluation of Protein Nutrition, passim.* Anderson et al., in their "Study of the Nutritional Status and Food Habits of Otomí Indians in the Mezquital Valley of Mexico," reach the conclusion that: "The region is arid and barren and, economically and culturally, one of the most depressed in the country. The inhabitants eat very few of the foods which are commonly considered as essential to a good nutrition pattern. Their consumption of meat, dairy products, fruits, and vegetables is exceedingly low. However, through the eating of tortillas, the drinking of pulque (the fermented unfiltered juice of the century plant), and the eating of every conceivably edible plant available, a fairly good diet is maintained." Guillermo Bonfil Batalla, in *Diagnóstico sobre el hambre en Sudzal, Yucatán* (pp. 133-135), indicates a daily consumption as typical not merely of Sudzal but also of "more than twenty communities all over the country" that would come to approximately 1,808 kilocalories daily, 1,466 coming from the ingestion of 419 grams of maize, approximately ½ liter.

consumed daily by an Indian peasant and of probable production in pre-Conquest central Mexico. Obviously anything we indicate here must be highly tentative. We have now indicated that the overwhelming majority of the Indians lived at a level of compensated undernutrition. Accordingly, our previously published estimate of probable daily consumption is too high. That estimate was based upon the allowance prescribed by the viceroy in 1555 for Indians conscripted for repair of the dikes of the lakes of the Valley of Mexico, and presumably reflected a customary ration. The allowance was one cuartillo of maize a day.[62] At 48 cuartillos in a fanega of 100 Castilian pounds (of 460 grams each, as against our pound of 453.6 grams), one cuartillo would be 958 grams of maize with a caloric value of approximately 3,350 kilocalories.[63] That is a generous ration, and when supplemented by other foodstuffs provided by the Indians themselves might reach a value of 3,800 or 4,000 kilocalories.

It is possible that the ration, even at that relatively early date after the Conquest, already corresponded to European ideas, which were more generous; but what evidence we have on European rations for men engaged in fairly strenuous physical activity would not come to so high a value.[64] Since the maize would be ground to meal and baked into tortillas for consumption, a service performed by women, we are inclined to suggest that the ration was for a man and his wife. Divided between them, it would come to the caloric values that we have indicated as probable. We shall return to these questions later in this essay. For the moment it is enough to suggest that the more

62. Borah and Cook, *The Aboriginal Population of Central Mexico on the Eve of the Spanish Conquest*, p. 90; but see the entire discussion, pp. 89–92.

63. We calculate 100 grams of maize as having 350 kilocalories. The value is a rough average of those given for various kinds of maize in Mercedes Hernández et al., *Valor nutritivo de los alimentos mexicanos; Tablas de uso práctico*, p. 6, and Juan Roca and Roberto Llamas, "Régimen alimenticio de los habitantes de la región de Izúcar de Matamoros (Puebla)," p. 584. For the maize of the sixteenth century, Roca and Llamas are probably nearer the true value at 341.81 kilocalories, since Hernández et al. deal with foods already greatly affected by the improvements of the Green Revolution—but the range from 341.81 to 366 is not great.

64. See the references in note 6; additionally, Cesáreo Fernández Duro, *La armada invencible*, I, pp. 248–320, esp. pp. 274–278; and Maria Cristina Silveira and Carlos Silveira, "A alimentação na 'Armada Invencível.'" The Silveiras base their calculations on a manuscript prepared by the Marqués de Santa Cruz, proposing supplies and rations for the Great Armada, the copy they consulted being in the Biblioteca Nacional, Lisbon. Fernández Duro publishes the manuscript.

normal allowance for an adult male commoner was closer to a range from one-third to one-half of a cuartillo of maize (319–479 grams), say from 1,120 to 1,676 kilocalories, the remainder of the day's consumption of foodstuffs and perhaps a far greater proportion of vitamins, proteins, and trace elements coming from fruits, nuts, frijoles, chile, pulque, small amounts of animal substance, etc. The amount of maize annually consumed by a peasant family might range from 10 to 20 fanegas, as suggested for the post-Conquest period in the Valley of Mexico by Charles Gibson.[65] For a family of average size before the Conquest, the likelier range would be 10 to 15 fanegas except in unusually favorable circumstances. The maize would be supplemented by a remarkable range of other foodstuffs.

The productivity of the pre-Conquest agriculture that provided this food is also difficult to estimate, since we have merely two sets of clues at this time and they are not easily reconciled. One set lies in the determinations of yields by Spanish tribute assessors in arriving at amounts and value of grain for tribute requirements set in plantings. Since such determinations occurred in the decades immediately succeeding the Conquest, we may assume that they reflect conditions substantially unchanged from aboriginal conditions. On an average, the determinations show a yield of 6.47 fanegas of maize for a planting of 1,000 square brazas,[66] or a harvest on the order of 1,060 kilograms of maize per hectare.[67] That average, which includes crops from irrigated and unirrigated land and from elevations from coast to plateau, is distinctly higher than the reported averages of Mexican agriculture just before the advent of the Green Revolution. We cannot exclude the possibility, therefore, that tribute maize was grown on the best land available to each town and was not representative of other yields.

65. Gibson, The Aztecs Under Spanish Rule, p. 311.
66. Cook and Borah, The Indian Population of Central Mexico, 1531–1610, p. 19.
67. Conversion of fanegas to kilograms is simple, since 1 fanega equals 46 kilograms. The braza is calculated at 1.6718 meters, the value given by Spain, Real Academia Española, Diccionario de la lengua española, from which we have taken the value for fanega. Sixteenth-century maize at this weight converts to dry measure at .83 kilograms per liter. These yields, which would work out to 14–16 bushels per acre, fall easily within the normal ranges indicated by Charles Gibson (The Aztecs Under Spanish Rule, pp. 309–310) for the Valley of Mexico in colonial times.

Our second set of clues on the probable yields of pre-Conquest agriculture is, of course, Mexican experience as recorded just before the remarkable changes that began in the 1940's and 1950's. In the first agricultural census of 1930, recording the agricultural year 1929-30, the range of yield for the states of central Mexico is enormous, from 472 to 1,237 kilograms of maize per hectare, and the returns subject to all the suspicions hovering around a new kind of statistical inquiry and one dependent upon thousands of respondents. The average for the states within the sedentary area of central Mexico as it was in 1520 is 633 kilograms per hectare, as against a countrywide average of 522. The countrywide average is for ejidos alone, 585, and for the private sector alone, 512. Productive units of one hectare and under were not asked to report.[68] Since one would normally expect the private sector to be more productive, we are inclined to suspect underreporting on a considerable scale. The 1940 agricultural census, reporting the 1939-40 agricultural year, has more favorable results: The area of central Mexico gave average maize yields of 679 kilograms per hectare, the returns being divided between productive units of more than 5 hectares, with an average of 665 kilograms, and those of 5 hectares and less, with an average of 699 kilograms per hectare.[69] So the two censuses, whatever the defects in them, indicate yields of maize for central Mexico ranging from 630 to 700 kilograms per hectare.[70]

68. Mexico, Dirección General de Estadística, *Primer censo agrícola-ganadero, 1930. Resumen general, cuadro* VIIIA, pp. 70-73. We have omitted Nayarit, Jalisco, Guanajuato, and Querétaro in our reconstitution of what was central Mexico in the sixteenth century, since they were then either sparsely settled or under the control of nomadic Indians. The 1930 census returns show an even greater range than the overall state averages indicate, since the average for ejidos in Puebla is 412 kilograms of maize per hectare, as against 1,424 kilograms for the Federal District.

69. Calculated from Mexico, Dirección General de Estadística, *Segundo censo agrícola-ganadero, 1940. Resumen general, cuadros* 2 and 4, pp. 54-186 and 201-242.

70. See also the annual averages of yields of maize per hectare from 1925 to 1937 in Mexico, Secretaría de Agricultura y Fomento, *Memoria*, 1937-1938, I, pp. 302-303, which show considerable fluctuation. If one turns to the 1950 agricultural census, the average yield per hectare for all of Mexico, after deduction of the crop of hybrid maize, was 786 kilograms. Land sowed to hybrid maize yielded on average 1,621 kilograms per hectare, but in that year so little was so sown that the average yield of maize of all types for all of the country was 790 kilograms per hectare. (Mexico, Dirección General de Estadística, *Censos agropecuarios. 1. Totales comparativos en 1930, 1940 y 1950. 2. Por entidades y distritos economico-agricolas en 1950*, p. 15.)

These returns may be low because of underreporting—but may be too low, further, for comparison with pre-Conquest agriculture, because of the havoc of four and a half centuries of erosion, continued cultivation of land without adequate preservation of fertility, and the adoption of the plow as against the digging stick. The plow gives higher yields per man-hour spent on agriculture, whereas the digging stick usually gives higher yields per unit of land.[71] Accordingly, we come to a range of probability: yields of maize for aboriginal agriculture may have been somewhere from 700 to 1,200 kilograms per hectare. That range of yield would have maintained the population we have postulated at the levels of nutrition postulated through cultivation of from 10 to 15% of the land.

4.

Let us turn now to the decades after the Spanish Conquest. That conquest deeply altered the forms and fabric of native life. One would suppose that it should have affected native production and consumption of food. The question is: In what respects, and how far, in the sixteenth and first half of the seventeenth century? The coming of the Europeans made available technology, plants, and animals previously unknown and capable of deeply altering Indian food production and diet. In addition, that coming unleashed other changes which were bound to have a profound effect upon native utilization of land and other resources. Among the new plants and crops introduced by the Europeans were grains, such as wheat, barley, oats; vegetables, such as lettuce, radishes, carrots, cabbage; fruits, such as apples, quinces, oranges, lemons, peaches, apricots; nuts, such as walnuts. Two fruits introduced by the Spaniards that have unusual interest were bananas, from Africa but strange to many Spaniards and so described by them as native to Mexico,[72] and guavas,[73] which came from the Antilles. A third European introduction of a non-European

71. See the comment by Gibson, *The Aztecs Under Spanish Rule*, pp. 309–310, and Francisco Javier Clavijero, *Historia antigua de México*, II, pp. 248–249.
72. For example, Relación de las minas de Sultepec, 5 March 1582, *PNE*, VII, p. 9; Pedro Martínez, *Descripción de la villa de Pánuco*, p. 4.
73. As in the Relación de Macuilsúchil, 9 April 1580, and the Relación de Chinantla, 1 November 1579, both in *PNE*, IV, pp. 103 and 65 respectively. The Relación de Chinantla correctly identifies guavas as coming from Hispaniola.

plant was the peanut, also from the Antilles, but given a Nahuatl name, *tlalcacahoatl*, little cacao—whence the present Mexican name *cacahuate*. In the sixteenth century it was raised in the region of Cuernavaca.[74] Among the new animals were almost the entire array of Old World domesticates, such as horses, donkeys, mules, cattle, sheep, swine, goats, chickens, and the stinging bee, with its greater production of honey. For food production, the most important items of technology were the pasturage and uses of livestock and the Roman plow.

Among the changes unleashed by the coming of the Europeans was the sharp decline of the native population, largely through the introduction of Old World diseases, which reduced the aboriginal numbers in central Mexico as of 1518 by approximately 97% in roughly a century; that is, by the 1620's the Indian population of central Mexico was about 750,000, 3% of what it had been in 1518. The drop varied with region and climate, being most catastrophic on the coasts and considerably less on the plateau.[75] Other changes were the insertion of the Spaniards as the new upper class; the relentless replacement of the native cult by Christian observances and clergy, but with a large underpinning of Indian assistants; demands for new services and products upon the Indian population by the Spanish overlords; the occupation of land and preemption of sources of water by the Spaniards for their own uses and purposes; and the beginning of the opening of the north to agricultural settlement, as the Spaniards applied the better European military technology to the problem of subduing the Chichimecs and settling the fine agricultural land thus made available.

The interaction of these factors made a complex pattern. The sharp and prolonged decline in Indian population made it impossible to cultivate large tracts of land. We know that very extensive tracts became waste, and that in consequence the availability of food through hunting, fishing, and gathering became correspondingly greater. We may further surmise that the Indian peasants of a town, forced to restrict cultivation to a much smaller part of their previous milpas and fields, would choose the better land for continued cultivation. Accordingly, the yield for effort spent on cultivation would improve; i.e., per

74. Hernández, *Historia natural*, I, p. 306.
75. See chap. 1 in this volume, and Cook and Borah, *The Indian Population of Central Mexico, 1531-1610*, pp. 46-56.

capita output would rise. With the large expanses of land returned to waste, the Spaniards could occupy substantial tracts without serious harm to the Indian population, except for desirable portions that the Indians might have wanted to retain but that the Spaniards wrested from them. A further source of pressure was control of water. Land and water nearest large centers of Spanish population, particularly Mexico City, would have been the most subject to Spanish seizure, despite native wish to continue occupation. The more serious countrywide problem was the spread of Old World livestock, which ranged freely over the waste and quickly became feral or nearly so. It was no respecter of legal lines, and preyed upon the Indians' milpas and gardens if they were accessible.[76] Had Old World livestock not moved into the ecological niche thus created, one may raise the question whether native species, such as deer, would not have multiplied with about the same result in harassing the Indians. Presumably deer and other wild species could be killed freely if found, whereas livestock had attached to them a presumptive Spanish property right.

One may measure the spread of Old World plants, animals, and technology through the reporting in tribute schedules, chronicles, land grants, and the Relaciones Geográficas. Although the Spanish attempted to persuade or force the Indians to raise wheat through requirement as tribute or other devices, the Indians found that the cultivation of wheat and other Old World cereals meant use of the plow, which in turn meant in the first years hiring a Spaniard and his work team of draft animals. They also found that the yield was less than that of maize, approximately 80% that of maize for the seed sown, and 70% for the area sown. Accordingly, there was persistent and substantial resistance to wholesale adoption of wheat. In more arid regions, where it had an advantage over maize, it was indeed used widely by the Indians, as in the Teotlalpan and the Mixteca Alta. Elsewhere, as the numerous references in the Relaciones Geográficas make clear, wheat was raised only in small quantities by the Indians. In general, the Hispanic com-

76. For abandonment of land, land appropriation by Spaniards, and the spread of livestock, see Simpson, *Exploitation of Land in Central Mexico in the Sixteenth Century, passim.* See also Gibson, *The Aztecs Under Spanish Rule,* pp. 257-299 and 405-408; and William B. Taylor, *Landlord and Peasant in Colonial Oaxaca,* pp. 67-257.

munity, demanding wheat bread through tradition and the prestige of the European, had to raise its own wheat, appropriating land and labor for the purpose.[77] Barley with its poorer yields was even less favored, and oats competing for use as fodder with the far more easily available and cheaper maize leaves and stalks were ignored by the Indians. The items of widest adoption among Old World plants were the fruits and vegetables, which were planted on a small scale for home use throughout much of central Mexico, climate and soil being suitable. In the warmer climates of the lower altitudes, two Old World plants had manifest advantage and were widely adopted. Bananas, with their prolific yield and small need for care, provided a warm-country staple that filled a genuine need and had no clear competition from native plants. Sugarcane, yielding a sweetener previously supplied only by honey or thickened maguey syrup, also filled a niche more fully than any previously available item.[78]

Of Old World animals, the adoptions by Indians in the sixteenth and early seventeenth century arose from their perception of usefulness and to a lesser extent pressure from the viceregal authorities and Spaniards. The animal most widely accepted was the chicken, which quickly spread throughout the country.[79] The adoption of the other animals may be traced in part through Lesley Simpson's study of viceregal land grants and permissions to raise livestock. The exact identification of use is somewhat obscured by the Spanish division of livestock into *ganado mayor* and *ganado menor*. Although it is certain that most *estancias de ganado menor* raised sheep, the term covered swine and goats as well. The mammalian domesticate most rapidly accepted by the Indians was sheep. Their interest was more likely the supply of wool than meat, for wool pro-

77. In addition to material in the Relaciones Geográficas, see Gibson, *The Aztecs Under Spanish Rule,* pp. 319–326; Cook and Borah, *The Indian Population of Central Mexico, 1531–1610,* p. 19; Borah, *New Spain's Century of Depression,* pp. 31–41.

78. In general, bananas seem to have been raised in almost every town with a suitable climate. Sugarcane was less widely diffused by the time of the Relaciones Geográficas, but still is mentioned sufficiently to indicate a considerable measure of adoption by the Indians.

79. By the time of the Relaciones Geográficas, chickens were present in virtually every town reporting. A few years later, Father Alonso Ponce and his companions were offered chickens for their food at almost every Indian town they came to. (*Relación breve y verdadera . . ., passim.*)

vided a far better fiber for cold-country use than any previously available, and enabled the plateau towns to make up the deficit of cotton that collapse of the tribute system of the Triple Alliance must have meant. According to Lesley Simpson's study, the overwhelming majority of grants to Indians were for sheep. A small proportion of grants were for raising horses and mules, and almost none were for raising cattle. The few such grants to Indians were on the eastern slopes of the plateau and in the north. In contrast, the majority of grants to Spaniards were for raising cattle, which spread rapidly throughout the country but were not in Indian ownership.[80] The extent to which swine and goats were adopted by the Indians is more difficult to trace. Certainly they were used to a far more limited extent. Except in marginal areas, goats have little advantage, if any, and the use of the pig as a scavenger may have developed somewhat slowly, since the chicken is a competitor. One other Old World animal was also adopted fairly widely by the Indians, namely, the Old World bee, with its superior production of honey.[81]

It is clear that the Indians in central Mexico adopted the plants, animals, and technology that made sense to them, and resisted the imposition of those items that meant a more expensive use of land and labor. The Roman plow, which meant the use of draft animals and the abandonment or destruction of steeply sloping land, spread very slowly.[82] Its advantage over the digging stick was dubious at best, and the crop most immediately linked to it, wheat, considerably less advantageous than maize in terms of food per unit of land. Moreover, preparation of wheat for consumption in the Spanish manner required grinding and processing in ways not easily available to an Indian

80. Simpson, *Exploitation of Land in Central Mexico, passim.*
81. Relaciones Geográficas, *passim.* Charles Gibson, *Tlaxcala in the Sixteenth Century,* pp. 150–154, indicates wide raising of pigs by Indians in Tlaxcala in the second half of the sixteenth century, but that province may be aberrant, since the Relaciones Geográficas and Ponce's *Relación breve y verdadera* do not confirm such raising for all of central Mexico, nor does Gibson himself indicate it for the Valley of Mexico (*The Aztecs Under Spanish Rule, passim*). See also Gómara's comment (II, p. 400): "Comen poca carne, creo que por tener poca, pues comen bien tocino y puerco fresco. No quieren carnero ni cabrón, porque les huele mal; cosa digna de notar, comiendo cuantas cosas hay vivas, y hasta sus mismos piojos...."
82. The spread of the plow among the Indians of central Mexico is clearly a story in itself that has never been explored. Clavijero (*Historia antigua,* II, pp. 248–249) indicates general adoption by the middle of the eighteenth century.

household. Equally slow was the spread of other crops dependent on the use of the plow. Chickens were an efficient scavenger, needing little care, able to fend for themselves, supplied eggs, and were a ready source of flesh in such small, inexpensive amounts that peasants could wring the neck of a chicken without reflecting upon the loss of revenue. Accordingly, they spread quickly. Sheep, with their special advantages in solving the needs of the Indians on the plateau, also spread quickly, although more slowly than chickens. The reasons for the slowness of the Indians to turn to raising cattle or pigs are less easily apparent. Cattle are more difficult to control than sheep, and perhaps more menace to milpas and gardens; they also represented a large investment without the annual yield of wool. Pigs may have looked less useful than chickens, a competing scavenger which both yielded eggs and came in smaller and more easily utilized units as flesh. On the other hand, pigs are the source of the highly prized cooking fat, lard, in a country which before the Spanish Conquest had no readily available, abundant supply of cooking fat or oil. Frying, one surmises, is essentially a post-Conquest culinary art. Finally, goats may have been considered less useful than sheep, yet in certain kinds of terrain their ability to browse on foliage instead of cropping grass allows them to survive where sheep cannot exist. Furthermore, goats are a good source of meat, and a rapid rate of reproduction is coupled with ready marketability.

Accordingly, in central Mexico, with the exception of a few of the more arid areas, Indian agriculture continued to raise maize, beans, squash, chile, tomatoes, as in the past, and the Indian diet continued to rely upon maize as a staple. What, then, did the Conquest bring in the way of change during the sixteenth and early seventeenth centuries?

First, the catastrophic shrinkage of the Indian population almost certainly meant that the survivors concentrated their efforts upon the better lands, and that average yields rose to correspond. So per capita output must have risen, and with it per capita consumption. Our study of prices of labor and of certain tribute commodities like maize indicates that in the second half of the sixteenth century wages rose more rapidly than commodity prices; that is, whatever the quirks of seasons, over the long term the wage of a day laborer tended to buy more maize. The main reason lay in the growing shortage of labor,[83] but the phenomenon is consonant as well with an improvement in per capita production and consumption.

A second change in food economy for which the Spanish Conquest was responsible was the pressure toward restriction of variety. It was economically more profitable under the European system to concentrate serious labor in the production of a few staple items, rather than to scatter energy in hunting and gathering types of food which were of diverse character and in the aggregate amounted to a great deal, but individually were trivial. Here would be found the snakes, insects, and algae. This reduction of multifarious natural sources occurred in the face of the introduction of new plants and animals, new grains, fruits, and vegetables. The latter species could be planted, harvested, and eaten under the supervision of the farmer, whereas the ancient resources flourished independently of any human control. Hence an apparent increase in resource range was actually accomplished by a canalization of effort which was more economical of effort than the old system and which actually furnished more edible material.

The further meaning of Old World animals for Indian food production and diet is distinctly more difficult to analyze. The Indian peasantry found a source of eggs and flesh in its chickens; in the end, the sheep and goats it raised would have made meat available, at least from old animals past any other usefulness. Furthermore, although the Indians did not take to raising cattle in the period we deal with, there is much testimony to the effect that they bought cattle for slaughter or bought beef from the Spaniards. Such beef was probably an item for the upper classes, and for the peasantry only on infrequent holidays.[84] Indeed, for the Indian upper classes the changes undoubtedly meant mere substitution, as in deference to European ideas they gave up consumption of human flesh and forewent protein from snakes and insects in favor of flesh from

83. Borah and Cook, *Price Trends*, pp. 39–46.

84. Gibson, *The Aztecs Under Spanish Rule*, pp. 346–347; Gibson, *Tlaxcala*, p. 153; Ponce, *Relación breve y verdadera, passim;* and Relaciones Geográficas, *passim.* The reports of the secretaries of Father Ponce would indicate a rather high consumption of beef by the Indians, but the Relaciones Geográficas, although also testifying to wide consumption of beef, indicate that ability to buy it played an important role in limiting consumption. See the detailed report by Juan Bautista Ponce in the Relación de Texcoco (García Icazbalceta, *Nueva colección*, III, pp. 49 and 54–55).

domesticated animals. For the lower classes the improvement was undoubtedly considerably less, but in an austere diet counted proportionately for far more. This improvement, in fact, constitutes the third probable change in food and nutrition referable to the Spanish invasion.

Although evidence is fragmentary, there are several bits which point to an increase in the average intake of both protein and kilocalories among the laborers and peasants of central Mexico in the decades from the middle of the sixteenth century to the middle of the seventeenth century. Our own examination of the wages of common labor in terms of purchasing power of maize indicates a rise in real wages after the first shock of the Conquest, a rise likely to have as one of its first effects an increase in consumption of basic foodstuffs. What evidence we have of rations and allowances of food point in the same direction. In September 1532 Lic. Maldonado, oidor of the Audiencia of Mexico, set the daily ration to be supplied by the town of Zicapuzalco to a slave gang working in the mines of Tasco at one cuartillo of maize, that is 1/48 of a fanega of 100 Castilian pounds, or 958 grams.[85] In November 1555, as we have already indicated, Viceroy Luis de Velasco proposed that the royal government furnish the Indian workmen to be drafted for repair of the dike system controlling the water levels in the lakes of Mexico, with a daily ration of one cuartillo of maize. He also proposed that the city of Mexico furnish meat for the workmen in a quantity that unfortunately cannot be determined, but must have envisaged an issue of several ounces daily or three times a week.[86] As we have already indicated, these were probably family rations.

Charles Gibson has assembled other evidence. According to him, in 1618 the standard ration for laborers on the Desagüe of the Valley of Mexico was one almud of maize per week, or 1/12 of a fanega. This means 12,880 kilocalories per week, or 1,840 kilocalories per day. Presumably other food was available to

85. Mexico, AGN, *El Libro de las tasaciones,* pp. 633–634. The slaves may have been given meat from another source. Presumably women made the tortillas and were fed from this ration without additional allowance.

86. Mexico (City), *Actas de cabildo . . .,* VI, pp. 192–193, session of 4 November 1555. The viceroy proposed that the city furnish 1,000 pesos de minas, which would buy meat for the 6,000 Indian workmen during a period of two months. Unfortunately we do not know the official price of beef at this time. If we estimate the ration at approximately 4 ounces daily, the price would have been 20 maravedís the arrelde of 4 pounds, a perhaps reasonable price for 1555, which was a year of scarcity. The city council, alleging poverty, refused to provide the meat.

supplement this allowance, so that the total caloric intake might have reached 2,200 or 2,300 kilocalories. Much later, in 1769, the standard ration for hacienda labor was, according to Gibson, 2 almudes of maize a week.[87]

These rations are high as allowances for a single man, even at hard labor. The question is pertinent whether this food was not intended for a man's family as well as for himself. There can be little doubt that such was the case on haciendas, where families were domiciled for long periods. We may also postulate the presence of women ministering to husbands working on the Desagüe, since the maize would have to be ground and baked into tortillas each day for consumption. Gibson mentions the presence of women tortilla-makers with the Desagüe labor drafts.[88]

The one instance where there is room for doubt concerns workers in the obrajes, who were usually kept confined. The ordinances for workers in obrajes, issued in 1579 by Viceroy Enríquez, set the daily ration at 2 Castilian pounds of tortillas, tamales, or bread, that is, approximately 920 grams of whichever was issued, to be given in three meals, and

... a medio día se les de un pedazo de carne los días que se pudiere comer, y a la noche tres o cuatro chiles; y el día que no fuere de carne se les de un cajete de frijoles o habas, y a la noche los chiles. . . .
(. . . at noon let them be given a chunk of meat on days when meat may be eaten, and at night three or four chiles; on days of abstinence let them be given a pot of frijoles or lima beans, and at night the chiles. . . .) [89]

We cannot be sure of the exact weight of a "chunk of meat," nor probably could the Spaniards of the time, but it must have meant at least 4 ounces of bone, fat, and muscle, a considerable nutritive addition to the 2 Castilian pounds of tortillas, tamales, or bread. The tortillas, tamales, or bread would have had a value of 2,100 to 2,200 kilocalories. The meat would have contributed at least 250 kilocalories, plus 20-odd grams of animal protein. The chiles, plus scraps which the persons might pick up

87. Gibson, *The Aztecs Under Spanish Rule*, p. 311.
88. *Ibid.*
89. Viceroy Enríquez, Mexico City, 7 November 1579, in Mexico, AGN, *Boletín*, XI (1940), p. 16. The ration was set in terms of weight to replace previous requirements that an Indian worker in an obraje be furnished daily 18 tortillas or 14 tamales and three times a week meat, on other days and in Lent frijoles, chile, or lima beans. Obraje owners either paid no attention or provided tortillas and tamales of small size and weight. *Habas* would normally mean horse beans, but in Mexican conditions were more likely lima beans.

from time to time, might add another 100 kilocalories,[90] so that
the total daily intake would have reached 2,450- 2,550 kilocalories. This is clearly a reasonably generous allowance for one
person engaged in moderate activity, if the obraje owner actually furnished it.

To sum up, definitive answers are precluded by a lack of
evidence; yet there is a strong presumption that the extremely
low nutritional levels endured by the Indians of pre-Conquest
central Mexico were mitigated significantly after the first shock
of the Spanish Conquest, that is, in a process that began by the
second half of the sixteenth century. This presumption finds
further support in the fact that the daily march of bearers under
full load, which was five leagues or hours of work in 1519,[91]
increased under the Spaniards to six.[92] Perhaps the strongest
support is in the testimony of the Relaciones Geográficas,
which repeatedly stress the austerity of life before the coming
of the Spaniards and the greater abundance and ease for the
commoner once the Spaniards had imposed their rule. The
respondents were trying to explain the shocking disappearance
of the Indian population; but their testimony, on the whole, is
firmly in favor of the idea that living conditions for commoners
had improved.

The Spaniards undoubtedly undertook to secure as much
native labor as possible as cheaply as possible. The fact that
they allowed their workers far more food than the latter had
been accustomed to in the aboriginal state is evidence first that
the food was available at low cost. This condition, in turn, is
referable to the economic and demographic changes induced by
the Conquest itself, and discussed here in a prior context. The
increase in ration is also probably due in considerable measure
to the opinion of the Spaniards on what constituted an adequate allowance. It must be remembered that the Spaniards
were thorough Europeans, and that 2 pounds of bread or the
equivalent and 4 ounces of meat, supplemented by some oil or
fat and vegetables, constituted a minimal adequate diet for a
working man, consistent with current Christian thought. We
doubt if they could conceive of steady labor being performed
when supported by a diet similar to that endured by the Mexica
and other Indians of central Mexico under aboriginal conditions.

90. Hernández et al., *Valor nutritivo*, pp. 6–16.
91. See note 48.
92. See the evidence assembled in Borah and Cook, *Price Trends*, pp. 41–42.

Chapter III

Mission Registers as Sources of Vital Statistics: Eight Missions of Northern California

1. THE MISSION REGISTERS

The Christian missions which the Roman Catholic Church established among aboriginal peoples in North America under the aegis of the Spanish Crown provide a rich and unusual source of demographic information. At the time of their conversion, the natives entered a written record that, so long as they and their descendants remained within the mission sphere of influence, kept track of them for an indefinite period thereafter, sometimes to the present day. As a result, we can find out a good deal about the aboriginal conditions of the natives as well as their behavior under the stress of European spiritual and material conquest. Despite great variation in time and place, there persists a certain uniformity in the response of the natives and in the clerical record of it which makes possible a study of the entire region on the northern border of colonial Mexico, that region which today is divided between two countries as the Mexican North and the American Southwest. At maximum, such a study can hope to trace the natives after conversion for two or three centuries. There is no need to examine the data on every locality and settlement. A series of samples should be quite adequate to the task.

The missions functioned also as parish churches for the non-Indian population, wherever it appeared, during the long periods that the missionaries were the only priests within the new-won territories. Accordingly, the mission records cover as well the so-called Hispanic population, the *gente de razón*. They were all of European culture, but more often than not of varied genetic stock—sometimes pure European, most likely mixed European and Indian, sometimes with an admixture of Negro, occasionally pure Indian from one of the native groups farther south. This melting-pot came into being as garrisons and mining and agricultural communities formed on what was initially a frontier.[1] The data on this population make possible a further set of studies for a group with different responses to what for them was often a remarkably favorable environment.

Selection of sample sets of data must depend upon their survival and availability. Here our own searches quickly disclosed that not all mission records have survived the ravages of time and indifference of man; further, that not all of those that have survived are readily available. The expectation of the Spanish Crown was that after the initial period of conversion and indoctrination, which might last for some generations, the mission population would be ready to enter normal parish life. At that time the missions would be secularized—that is, turned over to the secular clergy—and special endowments of lands and other productive wealth would be turned over to the natives or held in trust for them.[2] Accordingly, in normal course, as missions were secularized, their churches became parish churches and the registers of the missions continued as normal parochial registers. The earlier books of baptisms, marriages, burials, and all others should have remained in the parishes or have been transferred to a diocesan archive of some kind. Missions that were abandoned for lack of parishioners should have had their registers moved to another parish or to a local diocesan archive. Unfortunately, what happened was more complex. Many registers were lost through neglect; others have passed into private possession. There has been relatively little effort to trace mission by mission the fate of such records and the location of registers that do survive. For much of northern Mexico, we were unable to obtain information on the whereabouts of early mission registers or indeed much information of any kind. It is only now, under a widening impulse to cultivate local history and anthropology in new forms, which is being

1. See the discussion in "Racial Groups in the Mexican Population Since 1519," Cook and Borah, *Essays,* II, chap. 2, pp. 180–269.

2. The policy of secularization and the controversies it evoked may be traced in Mariano Cuevas, *Historia de la iglesia en México,* II–V, *passim,* and in Hubert Howe Bancroft, *History of Mexico,* III–IV, *passim.*

actively fostered by the National Institute of Anthropology and History in Mexico City, that inquiry is beginning into the whereabouts and state of such registers.[3] For Baja California, which long has excited interest on both sides of the international border—an interest that has extended particularly to the mission period—inquiries by a number of scholars indicate that few registers of the Jesuit period are known to survive, that considerably more of the Franciscan and Dominican period survive, and that there has been substantial dispersal of the materials.[4]

On the American side of the frontier, mission and parish registers for the Archdiocese of Santa Fe, covering the bulk of the Franciscan missionary zone of New Mexico, have been brought together in a central church archive, for which Fray Angélico Chávez, O.F.M., has published an excellent guide. From the guide, it is clear that all mission registers for the years prior to the Great Indian Uprising of 1680 have been lost, probably in 1680, and that much subsequent material has also disappeared. There remain, nevertheless, records and even runs of records for many missions and parishes, beginning, in general, at some time after the middle of the eighteenth century.[5] For another great Franciscan missionary province, California, there is still no up-to-date comprehensive guide. The registers are dispersed among the various dioceses, sometimes in a central diocesan archive, sometimes in the parish that succeeded the mission. The registers of Mission San Francisco de Solano are in

---

3. For example, Cynthia Radding de Murrieta, "Problemática histórica para estudios de población en la subregión de Álamos, Sonora," and her *Cátalogo del Archivo de la Parroquia de la Purísima Concepción* which give an inventory of the remaining parish registers of Álamos. Father Lino Gómez Canedo, O.F.M., has found a good many parish records surviving in the regions of Franciscan activity in northeastern Mexico. See his introduction to Ignacio del Río, comp., *A Guide to the Archivo Franciscano of the National Library of Mexico*, I, pp. xliii–xlviii.

4. The results of this inquiry are summarized in the discussion and table of Woodrow Borah, "Reflections on the Demographic History of the Peninsula of Baja California, 1534–1910." This paper is based on Hubert Howe Bancroft, *History of the North Mexican States and Texas*, I–II, *passim*; Zephyrin Engelhardt, *The Missions and Missionaries of California*, I, *Lower California, passim*; Peveril Meigs III, *The Dominican Mission Frontier of Lower California*, p. 181; Homer Aschmann, *The Central Desert of Baja California: Demography and Ecology* (IA 42), p. 276; Ellen C. Barrett, *Baja California, 1535–1956: A Bibliography of Historical, Geographical and Scientific Literature*, pp. xix–xx; George P. Hammond, ed. *A Guide to the Manuscript Collections of the Bancroft Library*, II, *passim*; and the filmed card catalogue of the library of the Genealogical Society of Utah, Salt Lake City.

5. Angélico Chávez, *Archives of the Archdiocese of Santa Fe, 1678–1900*, *passim*.

The eight northern California missions discussed in this book
and their approximate territories of conversion.

a civil deposit, the Bancroft Library of the University of California, Berkeley. Nevertheless, for the Alta California of the
Hispanic period, survival of records has been extraordinarily,
almost miraculously, good; and with the advent of microfilm,
consultation of the registers has become increasingly easier. A
thoroughly desirable further move to provide facilities for schol-

ars is under way in the concentration of microfilm of mission and parish registers for California, and the world as well, in the remarkable array of demographic materials of all kinds that is being assembled by the library of the Genealogical Society of Utah in Salt Lake City, with a branch library in Oakland, California.[6]

For the present paper, we chose as a sample the registers of eight missions in northern California, those situated in a continuous chain from San Luis Obispo in the south to Santa Clara in the north (see map). Listed in order of date of foundation, they are:[7]

San Carlos Borromeo, 3 June 1770
San Antonio de Padua, 14 July 1770
San Luis Obispo, 1 September 1772
Santa Clara, 12 January 1777
Santa Cruz, 28 August 1791
Nuestra Señora Dolorosísima de la Soledad, 9 October 1791 (We shall shorten this name to La Soledad.)
San Juan Bautista, 24 June 1797
San Miguel Arcángel, 25 July 1797

They fall by date of foundation into two groups, those founded between 1770 and 1777, and those founded between 1791 and 1797. The earlier group initiated the impact upon the aboriginal world of the California Indians from fourteen to twenty-one years before the second group; and to the extent that length of time was involved in the operation of this process, they were

6. An excellent attempt to give the location and coverage of California mission registers, now unfortunately obsolescent, is J. N. Bowman, "The Parochial Books of the California Missions: 1961." Moving the manuscript originals of some of the registers, consequent on changes in diocesan boundaries, has already rendered much of the article out-of-date, although it is still very useful. The best guide to the present whereabouts of the mission registers, so far as its coverage goes, is probably the card catalogue of the library of the Genealogical Society of Utah in Salt Lake City. We have consulted it in a filmed copy at the Oakland, Calif., branch of the library. That catalogue lists only what the society has been able to film. In 1976 it did not have the registers of the southernmost missions in the jurisdiction of San Diego, nor those in the Archdiocese of San Francisco. The early registers of Mission San Jose, for example, are not available in the filmed copies of the society, which do contain the later registers, because the former are in the care of the Archdiocese of San Francisco. We can only hope that the society ultimately will be able to secure film of all registers, and so for the first time make consultation of them relatively simple. For some idea of the general holdings of the library, see Larry T. Wimmer and Clayne L. Pope, "The Genealogical Society Library of Salt Lake City: A Source of Data for Economic and Social Historians."

7. Engelhardt, *The Missions and Missionaries of California*, II, pp. 74–78, 87–88, 103, 206, 216, 454, 494–496.

farther along in it by the time of secularization in 1834.[8]
Within the earlier group is San Carlos Borromeo in Carmel,
which served as parish church for the presidio and town at
Monterey, eventually the capital of Alta California. It was the
second mission established by Father Junípero Serra and was
one of the major foci of religious and political effort in the later
Spanish colonial empire. Its records also cover the longest span
of any of the eight missions. All of the missions continued as
parish churches after secularization.

Looked at in terms of native groups, the eight missions
covered the bulk of the territory occupied by the Costanoan
Indians, all of that occupied by the Esselen and Salinan linguistic bands, and at Mission San Luis Obispo incorporated the
northernmost villages of the Chumash. Despite linguistic diversity, all of these Indians, with the possible exception of the
Chumash, were basically of very similar culture.[9] The Costanoan
territory extended considerably northward, so that many Costa-
noans received religious administration from Mission San Jose
and Mission San Francisco de Asís (called alternatively, and
more usually, Nuestra Señora de los Dolores). Inclusion of those
missions in our sample would not, however, have given us a
more uniform group, for they ministered to large numbers of
coastal Miwok as well as other nearby groups. As Alfred Kroeber has commented, "Mission Dolores, at San Francisco, must
have contained an extraordinary jumble."[10] The fact is that
almost no mission dealt with a single linguistic or tribal group;
rather, each mission was forced by the Spanish strategic need
for a chain of posts along the coast, by slender resources in
personnel and supplies, and by the fragmentation of the native
population, to incorporate various linguistic groups into its
jurisdiction. For many of the missions in the north, the "jumble" was accentuated in the nineteenth century as Indians were
brought in from the Central Valley to replace the dying local
population. Substantial numbers of Yokuts thus were added to
the rolls.[11] Nevertheless, the eight missions do constitute a

8. *Ibid.*, III, pp. 473–477 and 501–532, gives a particularly bitter account of
secularization in California. Hubert Howe Bancroft, *History of California*, III, pp.
301–363, covers the plans, decrees, and eventual seizure of the mission lands.
9. Alfred L. Kroeber, *Handbook of the Indians of California*, pp. 347–350,
462–473, 544–568, and maps in those pages on approximate boundaries.
10. *Ibid.*, pp. 464–465.
11. *Ibid.* and pp. 474–543, for a description of the Yokuts.

relatively homogeneous sample in terms of culture of the local native population and of general geographic conditions.

Within the territory of the eight missions, there also came into being a relatively substantial population of European culture. In addition to the garrisons at the missions and ranches, there were three nuclei: the presidio and eventually town of Monterey, founded at the same time as the mission, 3 June 1770; the pueblo of San Jose, founded 29 November 1777, approximately two miles southeast of Mission Santa Clara; and the pueblo of Branciforte, founded in May or June 1797 at the northern end of Monterey Bay near Mission Santa Cruz.[12] The pueblo of San Jose was much closer to Mission Santa Clara than to Mission San Jose, so that it used the religious services of Mission Santa Clara even after the establishment of Mission San Jose. These three nuclei, and especially the two of the presidio at Monterey and the pueblo at San Jose, give a sample of the people of European culture.

We found that the registers needed for our inquiry, namely those of baptisms, marriages, and burials, on the whole, were extant for the eight missions, but with certain losses and certain difficulties of access. The first book of marriages for Mission San Miguel Arcángel, covering the years 1797-1853,[13] was not available, because it was stored in the mission itself rather than the diocesan archive. The first book of burials of Mission La Soledad, beginning about 1791 and continuing to the end of the Hispanic period, officially is lost. It may be in private possession, lie mislaid in some church deposit, or have been destroyed. A happier story is that of the first book of burials of Mission San Antonio de Padua, which at the time of our extraction of data also was considered lost. Somehow it had drifted into private hands, but has now been returned to the diocesan archive in Monterey.[14] Finally, the first book of marriages of Mission San Luis Obispo was destroyed in a fire on 29 Novem-

12. Bancroft, *History of California*, I, pp. 170-171, 311-313, and 568-571.
13. The second book of the register of marriages begins in 1879, but 6 marriage entries, covering the years 1854-1858, occur at the end of the first book of baptisms. For further information, see Bowman, pp. 309-315.
14. *Ibid.,* pp. 303-315. At some time before the First World War, Father Zephyrin Engelhardt (*Mission Nuestra Señora de la Soledad*, pp. 61-67) examined the first book of burials of Mission La Soledad; the book has disappeared since then. We are led to conjecture that it may have been mislaid, as was the first book of marriages of San Miguel Arcángel, or may have drifted into private hands, as happened to the first book of burials of San Antonio de Padua.

ber 1776, according to a notation by Father Junípero Serra in the new book he ordered prepared as replacement. The new book attempts to replace the lost entries from the *Status Animarum* or padron of the Indians and from popular knowledge. It was not possible to reconstruct the detail of the exact day, the witnesses, and much other information.[15] Thus approximately the first 45 entries lack as full information as the others, and for our purposes turned out to be unusable.

The three sets of mission registers that interest us here were part of a larger series of records kept at each mission under instructions from the parent Colegio de Propaganda Fide de San Fernando de México, which trained and supervised the early Franciscan missionaries in California. In addition to accounts, each mission was supposed to keep, and did keep, the following groups:

1. Register of Baptisms
2. Register of Confirmations
3. Register of Marriages
4. Register of Burials
5. The *Status Animarum*, or Padron, or census roll, which recorded the names of married adults, their children, widows, and widowers, with detail on date of birth, baptism, and origin or native village.
6. The *Libro de Patentes,* in which were transcribed documents of importance and circular letters of higher authorities, civil and ecclesiastical.

The books constituting each register were bound in flexible leather with sides that overlapped. The paper within, of good quality to take ink, measured approximately 8 by 11¾ inches. During the Hispanic period the books with blank paper were supplied by the Colegio de Propaganda Fide de San Fernando, and usually had from 300 to 350 leaves. The first and last leaves of each volume were usually left blank, the title being written on the obverse of the second folio. Invariably the first book of baptisms has, following the title page, a brief history of the founding of the mission; all volumes may have some leaves devoted to data that especially interested the missionaries and authorities. The entries are written in ink and signed by the priest who officiated at the rite. Usually a margin of perhaps an inch was left for a running number within each register, contin-

15. Engelhardt, *Mission San Luis Obispo in the Valley of the Bears,* p. 186.

ued into the following books of the same register. Within the margin the priests might note the names of the people baptized, married, or buried; whether Indian or gente de razón; if Indian, the village or ranchería; and so on.[16]

At best the information in the registers of baptisms, marriages, and burials is extensive. At a maximum, the baptismal entries give information for each individual which includes the date of birth, age when baptized, the Christian and sometimes the heathen name, the native village of the heathen Indian, the parents, their place of birth if known, and the nature of their relation to each other. The marriage entries give the name, the place of origin, the names of the parents, whether or not they were married, and the previous marital history of each of the new spouses. The burial entries list the name of the decedent, his village or tribal origin; sometimes the age and if not that, whether adult or child; the cause of death, if important; and religious information concerning last rites and burial. Clearly, if in every case the officiating clergyman collected and recorded all the data which was possibly pertinent, the vital record would be as voluminous and accurate as any contemporary registration system could devise. Regrettably, he was not always able or willing to do so. The entries as they are in the registers represent usually a transcription or enlargement from notes made at the time of the rite. Transcription permitted the priest to cast the entries in a more nearly common form, but pressure of ministration might delay transcription and, one suspects, in serious emergencies even lead to long delays and loss of notes. Moreover, within the requirements set by the Church, there was no fixed form which had to be adhered to. The individual priest wrote what he wished in the way he wished. In the vast spaces of California it was almost impossible to apply strict supervision, and the occasional *visitas,* which included inspection of the registers and the form in which they were kept, are invariably commendatory, regardless of what may have been said in private.

As we have already suggested, the mission registers permit us to examine the records of two distinct ethnic categories, although the format of the entries is the same for both. One

16. The system and format of mission registers are described with care in Engelhardt, *Mission San Carlos Borromeo (Carmelo),* p. 224, and *San Miguel Arcángel,* p. 40. See also Bowman, pp. 303–304.

group is the Indians, both as heathen at the moment of conversion and subsequently as neophytes in the mission. The other consists of what might loosely be called the white men, the gente de razón, predominantly Spaniards and Mexicans, who came with the missionaries and who supplied the manpower for the civil and military establishment. With them came their families. All were forced to rely upon the missionaries for religious services, for until the middle 1830's there were no parishes, and even after the secularization of the missions the former missionaries continued to function as parish priests. It was only in 1836, fifteen years after the independence of Mexico, that the Mexican national government decided to request the Pope to detach the Californias, Alta and Baja, from the Bishopric of Sonora. The formalities took four years and resulted in consecration of a bishop with see in San Diego.[17] Thereafter the American annexation led finally to the creation of a more elaborate arrangement of dioceses and the entrance of substantial numbers of new clergy. The process may be traced in the registers in the 1850's in the appearance of non-Hispanic priests, and a tentative choice of a language other than Spanish for the entries that eventually settled on Latin as the best compromise between Spanish and English. Thus, at first small in numbers, the people of European culture eventually came to outweigh the native element and to fill most of the pages of the mission books. At the end of the mission period and for two decades subsequently, the non-Hispanic people—that is, the Anglo-Americans, the French, the Irish, and other nationalities—began to make their numbers felt, despite the steady growth of the Hispanic population by natural increase and by immigration during the Gold Rush. During the 1850's they came to supersede the Hispanic component as the dominant ethnic group of European culture.

It is theoretically possible to make an analysis of the birth, marriage, and death status of the two fundamental racial groups, Indian and Caucasian, and to study also certain other parameters, such as racial fusion. Furthermore, we should be able to study the mixing of subcomponent groups within each of the dominant racial groups. However, in practice we are

17. Engelhardt, *The Missions and Missionaries of California,* IV pp. 90–91 and 195; Bancroft, *History of California,* IV, pp. 64–65.

restricted to the data which actually can be extracted from the registers. The restrictions are onerous. They vary greatly from mission to mission and within each book as new priests assumed responsibility and imposed their personal preferences and idiosyncracies. Nevertheless, they may be summarized in the following fashion:

To begin with, there are the usual technical difficulties, some of which have already been mentioned: illegible handwriting; poor copy because of the deterioration of the paper (perhaps most of all through overuse)[18] or penetration of ink to the other side of the leaf; all sorts of minor errors; and different formats, depending upon the priest and the exigencies of the moment. The result is that in all too many instances accessory information is lacking, such as identity of parents or birthplace of converts and couples being married. Even ages, where they are stated, are not exact. Usually the missionaries guessed at approximate age, given with the qualification "about" (*cerca de*) or as a range, e.g., 10-15 years. Naturally there was a great deal of heaping. Indeed, in the age groups over 40 years, the vast majority of persons were specified as being precisely 50, 60, or 70 years of age. Such imprecision in stating age is characteristic of similar records in the European world of the time.

More serious than inaccuracy in reporting, however, is the frequent and for some missions almost universal lack of any age statement at all. For Mission San Carlos Borromeo, one of the worst offenders in this regard, in both the marriage and burial registers indication of age beyond the categories of child and adult is completely missing. In the registers of other missions, there is a greater range of reporting age, up to very good. In consequence, direct tabulation of age at death is sometimes possible and sometimes impossible; for all deaths recorded in the registers of the eight missions, it is, of course, impossible. Baptismal data are better, for the entries in the baptismal registers of the eight missions do give ages for two groups of people, the heathen Indians at the time of conversion, and the

18. Virtually all holders of the mission registers now provide microfilm for the use of the public, as a result of the deterioration in the manuscripts brought about by much consultation. Unfortunately, the microfilm usually has been hastily made, without the care needed to make the film truly legible.

children of both Indians and gente de razón who were born under the auspices of the clergy. Since the Church insisted that a newly-born infant be baptized as quickly after birth as possible, we can be reasonably certain that a *párvulo* of any ethnic origin was, in general, no more than a few days or weeks old at the time of baptism. To be sure, baptism might be delayed even longer for reasons of health, distance from the mission, or long spells of inclement weather, but such instances are a small percentage of the baptisms of párvulos and more likely to be found among those of the children of the gente de razón than among those of the Indians, for the Indian settlements were either at the mission or visited fairly regularly and frequently by the missionaries.

The difficulty in securing adequate data on age at death would be insurmountable were it not for the custom, well developed in some missions but not in others, of writing in the margin of the entry of death in the register of burials the baptismal number of the person if he had been baptized in the same mission. It thus becomes feasible, at considerable labor, to check back to the number in the book of baptisms, where either the birth or the age at conversion ordinarily will be noted. Then the difference in dates permits the estimate of age at death. We have done so by full year rather than to month and day. If we assume that the age at baptism is correctly recorded, this estimate will be correct to within plus or minus one year, surely so in the case of newborn children, but much less so and with increasing error for higher ages in the case of converts. Even for newborn children the error is large by present-day standards; but the procedure is the best that can be obtained, because to calculate according to the month and the day of baptism or death would involve an inordinate additional amount of labor which, in most instances, would be wasted. We therefore, as a practical measure, are forced to rely upon averages by full year.

A number of our eight missions adhered faithfully to the custom of including the baptismal number in each death entry for which it was possible. Mission San Carlos Borromeo did not. Since its registers presented the worst problems for our study, we describe those problems in some detail. The registers of the other missions presented similar problems in varying but lesser degree. In the burial registers of Mission San Carlos Borromeo during the several blocks of years, representing different mission administrations, the baptismal numbers, with few exceptions, are omitted. In the remaining burial entries, the omissions of baptismal numbers occur frequently. The only sequence which is internally complete is that between 1799 and 1805 (nos. 1,287 to 1,604). The years from the foundation of the mission in 1770 to 1793 have been studied in detail by a previous investigator, almost certainly Monsignor James Culleton, who worked out the burials in detail. He wrote lightly in the margin the appropriate baptismal number beside the entry for each decedent, thus rectifying the omission of the missionary. Since these numbers are legible in the microfilm, which we consulted in lieu of the manuscript register, we were able to use them and here record our gratitude.

With these exceptions, the only way in which one may recover the age of decedents without baptismal number—and they constitute at least half the total at Mission San Carlos Borromeo—is to track them down one by one according to their Christian name. We had therefore to go through the pertinent sections of the burial register and write down the personal name and year of death of each decedent. Then the entire register of baptisms had to be examined within the years covered in our study, and each name checked against the list of those whose deaths were recorded in the mission.

For San Carlos Borromeo, close to 1,500 names were thus checked. Of these, 1,228 were found in the baptismal register. By difference, the age of death could be estimated for these to within one year. The remainder, 277 names, were not found in the baptismal register. The reasons for the deficiency are manifold. Many names were hopeless duplicates; others had undergone changes during the person's lifetime; in some instances the reconciliation was missed by sheer inadvertence. Indeed, the fact that nearly 82% of the missing ages at death were recovered must be counted something of an achievement.

Our final result for San Carlos Borromeo, however, leaves a good deal to be desired, for the aggregate number of ages at death obtained through all methods by no means equalled the number of Indian baptisms. This deficiency is demonstrated by certain totals obtained through examination of all the entries in the baptismal and burial registers of Mission San Carlos Borromeo for the years of our study. A direct count showed that 2,836 Indians were baptized between foundation of the mission and its secularization at the end of 1834.[19] Of these, 1,541 were converted gentiles and 1,295 were neophytes born in the mission. Of the former, the death entries for 1,117, or 72.5%, can be identified in the register of burials; of the latter, 893, or 69%. Collectively, of the 2,836 Indians baptized at Mission San Carlos Borromeo, 2,010, or 70.9%, have been identified as having died in the mission. Those 277 whose deaths are recorded but whose names have not been found in the baptismal record must be added to the identified dead, making 2,287 in all. There still remain, however, 549, or nearly that number, who were baptized but disappeared without trace from the mission record.

Several reasons for the shortage can be suggested. The first is that in some instances the priest was unable to or neglected to record the death. The latter contingency would have been very rare, but circumstances sometimes threw an almost unbearable load upon the missionaries. The epidemic of 1802 at Mission San Carlos was a case in point, for during several weeks the missionaries were so occupied with the care of the sick and the administration of the last rites to the dying that they were unable to keep the record up-to-date, and easily may have failed to record numerous deaths. A second source of loss derives from the fact that many of those Indians who entered the mission survived past secularization and were buried elsewhere. As is well known, all missions, including San Carlos Borromeo, underwent in the middle 1830's what in some instances amounted to complete disintegration.[20] The neophytes spread out into the surrounding countryside and merged with the civil population or, if they had been brought from a distance, returned to their native territory. When many of these people died, their decease was not recorded in the local mission register. Some may have moved to the jurisdiction of other missions, the registers of which do record their deaths, but such entries are even more difficult to track down.

19. The total of baptisms differs from any tabulated to date, as stated in Sherburne F. Cook, *The Population of the California Indians, 1769–1970*, p. 29. The reason lies in differing cut-off dates and, in part, in somewhat different criteria of selection. The same discrepancies will show up, in general, for all our data on baptisms, marriages, and burials for all eight of the missions. The data we adduce in this study are new assemblies based upon a new reading of the registers.

20. The plundering of the missions by civil administrators, and the exploitation of the Indians, may be traced in some detail in Bancroft, *History of California,* III–IV. Bancroft, although sympathetic to the concept of secularization, admits that it was a disaster in California (IV, pp. 43–44).

A third source of loss arises from those Indian neophytes who departed the missions even prior to secularization. They were the fugitives who caused so much trouble to the missionaries. Most of them preferred the old, primitive, free ways, and upon absconding from the mission reverted to their aboriginal mode of living. The burial register of Mission San Carlos Borromeo records several instances as early as 1780-1790 of neophytes who went to die in their old rancherías among the heathen. The volume of this kind of desertion was augmented notably in the last years of the missions, and undoubtedly accounts for a great many of the missing burial entries.

In any event, it is evident that we must deal with a sample of the total Indian population which, at San Carlos Borromeo, is of the order of 70%. With the converted gentiles, fugitivism or absenteeism in some form was the chief cause of loss. Although there may have been appreciable bias in favor of the younger adult age group, the effect probably was not serious, and the sample, therefore, would reflect more or less faithfully the response of the whole. Since very few heathen were admitted to the mission community at San Carlos Borromeo after 1804, the disintegration of mission society upon secularization at that mission would have affected the death records only of those persons older than 30 years. Hence, there might have been a reduction in the apparent number of deaths at the mature or older phases of life. It is impossible to state how severe this curtailment may have been.

The neophytes who were born in Mission San Carlos Borromeo were less likely to have absconded permanently than those who were accustomed to the heathen existence of their youth. Far more important for the participation of the former group in the demographic history of the mission is the fact that they were continuously produced from the earliest years to the end of the mission period. Hence in 1834, the surviving Indians born in the mission would show a spectrum of ages from newly-born to perhaps 60 years old. However, many of these survivors outlived mission supervision, and their deaths might never be recorded or might be recorded elsewhere. Hence, the sample available in the burial register includes only 70% of those who were born in the mission and were itemized in the baptismal entries. This problem is discussed further in the section below on the neophytes who were born in the mission.

In general, what we have stated about the data taken from

the registers of Mission San Carlos Borromeo applies to the data from the other missions. We estimate that we have been able to obtain approximately a 70% sample for each of the other five missions for which we have obtained information on burials. A problem of considerably lesser dimension than for the Mission San Carlos Borromeo registers arose for those burial registers which almost invariably identified baptismal number, in that some of the baptismal numbers turned out to be wrong and we were not always able to locate the correct entry. The effect was to reduce our identifications by something less than 1%. Perhaps the major difference in the data from some of the other missions and those from San Carlos Borromeo lies in the fact that upon exhausting the pool of local Indians within the mission territory—a circumstance that occurred at some time between 1804 and 1815 at different missions—a number of missions turned to the Central Valley for new converts, the so-called Tulareños or Tulares, who were almost all Yokuts, but were given their name in mission records because they came from the great reed swamps of the southern San Joaquin Valley. (The reeds were called *tules* in Mexican Spanish, from Nahuatl *tollin* or *tullin,* a reed; *tular* is a collective form.) The bringing in of the Tulareños meant a new population of somewhat different age distribution when it entered the mission records. At the time of secularization, the Tulareños still included substantial numbers of neophytes who could remember aboriginal life and were younger than similar groups among the local Indians. Accordingly, we have tried in our tabulations to keep data on the Tulareños or Tulares separate from the series for local gentiles. At the time of secularization, and afterwards for those who remained within the recording of the missions converted to parishes, the disintegration of both local and Tulareño Indians was bringing about a substantial amount of intermarriage, as the search for new marriage partners among widows and widowers broke down linguistic and cultural differences.

2. THE GENTILE COMPONENT OF MISSION INDIANS

We first examine data on the heathen Indians who were brought to Christianity at the missions. Our information for this section comes from the baptism and burial registers. We must segregate our data into the two distinct groups of heathen who were brought to the missions, the local gentiles (the missionary term), and the Tulares, for they came at different periods and had somewhat different characteristics. For the local gentiles, the process of conversion began as soon as the local mission was founded and lasted for periods ranging from 33 years to as little as 17 years after the foundation of the mission. At San Carlos Borromeo the period of conversion of local gentiles lasted from 1771 to 1804; at Santa Cruz, from 1791 to 1814; at San Juan Bautista, from 1797 to 1814. The changing content of the baptismal registers indicates clearly the ending of the initial period.

During the phase of conversion of the local population, the missionaries went out into the countryside in a continuing series of visits and brought to the mission those heathen who could be persuaded to come. Baptism came some time later, when the missionaries were persuaded that the Indians understood the rudiments of Christianity and were ready. If the selection of converts was entirely random with respect to age, and if the remaining population continued in a state of equilibrium, suffering merely the losses due to withdrawal to the mission, then the age distribution of the converts, regardless of the time involved, should be an accurate reflection of that of the aboriginal pool. Two circumstances render these assumptions untenable.

In the first place, the selection of converts may have been nearly random, but it was not quite so. For example, at Mission San Carlos Borromeo, of the first 50 baptisms, 4 were adults over 20 years of age, 9 were aged from 10 to 19, and the remaining 31 were children under 10 years. Later, groups of middle-aged or elderly adults were brought in. To be sure, these variations cancel out over a period of years, but short-term data are likely to be unreliable. In the second place, the residue of the native population was adversely affected. The social and economic balance, which even in a primitive society is delicate, was upset by the mere withdrawal of numerous individuals. Furthermore, the native community, close to and in contact with the mission, was exposed to the diseases introduced by the gente de razón and communicated with devastating effect to the neophytes.

Since conversion operated continuously upon a population steadily diminishing for other causes, the total conversions recorded by the missions could never equal the aboriginal total, even though the last native was swept up. How near it came to this total depended upon local circumstances. Cook has estimated elsewhere that the ratio of aboriginal population to conversions would be somewhere between 1.2 and 2.0.[21] For the eight missions here under study, the process of conversion went forward relatively smoothly: there was little physical conflict; there were no unusual epidemics. Hence a factor of 1.5 is possible. If so, and if 13,971 persons were converted, the pre-contact population of the area of our eight missions would have been approximately 21,000 just before 1770.[22]

Conversion of Indians from the Central Valley began only after the pool of local gentiles was exhausted. A series of expeditions to the Central Valley brought in Yokuts who had been persuaded or induced to come to the missions for conversion. Conversion of the Tulareños, a second phase of missionization, began sometime between 1805 and 1816 and was still under way at the time that the secularization of the missions brought it to an end. Three of our eight missions—San Carlos Borromeo, perhaps too far to the west, and San Miguel Arcángel and San Luis Obispo, the southernmost—did not participate in the conversion of the Tulares. San Antonio de Padua entered upon such conversion later than the other missions, since most of its baptisms of Tulares occurred in the years 1834–1838. Since the conversion of the Tulares was under way but far from completed at the end of the mission period, our figure of 4,020 Tulares baptized, which would indicate an aboriginal pool of perhaps 5,000 to 8,000, cannot be taken as an indication of the aboriginal numbers of the Yokuts. Cook has elsewhere estimated that as being of the order of 50,000.[23]

In Table 3.1 we list the percentages of local gentiles and Tulares baptized. For convenience, we give the total of such baptisms for all eight missions as well; the numbers for each mission are given in Table 3.2. The totals of baptisms for each category represent new counts and differ somewhat from those given in earlier work. Some of the difference arises from normal

21. Cook, *The Population of the California Indians, 1769–1970*, pp. 22–27.

22. With very small discrepancy, this total is in agreement with that in *The Population of the California Indians*, pp. 20–43. Our total here does not make provision for Mission San Francisco de Asís and Mission San Jose.

23. Cook, *The Aboriginal Population of the San Joaquin Valley, California*, *passim*, but esp. p. 70. The discussion does not separate out the Yokuts clearly, since it proceeds by area and subarea.

TABLE 3.1

Gentiles Baptized at Eight Missions
(Varying periods, 1770-1838)

PERCENT OF TOTAL

Mission	Local Gentiles (13,971)	Tulares (4,020)
Santa Clara	29.6	45.6
Santa Cruz	8.8	13.1
San Juan Bautista	10.7	27.2
San Carlos Borromeo	11.0	--
La Soledad	8.3	12.1
San Antonio de Padua	14.3	2.0^a
San Miguel Arcángel	8.0	--
San Luis Obispo	9.3	--
Total	100.0	100.0

^{a} Mostly 1834-1838

human disagreement on the totals of long counts; some because of the discarding of entries not giving the information wanted here; yet others because of differences in years included. In the case of Mission Santa Clara, for example, our figure for local gentiles baptized is 4,139. That is for the years 1777 to 1810 inclusive. We have omitted another 105 baptized in the years 1811 to 1834, since they fell outside the main period. If they are added to our total, we arrive at 4,244 local gentiles baptized, as compared with the figure 4,240 used by Cook in earlier work.[24] Our purpose in compiling Table 3.1 is to give an idea of the relative weight of each mission in conversions. Mission Santa Clara was the giant, accounting for 29.6% of local gentile and 45.6% of Tulare baptisms. The next most active mission in conversion of local gentiles (San Antonio de Padua) accounted for less than half as many. Mission San Juan Bautista, which was fourth in conversion of local gentiles, was second in conversions of Tulares. One can explain the differences in baptisms of local gentiles in terms of local numbers available, ease of access, and

24. Cook, *The Population of the California Indians, 1769-1970*, pp. 29-30.

the longer existence of some missions, but those terms do not
fully explain differences in the conversions of Tulares. One
would expect Mission Santa Clara and the easternmost missions
to have accounted for most, or all, of the Tulare baptisms, but
such an expectation cannot explain why Mission Santa Cruz
should be third in number of Tulare baptisms, nor does it fully
account for the role of Mission Santa Clara as the most prominent in such baptisms. One suspects that the Franciscan administration of the province, perhaps in consultation with civil
officials, made decisions on allocations.

In Table 3.2 we show the distribution of age among converts
at the eight missions at the time of baptism. The table is in the
format we use for all further tables in this essay: a summary,
followed by the data on each mission if available, the missions
being arranged not in the order of foundation but in geographical location from north to south. Where pertinent, this table is
divided into part A, local gentiles, and part B, Tulares, to test
differences that may show up. As we have already indicated, the
total usable baptisms of local gentiles come to 13,971, and
those of Tulares to 4,020. Ages are arranged by 5-year intervals
up to 24 years of age, and by 10-year intervals thereafter. The
data do not warrant finer subdivisions. In order to achieve
uniformity and to avoid heaping, the mean value of baptisms
per year of age is shown for each period of time. Finally, the
number of persons found in each age period is expressed as a
percentage of total baptisms, and the age periods are grouped in
larger units—0-9, 10-24, 25-64, and 65 plus—to discern
broader patterns of age distribution.

The two parts of the table indicate at once that there is
considerable variation in the data from the missions for both
local gentiles and Tulares. Furthermore, there is considerable
difference in the age distributions of local gentiles and Tulares.
In general, the local gentiles have high values for infants (but
Mission San Luis Obispo is a puzzling exception) and low
ones for aged, as one would expect. For the relatively small
proportion of local gentiles in the age group 10 to 14, particularly evident at Mission San Carlos Borromeo and Mission San
Antonio de Padua, we have no ready explanation; neither do we
have one for the lower proportions, on the whole, in the age
groups from 10 to 24. Otherwise, the age groups among the
local gentiles, if placed on a graph, would show a remarkably

TABLE 3.2

Age of Gentiles at Baptism

EIGHT MISSIONS

Age in Years	Total Number of Persons	Percent of Total Baptisms		Average Number of Persons Baptized Per Year of Age
A. Local Gentiles (1770-1819)				
0-4	3,452	24.7)	37.8	690.4
5-9	1,825	13.1)		365.0
10-14	1,078	7.7)		215.6
15-19	1,062	7.6)	22.7	212.4
20-24	1,032	7.4)		206.4
25-34	1,606	11.5)		160.6
35-44	1,550	11.1)		155.0
45-54	1,012	7.2)	35.6	101.2
55-64	811	5.8)		81.1
65-74	354	2.5)		35.4
75-84	132	1.0)	3.9	13.2
85 +	57	0.4)		5.7
Total	13,971	100.0		
B. Tulares (1805-1838)				
0-4	426	10.6)		85.2
5-9	493	12.3)	22.9	98.6
10-14	425	10.6)		85.0
15-19	372	9.2)	32.4	74.4
20-24	507	12.6)		101.4
25-34	895	22.3)		89.5
35-44	417	10.4)		41.7
45-54	237	5.9)	42.4	23.7
55-64	152	3.8)		15.2
65-74	78	1.9)		7.8
75-84	18	0.4)	2.3	1.8
85 +	0	0.0)		--
Total	4,020	100.0		

TABLE 3.2 (continued)

SANTA CLARA

Age in Years	Total Number of Persons	Percent of Total Baptisms	Average Number of Persons Baptized Per Year of Age
A. Local Gentiles (1777-1810)			
0-4	1,512	36.5)	302.4
5-9	465	11.2) 47.7	93.0
10-14	308	7.5)	61.6
15-19	248	6.0) 18.6	49.6
20-24	213	5.1)	42.6
25-34	362	8.8)	36.2
35-44	445	10.8)	44.5
45-54	278	6.7) 30.8	27.8
55-64	188	4.5)	18.8
65-74	74	1.8)	7.4
75-84	26	0.6) 2.9	2.6
85 +	20	0.5)	2.0
Total	4,139	100.0	
B. Tulares (1805-1830)			
0-4	152	8.3)	30.4
5-9	213	11.6) 19.9	42.6
10-14	201	11.0)	40.2
15-19	137	7.5) 32.2	27.4
20-24	252	13.8)	50.4
25-34	433	23.6)	43.3
35-44	204	11.1)	20.4
45-54	115	6.3) 45.1	11.5
55-64	75	4.1)	7.5
65-74	39	2.1) 2.7	3.9
75-84	11	0.6)	1.1
Total	1,832	100.0	

TABLE 3.2 (continued)

SANTA CRUZ

Age in Years	Total Number of Persons	Percent of Total Baptisms	Average Number of Persons Baptized Per Year of Age
	A.	*Local Gentiles (1791-1814)*	
0-4	217	17.6)	43.4
5-9	221	18.0) 35.6	44.2
10-14	140	11.4)	28.0
15-19	72	5.8) 24.6	14.4
20-24	91	7.4)	18.2
25-34	196	16.0)	19.6
35-44	146	11.9)	14.6
45-54	73	5.9) 37.7	7.3
55-64	48	3.9)	4.8
65-74	22	1.8)	2.2
75-84	3	0.2) 2.1	0.3
85 +	1	0.1)	0.1
Total	1,230	100.0	
	B.	*Tulares (1810-1835)*	
0-4	57	10.8)	11.4
5-9	47	8.9) 19.8	9.4
10-14	69	13.1)	13.8
15-19	74	14.1) 43.3	14.8
20-24	85	16.2)	17.0
25-34	96	18.2)	9.6
35-44	52	9.9)	5.2
45-54	30	5.7) 35.9	3.0
55-64	11	2.1)	2.1
65-74	3	0.6)	0.3
75-84	2	0.4) 1.0	0.2
85 +	0	0)	0
Total	526	100.0	

TABLE 3.2 (continued)

SAN JUAN BAUTISTA

Age in Years	Total Number of Persons	Percent of Total Baptisms		Average Number of Persons Baptized Per Year of Age
A.	*Local Gentiles (1797-1814)*			
0-4	316	21.0)		63.2
5-9	210	14.1)	35.3	42.0
10-14	122	8.2)		24.4
15-19	132	8.9)	24.8	26.4
20-24	116	7.8)		23.2
25-34	156	10.5)		15.6
35-44	176	11.8)		17.6
45-54	105	7.1)	37.0	10.5
55-64	115	7.7)		11.5
65-74	30	2.0)		3.0
75-84	9	0.6)	2.9	0.9
85 +	4	0.3)		0.4
Total	1,491	100.0		
B.	*Tulares (1816-1833)*			
0-4	151	13.8)		30.2
5-9	179	16.4)	30.1	35.8
10-14	83	7.6)		16.6
15-19	92	8.4)	25.4	18.4
20-24	103	9.4)		20.6
25-34	233	21.3)		23.3
35-44	115	10.5)		11.5
45-54	62	5.6)	41.3	6.2
55-64	42	3.8)		4.2
65-74	30	2.7)		3.0
75-84	5	0.5)	3.2	0.5
85 +	0	0.0)		--
Total	1,095	100.0		

TABLE 3.2 (continued)

SAN CARLOS BORROMEO

Age in Years	Total Number of Persons	Percent of Total Baptisms		Average Number of Persons Baptized Per Year of Age
A.	Local Gentiles (1771-1809)			
0-4	367	24.0)		73.4
5-9	252	16.5)	40.5	50.4
10-14	103	6.7)		20.6
15-19	163	10.6)	27.0	32.6
20-24	149	9.7)		29.8
25-34	162	10.6)		16.2
35-44	135	8.8)		13.5
45-54	86	5.6)	29.4	8.6
55-64	67	4.4)		6.7
65-74	27	1.8)		2.7
75-84	16	1.0)	3.1	1.6
85 +	5	0.3)		0.5
Total	1,532	100.0		

LA SOLEDAD

Age in Years	Total Number of Persons	Percent of Total Baptisms		Average Number of Persons Baptized Per Year of Age
A.	Local Gentiles (1791-1819)			
0-4	210	18.1)		42.0
5-9	107	9.2)	27.3	21.4
10-14	136	11.7)		27.2
15-19	123	10.5)	31.5	24.5
20-24	107	9.2)		21.4
25-34	136	11.7)		13.6
35-44	136	11.7)		13.6
45-54	119	10.3)	39.5	11.9
55-64	67	5.8)		6.7
65-74	17	1.5)		1.7
75-84	3	0.3)	1.7	0.3
85 +	0	0.0)		0.0
Total	1,161	100.0		

TABLE 3.2 (continued)

LA SOLEDAD

Age in Years	Total Number of Persons	Percent of Total Baptisms	Average Number of Persons Baptized Per Year of Age

B. Tulares (1806-1835)

Age	Total	Percent		Avg
0-4	66	13.6)		13.2
5-9	48	9.9)	23.4	9.6
10-14	61	12.5)		12.2
15-19	47	9.7)	33.1	9.4
20-24	53	10.9)		10.6
25-34	119	24.4)		11.9
35-44	41	8.4)		4.1
45-54	25	5.1)	42.7	2.5
55-64	23	4.7)		2.3
65-74	4	0.8)		0.4
75-84	0	0.0)	0.8	--
85 +	0	0.0)		--
Total	487	100.0		

SAN ANTONIO DE PADUA

A. Local Gentiles (1771-1814)

Age	Total	Percent		Avg
0-4	516	25.8)		103.2
5-9	266	13.3)	39.1	53.2
10-14	104	5.2)		20.8
15-19	139	6.9)	19.9	27.8
20-24	156	7.8)		31.2
25-34	248	12.4)		24.8
35-44	187	9.3)		18.7
45-54	150	7.5)	34.8	15.0
55-64	112	5.7)		11.2
65-74	71	3.5)		7.1
75-84	42	2.1)	6.2	4.2
85 +	11	0.5)		1.0
Total	2,002	100.0		

TABLE 3.2 (continued)

SAN ANTONIO DE PADUA

Age in Years	Total Number of Persons	Percent of Total Baptisms		Average Number of Persons Baptized Per Year of Age
B.	*Tulares (mostly 1834-1838)*			
0-4	--	--)		--
5-9	6	7.5)	7.5	1.2
10-14	11	13.8)		2.2
15-19	22	27.5)	58.8	4.4
20-24	14	17.5)		2.8
25-34	14	17.5)		1.4
35-44	5	6.3)		0.5
45-54	5	6.3)	31.3	0.5
55-64	1	1.2)		0.1
65-74	2	2.4)		0.2
75-84	--	--)	2.4	--
85 +	--	--)		--
Total	80	100.0		

SAN MIGUEL ARCÁNGEL

A. *Local Gentiles (1797-1819)*

Age in Years	Total Number of Persons	Percent of Total Baptisms		Average Number of Persons Baptized Per Year of Age
0-4	160	14.4)		32.0
5-9	124	11.1)	25.5	24.8
10-14	59	5.3)		11.8
15-19	51	4.6)	16.0	10.2
20-24	68	6.1)		13.6
25-34	166	14.9)		16.6
35-44	183	16.4)		18.3
45-54	98	8.8)	50.4	9.8
55-64	115	10.3)		11.5
65-74	62	5.5)		6.2
75-84	19	1.7)	8.1	1.9
85 +	10	0.9)		1.0
Total	1,115	100.0		

TABLE 3.2 (continued)

SAN LUIS OBISPO

Age in Years	Total Number of Persons	Percent of Total Baptisms		Average Number of Persons Baptized Per Year of Age
A.	Local Gentiles (1773-1809)			
0-4	154	11.8)		30.8
5-9	180	13.8) 25.7		36.0
10-14	106	8.2)		21.2
15-19	134	10.3) 28.6		26.8
20-24	132	10.2)		26.4
25-34	180	13.8)		18.0
35-44	142	10.9) 40.2		14.2
45-54	103	7.9)		10.3
55-64	99	7.6)		9.9
65-74	51	3.9)		5.1
75-84	14	1.1) 5.5		1.4
85 +	6	0.5)		0.6
Total	1,301	100.0		

smooth curve. There is little doubt that it represents the normal aboriginal condition among the native populations of the area—a high birth rate and a high death rate, which together result in a large youthful and a small aged population. The Tulares, in general, show larger values for the age groups 10 to 24, and so come nearer normal expectation in an aboriginal population, but on the other hand have considerably lower percentages than the local gentiles in the age groups 0-9. The deficiency is most marked in age group 0-4. Since they had to be brought considerable distances over rough terrain, the explanation may be that Yokuts with infants were more reluctant to attempt the journey or that, if they did, a substantial proportion of the infants died on the journey.

The next steps in our examination of data require some preceding reflection on the nature of the sample. First, we are dependent on the statement of age in the death entries, made by the missionaries. We have already commented on the problems in such statements. Second, we have noted that for only about 70% of those baptized is there an identifiable burial record. Any consideration of the mortality displayed by gentile converts in the missions must start with that fact, for one important result is that if we use only the 70% sample, as we must, the older age groups will be spuriously truncated progressively among those baptized during the later years of the mission period, since we cannot trace them past the middle 1830's. It therefore becomes mandatory for certain purposes to exclude the deaths which occurred beyond a relatively early age and to delete those gentiles who were baptized toward the end of the years of active conversion.

Basically we have here what is actually two distinct immigrant populations, a larger one and a smaller one, the entrance of both spread over a span of years. Accordingly, the formulation of ages cannot be considered a census. On the other hand, the deaths, within the limitations mentioned above, can be arranged in the form of a life table, where the age-specific death rates of the populations (q_x) can be shown, as well as the mean expectation of life (e_x) for each 10-year or 5-year age group. We have done so in Table 3.3. In this table the elimination of those gentiles who were baptized toward the end of the mission period has deleted the Tulares of all missions except Santa Clara. Hence the data shown are for local gentiles only, except for the division of the part of the table devoted to Mission Santa Clara into two parts, A for local gentiles and B for Tulares. For that reason, further, we do not repeat the data on the Tulares in the summary. The exact value of e_x at birth is very dubious, because there were abnormally few deaths in the first age group, 0–4 years, while the values for the older age groups are probably too high because of fugitivism and survival past 1834. Similarly, the value of e_x for the last age group should be regarded as a convention, since we have little evidence on which to calculate the true value. These features are also seen in the distribution of age at death (D_x). The Tulares at Mission Santa Clara show a distribution that is somewhat different from that of the local gentiles at the same mission, but actually nearer that of the local gentiles in general. The greater value of e_x for the age group 0–4 may well be due to deficiency of data.

TABLE 3.3

Age at Death of Local Gentiles Whose Deaths Were Identifiable,
1770-1834 (variable dates for each mission). Data Presented in Life Table.

SIX MISSIONS

Age Group	D_x	d_x	l_x	q_x	L_x	T_x	e_x
0-4	595	776	10,000	0.07763	48,060	354,309	35.43
5-9	475	620	9,224	0.06721	44,570	306,249	33.20
10-14	562	733	8,604	0.08519	41,188	261,679	30.41
15-19	557	727	7,871	0.09236	37,538	220,491	28.01
20-24	669	873	7,144	0.12220	33,538	182,953	25.61
25-34	1,165	1,520	6,271	0.24238	55,110	149,415	23.83
35-44	1,106	1,443	4,751	0.30372	40,295	94,305	19.85
45-54	952	1,242	3,308	0.37545	26,870	54,010	16.33
55-64	754	984	2,066	0.47628	15,740	27,140	13.14
65-74	482	630	1,082	0.58225	7,670	11,400	10.54
75-84	234	305	452	0.67477	2,995	3,730	8.25
85 +	113	147	147	1.00000	735	735	5.00

SANTA CLARA

Age Group	D_x	d_x	l_x	q_x	L_x	T_x	e_x

A. *Local Gentiles*

Age Group	D_x	d_x	l_x	q_x	L_x	T_x	e_x
0-4	345	1,381	10,000	0.13810	46,548	306,033	30.60
5-9	210	840	8,619	0.09745	40,995	259,485	30.11
10-14	207	828	7,779	0.10644	36,825	218,490	28.09
15-19	214	856	6,951	0.12314	32,615	181,665	26.14
20-24	215	860	6,095	0.14109	28,325	149,050	24.45
25-34	323	1,293	5,235	0.24699	45,885	120,725	23.06
35-44	298	1,193	3,942	0.30263	33,455	74,840	18.99
45-54	299	1,197	2,749	0.43543	21,505	41,385	15.05
55-64	188	752	1,552	0.48453	11,760	19,880	12.81
65-74	123	492	800	0.61500	5,540	8,120	10.15
75-84	51	204	308	0.66233	2,060	2,580	8.38
85 +	26	104	104	1.00000	520	520	5.00

TABLE 3.3 (continued)

SANTA CLARA

Age Group	D_x	d_x	l_x	q_x	L_x	T_x	e_x
			B.	*Tulares*			
0-4	31	301	10,000	0.03012	49,248	342,927	34.29
5-9	45	437	9,699	0.04505	47,403	293,679	30.28
10-14	74	719	9,262	0.07762	44,513	246,276	26.59
15-19	104	1,011	8,543	0.11834	40,188	201,763	23.62
20-24	143	1,390	7,532	0.18454	34,185	161,575	21.45
25-34	211	2,051	6,142	0.33393	51,165	127,390	20.74
35-44	143	1,390	4,091	0.33977	33,960	76,225	18.63
45-54	113	1,098	2,701	0.40651	21,520	42,265	15.65
55-64	69	670	1,603	0.41796	12,680	20,745	12.94
65-74	68	661	933	0.70846	6,025	8,065	8.64
75-84	21	204	272	0.75000	1,700	2,040	7.50
85 +	7	68	68	1.00000	340	340	5.00

SANTA CRUZ

Age Group	D_x	d_x	l_x	q_x	L_x	T_x	e_x
			Local Gentiles				
0-4	50	490	10,000	0.04900	48,775	304,992	30.50
5-9	83	815	9,510	0.08569	45,513	256,217	26.94
10-14	125	1,227	8,695	0.14111	40,408	210,704	24.23
15-19	90	883	7,468	0.11823	35,133	170,296	22.80
20-24	102	1,001	6,585	0.15201	30,423	135,163	20.53
25-34	178	1,747	5,584	0.31285	47,105	104,740	18.76
35-44	182	1,786	3,837	0.46546	29,440	57,635	15.02
45-54	92	903	2,051	0.44027	15,995	28,195	13.75
55-64	66	648	1,148	0.56445	8,240	12,200	10.63
65-74	39	383	500	0.76600	3,085	3,960	7.92
75-84	9	88	117	0.75213	730	875	7.48
85 +	3	29	29	1.00000	145	145	5.00

TABLE 3.3 (continued)

SAN JUAN BAUTISTA

Age Group	D_x	d_x	l_x	q_x	L_x	T_x	e_x
			Local Gentiles				
0-4	44	407	10,000	0.04070	48,982	344,685	34.47
5-9	76	702	9,593	0.07317	46,210	295,703	30.82
10-14	89	823	8,891	0.09256	42,398	249,493	28.06
15-19	100	924	8,068	0.11452	38,030	207,095	25.67
20-24	98	906	7,144	0.12689	33,455	169,065	23.67
25-34	200	1,848	6,238	0.29624	53,140	135,610	21.74
35-44	155	1,433	4,390	0.32642	36,735	82,470	18.79
45-54	118	1,091	2,957	0.36895	24,115	45,735	15.47
55-64	107	988	1,866	0.52947	13,720	21,620	11.59
65-74	66	610	878	0.69476	5,730	7,900	9.00
75-84	20	185	268	0.69029	1,755	2,170	8.10
85 +	9	83	83	1.00000	415	415	5.00

SAN CARLOS BORROMEO

Age Group	D_x	d_x	l_x	q_x	L_x	T_x	e_x
			Local Gentiles				
0-4	91	813	10,000	0.08130	47,968	341,454	34.15
5-9	62	554	9,187	0.06030	44,550	293,486	31.94
10-14	81	723	8,633	0.08325	41,358	248,936	28.83
15-19	87	777	7,910	0.09823	37,608	207,578	26.24
20-24	131	1,170	7,133	0.16403	32,740	169,170	23.82
25-34	163	1,456	5,963	0.24417	52,350	137,230	23.01
35-44	161	1,438	4,507	0.31906	37,880	84,880	18.83
45-54	135	1,206	3,069	0.39296	24,660	47,000	15.31
55-64	119	1,063	1,863	0.57058	13,315	22,340	11.99
65-74	46	411	800	0.51375	5,945	9,025	11.28
75-84	30	268	389	0.68894	2,500	3,080	7.91
85 +	13	116	116	1.00000	580	580	5.00

LA SOLEDAD

(The burial register of Mission Nuestra Señora de la Soledad has been lost. Hence it is impossible to formulate any data regarding deaths, whether Indian or gente de razón, nor can survival be calculated.)

SAN ANTONIO DE PADUA

(The burial register for Mission San Antonio de Padua was not available.)

TABLE 3.3 (continued)

SAN MIGUEL ARCÁNGEL

Age Group	D_x	d_x	l_x	q_x	L_x	T_x	e_x
			Local Gentiles				
0-4	38	426	10,000	0.04260	48,935	475,367	47.54
5-9	30	336	9,574	0.03510	47,030	426,432	44.54
10-14	33	370	9,238	0.04005	45,265	379,402	41.07
15-19	21	235	8,868	0.02650	43,753	333,777	37.64
20-24	46	516	8,633	0.05977	41,875	290,024	33.59
25-34	115	1,289	8,117	0.15880	74,725	248,169	30.57
35-44	123	1,379	6,828	0.20196	61,385	173,424	25.40
45-54	125	1,402	5,449	0.25729	47,480	112,039	20.56
55-64	135	1,514	4,047	0.37410	32,900	64,559	15.95
65-74	106	1,188	2,533	0.46901	19,390	31,659	12.50
75-84	75	841	1,345	0.62528	9,245	12,269	9.12
85 +	45	504	504	1.00000	2,520	2,520	5.00

SAN LUIS OBISPO

Age Group	D_x	d_x	l_x	q_x	L_x	T_x	e_x
			Local Gentiles				
0-4	27	256	10,000	0.02560	49,360	438,569	43.86
5-9	14	133	9,744	0.01364	48,388	389,269	39.95
10-14	27	256	9,611	0.02655	47,415	340,821	35.46
15-19	45	427	9,355	0.04564	45,708	293,406	31.36
20-24	77	731	8,928	0.08187	42,813	247,698	27.74
25-34	186	1,766	8,197	0.21544	73,140	204,885	25.00
35-44	187	1,776	6,431	0.27616	55,430	131,745	20.49
45-54	183	1,738	4,655	0.37336	37,860	76,315	16.39
55-64	139	1,320	2,917	0.45251	22,570	38,455	13.18
65-74	102	969	1,597	0.60676	11,125	15,885	9.95
75-84	49	466	628	0.74203	3,950	4,760	7.58
85 +	17	162	162	1.00000	810	810	5.00

There is little value in attempting to set this pseudo-life table alongside the many models available in the literature, for it is established by the peculiar and individual circumstances surrounding the Christianization of these particular Indians. It is, however, of value for the purpose of comparison among the eight missions and with other missions within the same province and elsewhere.

An alternative approach to the problem of mortality among the converted Indians is through an examination of survivorship in the missions. The essential point is that, whereas in constructing a normal or ordinary life table we reckon the age at death from birth of each person, here we take the difference in years between age at death and age at conversion. Thus we deal with the number of years the neophyte lived after entering the new environment, an event which was signalized by the ceremony of baptism. It may be noted that this examination of survivorship under altered conditions can be applied to any segment of a population which has been generated by mass migration so as to form a new demographic entity. Furthermore, since we use the interval of two events recorded as each occurred, and make that calculation of interval ourselves, the data are free from the inaccuracies of missionary knowledge or estimate of age.

Table 3.4A shows the number of years survived, in intervals of five years each, by the gentiles who were baptized in the decades between 1770 and 1809. We have data for six missions. For two missions, San Juan Bautista and San Miguel Arcángel, we have included data to 1815. The main table deals only with local gentiles, but we have included an appendix on the Tulares at Santa Clara with data from 1805 to 1834. The earlier the decade, the more complete the data. Our data, with very few exceptions, have a definite cut-off, manifest for those who lived to the period of secularization. This feature is evident in the lack of data, in general, for survivors in the 1800–1809 group of more than 30 years and in the 1790–1799 group of more than 40 years. We have attempted to minimize the difficulties arising from the cut-off date by calculating the percentages and medians for those who survived less than 30 years in the missions, as well as for those who survived to the full 49 years provided in the categories of the table. The error introduced by our inability to trace survivors after secularization is of an order at which we can only guess. We estimate 2 to 3%—a magnitude which is considerable, especially since it weighs upon the longer terms of years of survival, but in the circumstances is not fatal.

Table 3.4A exhibits certain features easily noticeable. In general, there is a progressive gradation in survival regardless of age at baptism and calendar year of conversion. Even more striking is the degree of variation in the experience at each mission, which is smoothed out in the summary. Mission San

Carlos Borromeo shows a comparatively uniform picture, with little change during the mission period. The median span of years for all local gentiles surviving less than 30 years at the mission was close to 8.9 years, and for the entire group surviving up to 49 years, the median was close to 10.2. The best record in terms of survivorship was that of Mission San Luis Obispo, at which the median span of years for local gentiles surviving less than 30 years after baptism was 12.7, and for the entire group surviving up to 49 years, 15.62 years. The other missions show considerably poorer records, with sharp variation in the experience of those baptized in one decade from that of those baptized in other decades. At Mission Santa Clara, for example, those baptized in the decade 1780-1789 show a median experience of 8.41 years of survival for those who survived less than 30 years after baptism and 9.61 for those who survived up to 49 years after baptism. For those baptized in the decade 1790-1799, the medians fell respectively to 4.22 and 4.35. In terms of survival after baptism, there was very real good or bad fortune according to the mission the local gentile was in. The difference in experience shows up very clearly in the totals for each mission and in the degree of variation among the cohorts. Experience for the Tulares at Mission Santa Clara, incidentally, appears to have been slightly more favorable than for local gentiles, but the differences may be more apparent than real because of greater nearness to the cut-off years of secularization. We are at this time unable to account for the high degree of variation in the experience of most missions and for the great variability from mission to mission. We can only suggest that a reexamination of the history of these missions with this table in mind may well yield new and perhaps unexpected insights.

One question of considerable interest concerns the length of time the same Indians would have survived if they had remained in their aboriginal culture and had not been gathered into missions—even more if they had not had any contact with the Europeans. There is, of course, no basis at this time for an answer. The unavoidable establishment of contact with Europeans would have brought the diseases of the Old World in any event. If the coastal Indians of central California had not experienced the perhaps benign regime of the Franciscan missions, their fate might have been even harsher under a civil regime of some kind, or under another European subculture.

TABLE 3.4A

Years Survived after Baptism by Converts, 1770-1809

Two age groups are shown: 0-29 and 30-49 years of survival in the mission after baptism. Jointly they form the group which survived 0-49 years and whose deaths were identifiable.

SIX MISSIONS

Number of Years Survived	Number Baptized				Total	Percent	
	1770-1779	1780-1789	1790-1799	1800-1809		0-29 Years	0-49 Years
0-4	106	318	1,221	1,091	2,736	39.4	36.6
5-9	154	200	410	707	1,471	21.2	19.7
10-14	82	133	326	451	992	14.3	13.3
15-19	93	130	208	331	762	11.0	10.2
20-24	75	113	135	248	571	8.2	7.6
25-29	61	74	93	190	418	6.0	5.6
0-29	571	968	2,393	3,018	6,950	100.0	93.0
Median	11.55	9.15	4.90	7.96	7.51		
30-34	35	58	64	130	287		3.8
35-39	22	48	41	36	147		2.0
40-44	13	23	15	8	59		0.8
45-49	16	16	1	—	33		0.4
0-49	657	1,113	2,514	3,192	7,476		100.0
Median	14.18	11.45	5.44	8.57	8.41		

TABLE 3.4A (continued)

SANTA CLARA (1780-1809)[a]

Number of Years Survived	Number Baptized				Percent	
	1780-1789	1790-1799	1800-1809	Total	0-29 Years	0-49 Years
0-4	158	732	230	1,120	48.63	46.74
5-9	110	162	148	420	18.24	17.53
10-14	56	140	86	282	12.24	11.77
15-19	60	101	72	233	10.12	9.72
20-24	45	57	45	147	6.38	6.14
25-29	37	44	20	101	4.39	4.21
0-29	466	1,236	601	2,303	100.00	96.11
Median	8.41	4.22	7.38	5.38		
30-34	23	24	3	50		2.09
35-39	17	11	--	28		1.17
40-44	7	2	--	9		0.38
45-49	6	--	--	6		0.25
0-49	519	1,273	604	2,396		100.00
Median	9.61	4.35	7.43	5.93		

a Some local gentiles were baptized between 1811-13, 1824-27, 1831-34 (105 in all); three people lived over 50 years after baptism. These 108 individuals do not appear in the above table.

TABLE 3.4A (continued)

SANTA CRUZ (1791-1809)

Number of Years Survived	Number Baptized			Percent	
	1791-1799	1800-1809	Total	0-29 Years	0-49 Years
0-4	310	150	460	46.27	45.14
5-9	158	83	241	24.25	23.65
10-14	106	42	148	14.89	14.52
15-19	48	19	67	6.74	6.58
20-24	42	20	62	6.24	6.08
25-29	11	5	16	1.61	1.57
0-29	675	319	994	100.00	97.54
Median	5.87	5.57	5.77		
30-34	10	2	12		1.18
35-39	10	--	10		0.98
40-44	3	--	3		0.30
45-49	--	--	--		0.00
0-49	698	321	1,019		100.00
Median	6.23	5.63	6.03		

TABLE 3.4A (continued)

SAN JUAN BAUTISTA (1797-1815)

Number of Years Survived	Total	Percent	
		0-29 Years	0-49 Years
0-4	388	36.95	35.86
5-9	307	29.24	28.37
10-14	153	14.57	14.14
15-19	88	8.38	8.13
20-24	63	6.00	5.82
25-29	51	4.86	4.71
0-29	1,050	100.00	97.54
Median	7.23		
30-34	28		2.59
35-39	3		0.28
40-44	1		0.09
45-49	--		0.00
0-49	1,082		100.00
Median	7.49		

215

TABLE 3.4A (continued)

SAN CARLOS BORROMEO (1770-1809)

Number of Years Survived	Number Baptized				Total	Percent	
	1770-1779	1780-1789	1790-1799	1800-1809		0-29 Years	0-49 Years
0-4	74	122	81	28	305	30.81	27.60
5-9	130	68	37	7	242	24.44	21.90
10-14	58	61	33	16	168	16.97	15.20
15-19	51	41	21	18	131	13.23	11.85
20-24	21	37	16	5	79	7.98	7.14
25-29	21	20	19	5	65	6.57	5.88
0-29	355	349	207	79	990	100.00	89.57
Median	8.98	8.86	8.04	11.40	8.93		
30-34	16	26	13	--	55		4.98
35-39	11	20	5	--	36		3.26
40-44	3	10	--	--	13		1.18
45-49	7	4	--	--	11		1.01
0-49	392	409	225	79	1,105		100.00
Median	9.70	11.19	9.25	11.40	10.15		

TABLE 3.4A (continued)

SAN MIGUEL ARCÁNGEL (1797–1815)

Number of Years Survived	Total	Percent		
		0-29 Years	0-49 Years	
0-4	241	31.25	27.54
5-9	123	16.21	14.06
10-14	121	15.94	13.83
15-19	106	13.97	12.11
20-24	89	11.73	10.17
25-29	79	10.41	9.03
0-29	759	100.00	86.74
Median	10.75		
30-34	79		9.03
35-39	32		3.66
40-44	5		0.57
45-49	—		0.00
0-49	875		100.00
Median	13.12		

TABLE 3.4A (continued)

SAN LUIS OBISPO (1770-1809)

Number of Years Survived	Number Baptized					Percent	
	1770-1779	1780-1789	1790-1799	1800-1809	Total	0-29 Years	0-49 Years
0-4	37	38	98	54	227	26.42	22.61
5-9	24	22	53	39	138	16.07	13.75
10-14	24	16	47	33	120	13.97	11.95
15-19	42	29	38	28	137	15.95	13.65
20-24	54	31	20	26	131	15.25	13.05
25-29	40	17	19	30	106	12.34	10.56
0-29	221	153	275	210	859	100.00	89.57
Median	18.04	15.86	8.72	11.82	12.69		
30-34	19	9	17	18	63		6.27
35-39	11	11	15	1	38		3.78
40-44	10	6	10	2	28		2.79
45-49	9	6	1	--	16		1.59
50-54	7	4	--	--	11		--
55-59	7	--	--	--	7		--
60-64	1	--	--	--	1		--
0-64	285	189	318	231	1,023		100.00
Median 0-49					15.62		

TABLE 3.4A *(continued)*

Years Survived by Tulare Converts at Santa Clara *(1805-1834)*

Number of Years Survived	Number Baptised			Total	Percent 0-29 Years
	1805-1814	1815-1824	1825-1834		
0-4	113	193	56	362	35.7
5-9	131	163	51	345	34.0
10-14	94	78	10	182	17.9
15-19	66	15	--	81	8.0
20-24	33	--	--	33	3.3
25-29	11	--	--	11	1.1
0-29	448	449	117	1,014	100.0
Median	9.24	5.97	5.25	7.10	

In Table 3.4B the data from Table 3.4A for the total number of gentiles of all ages baptized from 1770–1809, for whom we also have death entries, have been recast in the form of a life table. Since we have data on local gentiles for six missions in Table 3.4A, we have data for them for the same missions in Table 3.4B, plus an appendix on the Tulares of Mission Santa Clara. The critical columns are q_x and e_x. The variability of experience in the six missions in Table 3.4A shows up again in Table 3.4B. Column e_x tells us that the expectancy of survival of a gentile upon conversion to Christianity was highest at Mission San Luis Obispo, with 17.4 years; next best at San Miguel Arcángel, with 14.9 years, and third best at Mission San Carlos Borromeo, with 13.3 years. It was poorest at Mission Santa Cruz, with 8.6 years. For all six missions it was 11.6 years. At Santa Clara, it was 9.6 for local gentiles and 7.8 for Tulares, a difference that is to be explained in part by the shorter run of data on the Tulares and our inability to trace many of the longer-lived converts. The differences in values between these figures and the medians shown in Table 3.4A are due to the differences in weighting of the older members of the population.

TABLE 3.4B

Years Survived in the Missions by Converts

The data are tabulated in life table form. The first column represents not age but survival time in years lived after conversion. Data from Table 3.4A.

Years survived	D_x	d_x	l_x	q_x	L_x	T_x	e_x
			SIX MISSIONS				
0-4	2,741	3,664	10,000	0.36639	40,840	116,242	11.62
5-9	1,471	1,966	6,336	0.31029	26,765	75,402	11.90
10-14	992	1,326	4,370	0.30343	18,535	48,637	11.13
15-19	762	1,019	3,044	0.33475	12,673	30,102	9.89
20-24	571	763	2,025	0.37679	8,218	17,429	8.61
25-29	418	559	1,262	0.44294	4,913	9,211	7.30
30-34	287	384	703	0.54623	2,555	4,298	6.11
35-39	147	196	319	0.61442	1,105	1,743	5.46
40-44	59	79	123	0.64227	418	638	5.19
45-49	33	44	44	1.00000	220	220	5.00

TABLE 3.4B (continued)

Years survived	D_x	d_x	l_x	q_x	L_x	T_x	e_x
			SANTA CLARA				
0-4	1,120	4,674	10,000	0.46744	38,315	95,994	9.60
5-9	420	1,753	5,326	0.32914	22,248	57,679	10.83
10-14	282	1,177	3,573	0.32914	14,923	35,431	9.92
15-19	233	972	2,396	0.40567	9,550	20,508	8.56
20-24	147	614	1,424	0.43117	5,585	10,958	7.70
25-29	101	421	810	0.51975	2,998	5,373	6.63
30-34	50	209	389	0.53727	1,423	2,375	6.11
35-39	28	117	180	0.65000	607	952	5.29
40-44	9	38	63	0.60317	220	345	5.48
45-49	6	25	25	1.00000	125	125	5.00
			SANTA CRUZ				
0-4	460	4,514	10,000	0.45140	387,150	854,780	8.55
5-9	241	2,365	5,486	0.43109	215,175	467,630	8.52
10-14	148	1,452	3,121	0.46523	119,750	252,455	8.09
15-19	67	658	1,669	0.39424	67,000	132,705	8.95
20-24	62	608	1,011	0.60138	35,500	65,705	6.50
25-29	16	157	403	0.38957	16,225	30,355	7.53
30-34	12	118	246	0.47967	9,350	14,130	5.74
35-39	10	98	128	0.76562	3,950	4,780	3.73
40-44	3	29	30	0.96666	775	800	2.67
45-49	--	1	1	1.00000	25	75	--
			SAN JUAN BAUTISTA				
0-4	388	3,586	10,000	0.35860	410,350	980,595	9.81
5-9	307	2,837	6,414	0.44231	249,775	570,245	8.89
10-14	153	1,414	3,577	0.39530	143,500	320,470	8.96
15-19	88	813	2,163	0.37586	87,825	176,970	8.18
20-24	63	582	1,350	0.43110	52,950	89,145	6.60
25-29	51	471	768	0.61328	26,625	36,195	4.71
30-34	28	259	297	0.87205	8,375	9,570	3.22
35-39	3	28	38	0.73684	1,150	1,195	3.4
40-44	1	9	9	1.00000	45	45	--
45-49	--	--	--	---	--	--	--

TABLE 3.4B (continued)

Years survived	D_x	d_x	l_x	q_x	L_x	T_x	e_x
			SAN CARLOS BORROMEO				
0-4	305	2,760	10,000	0.27600	431,000	1,333,420	13.33
5-9	242	2,190	7,240	0.30248	307,250	902,420	12.46
10-14	168	1,520	5,050	0.30099	214,500	595,170	11.79
15-19	131	1,185	3,530	0.33569	146,875	380,670	10.78
20-24	79	714	2,345	0.30447	99,400	233,795	9.97
25-29	65	588	1,631	0.43203	66,850	134,395	8.24
30-34	55	497	1,043	0.47651	39,725	67,545	6.48
35-39	36	325	546	0.59523	19,175	27,820	5.10
40-44	13	117	221	0.52941	8,125	8,645	3.92
45-49	11	99	99	1.00000	520	520	--
			SAN MIGUEL ARCÁNGEL				
0-4	241	2,754	10,000	0.27540	42,865	149,012	14.90
5-9	123	1,406	7,246	0.19403	32,715	106,147	14.65
10-14	121	1,383	5,840	0.23681	25,743	73,432	12.57
15-19	106	1,211	4,457	0.27170	19,257	47,689	10.70
20-24	89	1,017	3,246	0.31330	13,687	28,432	8.76
25-29	79	903	2,229	0.40511	8,887	14,745	6.62
30-34	79	903	1,326	0.68100	4,373	5,858	4.42
35-39	32	366	423	0.86524	1,200	1,485	3.51
40-44	5	57	57	1.00000	285	285	2.50
45-49	--	--	--	---	--	--	--
			SAN LUIS OBISPO				
0-4	227	2,219	10,000	0.22190	444,525	1,742,650	17.43
5-9	138	1,349	7,781	0.17337	355,325	1,298,125	16.68
10-14	120	1,173	6,432	0.18236	292,275	942,860	14.66
15-19	137	1,339	5,259	0.25461	229,475	650,525	12.37
20-24	131	1,281	3,920	0.32678	163,975	421,050	10.74
25-29	106	1,036	2,639	0.39257	105,050	257,075	9.74
30-34	63	616	1,603	0.38427	64,750	151,025	9.42
35-39	38	371	987	0.37588	40,075	80,275	8.13
40-44	28	274	616	0.44480	23,950	46,200	7.50
45-49	16	156	342	0.45614	13,200	22,250	6.51
50-54	11	108	186	0.58064	6,600	9,050	4.87
55-59	7	68	78	0.87179	2,200	2,450	3.14
60-64	1	10	10	1.00000	250	250	---

TABLE 3.4B (continued)

Years survived	D_x	d_x	l_x	q_x	L_x	T_x	e_x
			APPENDIX				
		Years Survived by Tulare Converts at Santa Clara					
0-4	413	4,073	10,000	0.40729	39,818	78,434	7.84
5-9	304	2,998	5,927	0.50582	22,140	38,616	6.52
10-14	172	1,696	2,929	0.57903	10,405	16,476	5.63
15-19	81	799	1,233	0.64801	4,168	6,071	4.92
20-24	33	325	434	0.74884	1,358	1,903	4.38
25-29	11	109	109	1.00000	545	545	(5.00)

The value of e_x for survivorship is, of course, much less than the corresponding expectation of life at birth found in Table 3.3. In general, the values for e_x move downward in a smooth curve for the groups showing longer survivorship, except for Mission Santa Clara, where the value for the group surviving 0-4 years is markedly less than that for survivors 5-9 years and slightly inferior to survivors 10-14 years; and Mission San Juan Bautista, where the value for survivors 5-9 years is slightly inferior to that for survivors 10-14 years. The anomaly at Mission San Juan Bautista may be dismissed as a random variation of small significance, but that at Mission Santa Clara points to heavier mortality in the first years after baptism than at other missions.

If we turn our attention to column q_x, we find a numerical expression of the very high death rate, which, with some variation, rises slowly, but is relatively stable for most missions at between 300 and 400 per thousand up to 25 years after baptism. The better chance for survival at Missions San Luis Obispo and San Miguel Arcángel is evident in distinctly lower death rates up to the group of 25-29 years of survival.

It is of further interest to discover whether length of survival in the mission varied with the age at conversion. In order to do this, we re-sort the data by specific age at conversion, in particular of the younger component. The first is 0-1 years. The double year is necessary because only the full year is used for age determination, and baptism did not necessarily coincide with birth. If a child was born on 31 December 1779 and died on 2 January 1780, he would have lived less than one year, or 0 years, but he would be recorded as having been 1 year of age. If he was born on 2 January 1779 and died on 31 December 1780, he would still be recorded as only 1 year of age. On the other hand, if both baptism and death fell within the same year, the age would be 0 years. The second age group will be 2-4, the third 5-9, and so on.

The numbers are given in Table 3.5, together with the mean and median age of survival for each age group of converts. We have data on the local gentiles for six missions and on the Tulares for Mission Santa Clara, the latter placed in an appendix as in the preceding tables. Table 3.5 also shows the percentage of each age group who survived less than 2 full years. These values are calculated for the converts who survived as long as 29 years, and for those who survived as long as 49 years. Since we use the same data as for Tables 3.4A and 3.4B, there will be, in general, the same variability among missions, even though the data have been arranged in another way.

TABLE 3.5

Years of Survival of Converts

Years survived according to age of convert at baptism.
Table in two parts, 0-29 and 0-49 years survived.

Years survived	Age of Converts							
	0-1	2-4	5-9	10-14	15-24	25-44	45-64	65 +
SIX MISSIONS								
0-1	323	83	99	64	135	247	229	126
2-4	184	120	177	106	219	356	227	70
5-9	132	150	197	135	233	372	214	57
10-14	93	87	137	86	151	285	143	34
15-19	74	91	114	64	122	204	106	12
20-24	56	65	86	53	109	147	63	8
25-29	58	38	71	30	66	107	40	3
Total 0-29	920	634	881	538	1,035	1,718	1,022	310
Mean	7.90	10.75	11.11	10.52	10.57	10.28	8.60	5.47
Median	4.23	8.80	9.18	8.67	8.51	8.44	6.29	3.24
Percent surviving less than 2 years	35.1	13.1	11.2	11.9	13.0	14.4	22.4	40.6
30-34	30	43	51	28	45	68	24	1
35-39	20	15	26	15	34	37	5	0
40-44	8	5	16	10	12	10	1	0
45-49	9	4	11	2	4	6	0	0
Total 0-49	987	701	985	593	1,130	1,839	1,052	311
Mean	9.89	13.09	13.83	12.90	12.72	11.95	9.31	5.56
Median	4.78	9.92	10.71	9.69	9.53	9.25	6.63	3.26
Percent surviving less than 2 years	32.7	11.8	10.1	10.8	11.9	13.4	21.8	40.5

TABLE 3.5 (continued)

Years survived	Age of Converts							
	0-1	2-4	5-9	10-14	15-24	25-44	45-64	65 +
			SANTA CLARA					
0-1	207	25	31	26	62	117	81	33
2-4	115	51	64	41	60	124	89	20
5-9	77	52	40	34	54	91	63	18
10-14	63	35	35	23	23	80	41	6
15-19	54	35	31	19	29	52	31	2
20-24	34	21	12	17	24	33	15	1
25-29	30	8	11	9	15	23	10	0
Total 0-29	580	227	224	169	267	520	330	80
Mean	7.98	8.57	9.41	9.91	9.08	8.69	7.67	4.63
Median	4.17	8.61	7.13	7.57	6.06	6.04	4.83	3.05
Percent surviving less than 2 years	35.7	11.0	13.8	15.4	23.2	22.5	24.5	41.3
30-34	15	10	8	8	5	6	3	0
35-39	8	5	3	4	6	5	0	0
40-44	3	1	2	2	2	1	0	0
45-49	4	1	2	0	0	0	0	0
Total 0-49	610	244	239	183	280	532	333	80
Mean	9.39	10.45	11.13	11.85	10.34	9.29	7.90	4.63
Median	4.56	9.42	8.06	8.60	6.67	6.37	4.88	3.05
Percent surviving less than 2 years	33.9	10.2	13.0	14.2	22.1	22.0	24.3	41.3
			SANTA CRUZ					
0-1	20	18	28	20	22	49	19	6
2-4	11	25	51	34	42	80	28	7
5-9	7	21	35	30	34	75	31	4
10-14	11	13	24	16	20	49	13	3
15-19	2	8	18	10	12	15	7	0
20-24	6	6	15	6	8	15	4	0
25-29	1	1	4	1	0	2	0	0
Total 0-29	58	92	175	117	138	285	102	20
Mean	7.69	7.91	8.75	7.71	7.71	7.58	7.10	4.90
Median	4.45	5.71	6.26	5.75	5.74	5.90	5.65	3.71
Percent surviving less than 2 years	34.5	19.6	16.0	17.1	15.9	17.2	18.6	30.0
30-34	2	1	4	1	0	2	0	0
35-39	1	3	3	1	1	2	1	0
40-44	0	2	0	1	0	0	0	0
45-49	0	0	0	0	0	0	0	0
Total 0-49	61	98	182	120	139	289	103	20
Mean	8.99	9.78	9.75	8.45	7.92	7.96	7.40	4.90
Median	4.86	6.43	6.71	6.00	5.81	6.03	5.73	3.71
Percent surviving less than 2 years	32.8	18.4	15.4	16.7	15.8	17.0	18.4	30.0

TABLE 3.5 (continued)

Years survived	Age of Converts							
	0-1	2-4	5-9	10-14	15-24	25-44	45-64	65 +
SAN JUAN BAUTISTA								
0-1	19	8	11	3	16	22	26	11
2-4	19	16	30	19	60	72	41	12
5-9	21	34	45	32	56	66	40	7
10-14	8	11	18	15	30	40	28	1
15-19	3	7	12	8	12	27	15	2
20-24	1	9	6	9	16	14	9	0
25-29	7	10	13	3	6	12	2	1
Total 0-29	78	95	135	89	196	253	161	34
Mean	6.90	11.12	10.23	10.35	8.96	9.43	8.32	5.31
Median	5.24	8.46	7.95	8.52	8.75	7.46	6.69	4.50
Percent surviving less than 2 years	24.4	8.4	8.2	3.4	8.2	8.7	16.2	32.3
30-34	3	6	8	2	5	3	1	0
35-39	0	1	0	0	0	2	0	0
40-44	0	0	0	1	0	0	0	0
45-49	0	0	0	0	0	0	0	0
Total 0-49	81	102	143	92	201	258	162	34
Mean	7.85	12.64	11.48	11.19	9.54	9.92	8.47	5.31
Median	5.60	8.97	8.39	8.75	8.98	7.65	6.75	4.50
Percent surviving less than 2 years	23.5	7.9	7.7	3.3	8.0	8.5	16.1	32.3
SAN CARLOS BORROMEO								
0-1	47	16	15	5	23	16	33	14
2-4	25	17	12	5	35	24	14	5
5-9	19	28	55	23	44	58	29	6
10-14	5	17	31	10	35	47	18	7
15-19	6	22	24	4	35	31	9	2
20-24	7	9	14	9	17	21	3	0
25-29	7	6	12	3	12	17	2	0
Total 0-29	116	115	163	59	201	214	108	34
Mean	6.55	10.87	11.79	11.44	11.13	12.17	7.45	5.55
Median	3.32	9.38	9.95	9.24	9.82	10.86	5.21	3.80
Percent surviving less than 2 years	40.5	13.9	9.2	8.5	11.5	7.5	30.6	41.2
30-34	3	12	10	7	13	9	3	0
35-39	3	1	10	5	9	8	1	0
40-44	1	0	3	1	3	4	0	0
45-49	2	0	5	0	2	2	0	0
Total 0-49	125	128	191	72	228	237	112	34
Mean	9.14	13.11	15.64	15.73	14.13	14.61	8.39	5.55
Median	3.86	10.88	12.18	11.75	11.71	12.18	5.55	3.80
Percent surviving less than 2 years	37.6	12.5	8.6	7.0	9.9	6.7	29.5	41.2

TABLE 3.5 (continued)

Years survived	Age of Converts							
	0-1	*2-4*	*5-9*	*10-14*	*15-24*	*25-44*	*45-64*	*65 +*
	SAN MIGUEL ARCÁNGEL							
0-1	17	11	10	3	3	23	26	27
2-4	8	7	15	3	9	30	30	19
5-9	4	10	11	6	14	41	22	15
10-14	3	1	15	10	18	39	23	12
15-19	1	10	11	7	8	42	23	4
20-24	3	8	7	6	10	30	22	3
25-29	8	5	10	4	6	27	18	1
Total 0-29	44	52	79	39	68	232	164	81
Mean	9.42	11.77	12.02	14.08	13.08	13.20	11.97	6.32
Median	3.87	9.00	11.17	13.75	12.22	12.82	10.87	8.56
Percent surviving less than 2 years	38.6	21.2	12.7	7.7	4.4	9.9	15.9	33.3
30-34	6	7	7	1	9	32	16	1
35-39	5	4	3	1	4	13	2	0
40-44	0	1	3	0	0	0	1	0
45-49	0	0	0	0	0	0	0	0
Total 0-49	55	64	92	41	81	277	183	82
Mean	14.48	16.13	15.42	15.13	16.45	16.57	13.97	6.64
Median	8.43	17.00	13.33	14.25	14.03	15.65	12.93	8.68
Percent surviving less than 2 years	30.9	17.2	10.9	7.3	3.7	8.3	14.2	33.0

TABLE 3.5 (continued)

Years survived	Age of Converts							
	0-1	*2-4*	*5-9*	*10-14*	*15-24*	*25-44*	*45-64*	*65 +*
			SAN LUIS OBISPO					
0-1	13	5	4	7	9	20	44	35
2-4	6	4	5	4	13	26	25	7
5-9	4	5	11	10	31	41	29	7
10-14	3	10	14	12	25	30	20	5
15-19	8	9	18	16	26	37	21	2
20-24	5	12	32	6	34	34	10	4
25-29	5	8	21	10	27	26	8	1
Total 0-29	44	53	105	65	165	214	157	61
Mean	11.10	15.60	17.99	14.37	15.49	13.59	8.91	5.30
Median	8.75	16.39	20.78	14.79	15.87	13.33	6.64	4.36
Percent surviving less than 2 years	29.5	9.4	3.8	10.8	5.7	9.3	28.0	57.4
30-34	2	7	14	9	13	19	1	0
35-39	3	1	7	4	14	9	0	0
40-44	2	1	8	4	7	5	1	0
45-49	3	3	4	2	2	4	0	0
50-54	1	2	1	0	4	2	0	0
55-59	0	0	4	0	3	0	0	0
60-64	0	0	0	0	1	0	0	0
Total 0-49	54	65	139	84	209	253	159	61
Mean	16.55	19.65	22.73	19.54	18.64	16.86	9.27	5.30
Median	15.62	19.73	22.66	17.81	20.73	16.28	6.81	4.36
Percent surviving less than 2 years	24.1	7.7	2.9	8.3	4.3	7.9	27.7	57.4

APPENDIX

Years of Survival of Tulare Converts at Santa Clara

Years survived	Age of Converts							
	0-1	*2-4*	*5-9*	*10-14*	*15-24*	*25-44*	*45-64*	*65 +*
0-1	16	5	16	25	47	32	19	2
2-4	8	18	17	25	77	75	28	6
5-9	0	10	16	37	64	108	62	12
10-14	1	8	26	21	30	53	27	6
15-19	1	8	9	8	13	29	12	2
20-24	2	3	3	6	5	5	8	1
25-29	0	2	0	2	4	3	1	0
Total 0-29	28	54	87	124	240	305	157	29
Mean	4.25	9.36	8.57	7.92	6.96	8.10	8.52	8.47
Median	1.75	7.00	8.28	6.62	4.84	7.11	7.54	7.71
Percent surviving less than 2 years	57.1	9.3	18.4	20.2	19.6	10.5	12.1	6.9

From Table 3.5 we may draw three conclusions. First, the survival time was very short among the youngest converts, those under 2 years of age. Second, after the age of 2 years, the survival time for the local gentiles in the summary for the six missions shows a consistent mean of 10 to 14 years for those who were from 3 to 44 years of age at the time of baptism. The medians for the same age groups are somewhat lower. This phenomenon is illustrated also in Table 3.4A, where persons of all ages are consolidated. The summary sheet averages out, of course, considerably wider variation in the means for each mission; but, in general, for each mission there is the same pattern, although the exact range of the means and medians varies. Third, the survival time became much shorter in the two groups aged 45–64 and 65 and over at the time of baptism. This finding is, of course, to be expected, for the duration of life under any circumstances is truncated severely in this range of years. In general, then, if we omit from consideration a high infant mortality and the normal curtailment of life at what was then great age, we find the average survival time of converts among local gentiles to be remarkably uniform in a series of ranges varying for each mission, but which for all six missions show a value not far from 10 years if survival is limited to 29 years and 12 years if survival time is extended to 49 years. The Tulares, because of paucity of data and the special circumstances of their entrance into mission life, present a case apart, which nevertheless had somewhat higher values of survival in the aggregate than those for the local gentiles at Mission Santa Cruz. There may have been a weeding out of some of the weaker individuals in the selection of converts and in the long journey from the Central Valley to the coastal missions.

3. THE NEOPHYTES BORN IN THE MISSIONS

The children born to Indian parents who were converts constitute for our purposes the first generation of native-born, corresponding to the children born in the new environment to any group of immigrants. Since they were baptized immediately or almost immediately after birth, their age at baptism may be taken uniformly as 0 years, and indeed can be allocated to categories expressed in days or weeks. Their lives were spent in the missions or under the influence of the missionaries. They resorted relatively little to fugitivism, and most of their deaths which occurred prior to secularization may be found in the burial register. Our overall sample is excellent, since we have the age at death for approximately 70% of those baptized. The majority of the 30% whose names are not in the burial registers survived the final dissolution of the missions in the middle 1830's.

At each mission, gentile conversions ceased after a span of years, varying from mission to mission, as the pool of local gentiles was exhausted. Births at the mission, on the contrary, continued up to and indeed beyond the final years. Consequently, there is a progressively diminishing age beyond which one would not expect to find the deaths of those born in the mission because of the scattering of the neophytes upon secularization. Our best information on age at death is on the first few cohorts born at the missions, since the life spans of those cohorts were by and large concluded by the end of the mission period. For example, for the cohort born in the years 1775-1779, our first, we have the age at death for 119 of the 135 recorded as baptized, that is, for 88.1%. In general, the proportion of deaths known to baptisms recorded declines as the cohorts move toward 1834. For the cohort born in 1825-1829, our information on age at death covers 63.4%, but for the cohort 1830-1834, the last, we have age at death only for 31.1%. This fact puts a limit on the parameters in vital statistics which may be analyzed for this population. We cannot plot the distribution of age at death; we cannot formulate a proper life table; we cannot determine the survival time of those born in the mission. There are left, however, two possibilities for studying the births which occurred in the missions. One of these is an analysis of the cohorts as they came into being with the passage of the years. The other is through the annual reports of the missionaries at each mission listing the total number of neophytes, since through those we can estimate the approximate crude birth rate. We first discuss the former possibility.

In Table 3.6 we present the data on 5-year cohorts of Indians born in the mission, beginning with the quinquennium 1775-1779. Prior to 1775, only 9 were baptized, 6 at San Carlos Borromeo and 3 at San Luis Obispo; we have omitted them as too small a number to consider. From the quinquennium 1775-1779, increasing numbers of neophytes were born in the missions, the total for all missions rising from 135 in 1775-1779 to 918 in 1805-1809, when it reached an all-time peak. Thereafter the total fell to 778 in 1810-1814 but rose to 901 in 1820-1824. The total of baptisms for 1825-1829 represents a marked drop, and that of 499 for 1830-1834 an even larger one, but by then the missions were already under pressure from the state and the civil population. The numbers of baptized, essentially those born, in each 5-year period are shown in the table, together with information on age at death arranged by age group from birth to a maximum of 54 years. It is probable that infants and very young children were kept at the mission and that their deaths were quite consistently recorded. Consequently, these groups provide perhaps the only stable basis for a direct estimate of mortality in the missions. If we attempt to include the deaths of those who reached more advanced years, we at once encounter the difficulty that each cohort differs from its predecessors and followers because of the universal cut-off date in the middle 1830's. This condition may be appreciated by considering the recorded deaths of persons over 4 years old as given for the cohorts in Table 3.6. The increase in totals of baptisms by quinquennium and the corresponding increase in deaths of people from 5 on give a rising total of deaths until the quinquennium 1805-1809. They fall thereafter to 12 in 1825-1829 and 1 in 1830-1834. The difficulty is even more apparent by a simple glance at the blanks in the data for the more advanced age groups, for beginning in 1790-1794 we have no information on deaths for people over 44, and that gap moves into progressively lower age groups until for the cohort born in 1830-1834 it reaches the age group 5-9, for which we have only 1 recorded death. These deficiencies in our data make suspect the apparent improvement in infant mortality shown for the cohort born in 1830-1834.

The persons in the age group 0-4 years show values for crude mortality which are quite erratic when the recorded deaths are expressed as a percentage of the number baptized. (See Table 3.6.) In the summary for the six missions for which we have burial as well as baptismal data, the values for the cohorts born in 1785-1789 and 1800-1804 are relatively low, that for 1785-1789 very much so. We know that the quinquennium 1800-1804 was marked by a number of epidemics and that in one, at San Carlos Borromeo, the missionary in charge noted in

TABLE 3.6

Baptisms and Recorded Deaths of Local Indians Born in the Missions According to Cohorts

SIX MISSIONS

Total Baptisms	135	232	344	433	625	772	918	778	810	901	602	499	7,055
Age Group for Deaths	1775 -79	1780 -84	1785 -89	1790 -94	1795 -99	1800 -04	1805 -09	1810 -14	1815 -19	1820 -24	1825 -29	1830 -34	Totals
0	22	57	68	164	208	212	289	211	227	257	166	97	1,978
1-4	35	27	55	133	178	209	315	251	259	287	204	60	2,013
5-9	12	7	16	15	20	40	40	39	49	61	10	1	310
10-14	2	7	7	5	9	17	21	23	24	14	2		131
15-19	4	10	13	8	10	18	25	46	16	1			151
20-24	6	12	14	12	12	15	35	31	12				149
25-29	10	6	16	6	15	18	12	5					88
30-34	12	4	9	5	6	8	2						46
35-39	5	1	3	6	4	1							20
40-44	5	6	8	5	1								25
45-49	3	3	2										8
50-54	3	8	1										12
Totals	119	148	212	359	463	538	739	606	587	620	382	155	4,931
Percent of those baptized who died at 0 years of age	16.3	24.6	19.8	37.9	33.3	27.5	31.5	27.1	28.0	28.5	27.6	19.3	28.0
Percent of those baptized who died at 0-4 years of age	42.2	36.2	35.8	68.6	61.8	54.5	65.8	59.4	60.0	60.4	61.5	31.3	56.6

TABLE 3.6 (continued)

SANTA CLARA

Total Baptisms	1	62	62	126	228	193	214	196	161	185	163	102	1,693
0			1	40	66	19	48	52	32	40	42	9	349
1–4			6	40	68	65	86	69	67	72	75	14	562
5–9			1	3	2	2	15	14	10	12	2		61
10–14				1	2	3	6	7	3	2			24
15–19		1	3	2	4	5	6	9	1				31
20–24		1	3		1	2	9	4					20
25–29		1	4		5	1							11
30–34		1	1	1	2								5
35–39			1										1
40–44			1										1
50–54													1
Totals	4	21	87	150	97	170	155	113	126	119	23	1,065
Percent of those baptized who died at 0 years of age	0.0	1.6	31.7	28.9	9.8	22.4	26.5	19.9	21.6	25.8	8.8	20.6
Percent of those baptized who died at 0–4 years of age	0.0	11.3	63.5	58.8	43.5	62.6	61.7	61.5	60.6	71.8	22.5	53.8

233

TABLE 3.6 (continued)

SANTA CRUZ

Total Baptisms	16	72	57	57	53	62	89	51	49	506
0	5	29	26	33	27	23	34	8	9	194
1-4	7	27	19	11	6	19	17	2	3	111
5-9		2	2			2	1	2		9
10-14				1			1			2
15-19	1		1	1						2
20-24	1	2			3					6
25-29					1					1
30-34		1	1							2
Totals	14	61	48	46	37	44	53	12	12	327
Percent of those baptized who died at 0 years of age	31.3	40.3	45.6	58.0	51.0	37.1	38.2	15.7	18.4	38.3
Percent of those baptized who died at 0-4 years of age	75.0	77.8	79.0	77.2	62.3	67.8	57.3	19.6	24.5	60.3

234

TABLE 3.6 (continued)

SAN JUAN BAUTISTA

Total Baptisms	34	135	215	141	170	283	157	167	1,302
0	16	35	57	17	48	83	43	35	338
1-4	6	51	87	78	61	110	60	10	466
5-9	5	12	4	6	15	24	3		69
10-14		3	5	4	5	1			18
15-19		3	5	7	1				16
20-24	1	1	8	3					13
25-29	1	1							2
30-34									
Totals	29	113	166	115	130	218	106	45	922
Percent of those baptized who died at 0 years of age	47.0	28.9	25.5	12.1	28.2	29.3	36.5	21.0	26.0
Percent of those baptized who died at 0-4 years of age	64.7	69.9	67.0	67.4	64.2	68.2	65.6	27.0	61.8

TABLE 3.6 (continued)

SAN CARLOS BORROMEO

Total Baptisms	73	85	153	178	153	105	105	91	119	85	74	68	1,289
0	11	30	25	59	24	7	43	24	26	23	13	6	291
1-4	21	17	31	67	56	19	27	31	42	31	37	5	384
5-9	9	3	11	8	7	12	7	6	6	6			75
10-14	1	4	2	2	6	4	4	5	5	1			34
15-19	1	2	3	4	3	1	4	7	3				28
20-24	2	4	4	5	7	5	2						29
25-29	4	1	3	4	3	1							16
30-34	7	1	5	3	1								17
35-39	3		1	1	1								6
40-44	1	5	1										7
45-49	2	2											4
50-54	2												2
Totals	64	69	86	153	108	49	87	73	82	61	50	11	893
Percent of those baptized who died at 0 years of age	15.0	35.3	16.3	33.2	15.7	6.7	41.0	26.4	21.8	27.1	17.6	8.8	22.6
Percent of those baptized who died at 0-4 years of age	42.4	55.3	36.6	70.8	52.3	24.8	66.7	60.4	57.1	63.5	67.6	16.2	52.4

TABLE 3.6 (continued)

SAN MIGUEL ARCANGEL

	18	116	182	170	186	182	132	93	1,079
Total Baptisms									
0	10	47	51	51	55	52	48	26	340
1–4	2	24	56	30	47	37	29	25	250
5–9	1	3	11	11	9	13	3	1	52
10–14		3	3	6	9	7	1		29
15–19		6	6	16	7	1			36
20–24	1	5	15	16	10				47
25–29	2	9	9	4					24
30–34		4	1						5
35–39		1							1
40–44	1								1
45–49									
50–54									
Totals	17	102	152	134	137	110	81	52	785
Percent of those baptized who died at 0 years of age	55.6	40.5	28.0	30.0	29.5	28.6	36.3	28.0	31.5
Percent of those baptized who died at 0–4 years of age	66.7	61.2	58.8	47.6	54.8	48.9	58.3	54.8	54.7

TABLE 3.6 (continued)

SAN LUIS OBISPO

Total Baptisms	61	85	129	113	120	166	145	127	112	77	25	23	1,186
0	11	27	42	60	63	74	57	40	43	25	12	12	466
1-4	14	10	18	19	19	28	48	37	23	20	1	3	240
5-9	3	4	4	4	3	9	3	2	7	5			44
10-14	1	3	5	2	1	4	2	1	2	2	1		24
15-19	3	7	7	1	3	3	3	7	4				38
20-24	4	7	7	6		2	1	5	2				34
25-29	6	4	9	2	4	6	3						34
30-34	5	2	3	1	2	3	1						17
35-39	2	1	1	5	3								12
40-44	4	1	6	5									16
45-49	1	1	2										4
50-54	1	8	1										10
55-59	1												1
60-64			1										1
Totals	56	75	105	105	98	129	118	92	81	52	14	15	941
Percent of those baptized who died at 0 years of age	18.0	31.8	32.6	53.1	52.5	44.6	39.2	31.5	38.3	32.5	47.8	52.2	39.3
Percent of those baptized who died at 0-4 years of age	41.0	43.5	46.5	69.9	68.3	61.4	72.5	60.6	58.9	58.4	52.0	65.2	59.5

238

the burial book that he simply did not have the time to keep a proper record. Hence it is likely that the low value of deaths for that period is spurious at San Carlos and also at Santa Clara, which shows an even lower value. For the anomaly of the low values for the cohort of 1785-1789, we have at this time no firm explanation but are inclined to attribute it to under-reporting of some kind rather than unusually beneficent conditions of health. We should notice, however, that in the summary for the six missions the value of infant mortality for the cohort born in 1800-1804 is slightly higher than that for the cohort born in 1810-1814.

Whatever the difficulties in our data, it is evident that child mortality, expressed as deaths from 0 to 4 years of age, ran an erratic course at high values throughout the mission period. The range in the summary sheet is approximately from 36 to 66%, or from 360 to 660 deaths per 1,000 births. If we made some adjustment for reporting in our low quinquennia, we should think in terms of 400 to 700 deaths per 1,000 births. In other words, throughout the 60 years of the mission period more than half of the neophytes born in the mission died before they reached their fifth birthday. The mean value, excluding 1830-1834, is 584 deaths per 1,000 births. Adjustment for suspected or known periods of underreporting will raise the proportion.

A further refinement is possible because the missionaries were able to state the exact date of birth and of death for those children who were born in the missions and died there within one or two years. Hence we have the infant mortality when this parameter is defined as the relative number of those born who die before reaching their first birthday. The data are in Table 3.6. The values in the summary for the various cohorts are about as erratic as those for the larger group who lived 0-4 years. They reached a maximum in the decade from 1790-1799; and thereafter, even with some allowance for the adjustment that may be needed for the value in the quinquennium 1800-1804 and perhaps that of 1810-1814, reached a plateau at roughly 270 to 320 deaths per 1,000 births. There is no evidence of improvement beyond that. The values for deaths at ages 0-4, necessarily higher, show a not too dissimilar picture, but with wider variations in the number of deaths per 1,000 births.

It is possible that any improvement in infant mortality is masked by the inclusion, in the summary of the table, of data from missions founded in two groups, with a considerable interval of years between the two sets of foundations. If there were longer-trend factors operating that would bring improvement in infant mortality, they might appear in the older missions, but their appearance would be obscured by inclusion of data from the newer ones. The arrangement of Table 3.6 permits an easy test, since the data for the individual missions are there. Examination of the data for the three oldest missions, San Carlos Borromeo, San Luis Obispo, and Santa Clara, indicates that there may have been the beginnings of improvement at San Carlos Borromeo and at Santa Clara, although the improvement was slight, and that there was none at San Luis Obispo.

If we use the age group under one year as a base, and omit the data for 1830–1834, the mean mortality was 287 deaths per 1,000 births. As a measure of comparison, the death rate for the group under one year in the United States during the decade 1951–1960 was 27.0 per 1,000 live births. In 1960 it was 26.1. The mortality of infants in the first year of life was therefore less than one-tenth its level among those born in the missions. Of course a comparison between mortality in a population living in the much poorer conditions of public health and medical knowledge that prevailed in most areas in earlier generations, and the present one in the United States, with its far better levels of public health and medical care, is not a truly meaningful one for our purpose. Even in the United States in 1840, infant mortality was of the order of 185.6 per 1,000 live births. As late as 1915 and 1916, the rate was 99.9 and 101.0 per 1,000 live births respectively, and in 1918 it rose to 100.9.[25] We turn, then, to populations which may be considered more nearly comparable. French studies of Breton parishes in the eighteenth century indicate a rate of infant mortality to

25. World Health Organization, "Special Subject: Infant Mortality," p. 788; U. S. Department of Health, Education and Welfare, *Vital Statistics of the United States, 1960*, II, part A, table 2–1 (Abridged Life Tables for Total, Male, Female Population: United States, 1960), pp. 2–7; U. S. Department of Commerce, Bureau of the Census, *Historical Statistics of the United States, Colonial Times to 1957*, Table B 101–112 (Foetal Death Rates; Neonatal, Infant, and Maternal Mortality Rates), p. 25; Paul H. Jacobson, "Cohort Survival for Generations Since 1840," part 1, pp. 38–43.

births falling in a range from 285 to 237 deaths per 1,000 births. The average would be 255.[26] These rates are not much better than those for the California mission Indians. Brittany was one of the poorest regions of France at the time but, although studies for some other parts of the kingdom show lower rates, those for the Paris basin, in general, do not.[27]

All these comparisons may be objected to on the ground that they deal with the experience of European populations, who lived in considerably different conditions and did not have a substantial Indian genetic component. Our best comparison, accordingly, is Mexico, which has a population with a large proportion of Indian genetic stock and is much more like that of the California mission Indians. Unfortunately, the earliest statistics we have for Mexico are for the Díaz period and to some extent reflect the introduction of advanced medical practices into the larger cities. Nevertheless, the rate of infant mortality in the first year of life, per 1,000 births, as reported in the admittedly defective Porfirian statistics, was high, as follows:

1896–1898	324.2	1904–1905	290.6
1899–1901	288.6	1908–1910	301.8

The range of annual rates was from 266.4 deaths per 1,000 live births in 1901 to 376.7 in 1897. The mean of the annual rates for the years 1896–1910 was 304.6.[28] Eduardo Arriaga's reworking of the Mexican national census of 1895 would indicate a rate of infant mortality for 1894–1895 of 276.7.[29] These national averages conceal wide variation in which infant mortality was far worse in a rural and Indian state such as Oaxaca.[30] When compared with such data, infant mortality in the California missions studied here, shocking though it is by present-day

26. Pierre Goubert, "Legitimate Fecundity and Infant Mortality in France During the Eighteenth Century: A Comparison," pp. 598–602, esp. p. 599. A study by A. LeGoff, "Bilan d'une étude de démographie historique," pp. 223–225, shows values in the same range for yet another Breton settlement.

27. LeGoff, pp. 223–225, and Louis Henry, "Historical Demography," p. 392; Jacques Dupâquier, "Villages et petites villes de la généralité de Paris; Introduction"; Pierre Goubert, Beauvais et le Beauvaisis, pp. 39–40.

28. El Colegio de México, Centro de Estudios Económicos y Demográficos, Dinamica de la población de Mexico, pp. 24–25; Enrique Cordero, "La subestimación de la mortalidad infantil en México," p. 47.

29. Eduardo E. Arriaga, New Life Tables for Latin American Populations, pp. 170–171.

30. Cordero, pp. 56–59 et passim.

standards, was no worse than in comparable societies in the eighteenth and nineteenth centuries.

According to Table 3.6, mortality in the age group 0–4—that is, in the first 5 years of life—averaged 567 per 1,000 births. If we delete the data for 1830–1834, the rate is even worse, 584 deaths per 1,000 births. Mortality in the United States in 1960 for that group was 30.2 deaths per 1,000 births. Again, comparison with a population enjoying present-day levels of public health is not truly meaningful, except perhaps to make us thankful that we live now rather than in former times. In 1840 in the United States the mortality in the age group 0–4 ran 324.7 per 1,000 live births.[31] We therefore adduce data on populations more nearly comparable. In the parishes of Brittany mentioned above, in the eighteenth century roughly half the children died before their tenth year. For the parishes of the Paris basin that have been studied, experience was comparable. That is distinctly better than the experience of the six California missions, even for age groups 0–4. For other parts of eighteenth-century France, studies indicate a somewhat lower mortality.[32] For Porfirian Mexico in the study of Arriaga, the census of 1895 indicates a mortality in the first 5 years of life of 410.6 per 1,000 births, and the census of 1900 one of 406.5.[33] The rates resemble those of eighteenth-century France, and are distinctly more favorable than that of the Indians in the six missions. We conclude, then, that the major difference in the mortality among neophytes born in the six missions relative to comparable populations elsewhere lay less in the first year of life than in the years immediately succeeding.

We may make one further comment on Table 3.6. Examination of the data for individual missions indicates that the experience of the various missions in deaths of neophytes born in the mission showed some variation from mission to mission, but that that variation was considerably less than in life expectancy after conversion for local gentile converts. San Luis

31. U. S. Department of Health, Education and Welfare, *Vital Statistics of the United States, 1960*, II, part A, table 2–1, pp. 2–7; Jacobson, "Cohort Survival," p. 44.

32. Goubert, "Legitimate Fecundity," pp. 599–600, and Henry, "Historical Demography," p. 392; Goubert, *Beauvais et le Beauvaisis*, pp. 39–40; Dupâquier, "Villages et petites villes"; and LeGoff, pp. 223–225.

33. Arriaga, pp. 170–173.

Obispo and San Miguel Arcángel, which were among the most healthful missions for converts, were not so for neophytes born in the mission. San Carlos has a distinctly more favorable set of data, and Santa Clara, the record of which for local gentile converts was relatively poor, emerges as a much more favorable environment for neophytes born in the mission. Mission Santa Cruz continues to figure among the worst mission in terms of mortality and life expectancy. We have no explanation for these variations, but again suggest that these findings indicate the need for new research into the environments provided by the individual missions.

For the mission-born, the life-table approach is not applicable save for one and perhaps two exceptions. The earliest cohorts, those born in 1775-1779 and 1780-1784, had almost run their course by 1834, although there may have been a few survivors at that year. During the ten-year period, only two missions, namely, San Carlos Borromeo and San Luis Obispo, were in operation long enough to provide data. The total of mission-born Indians baptized in them in that period was 304, of whom we are able to trace 263 in the death registers, or 84.6%. Their probability of death and expectation of life may be compared roughly with those of the local Indians who had been converted and who lived side by side with them in the missions. Table 3.7 shows the result of treating these two consolidated cohorts born in the missions according to life-table procedure. We have separated the age group 0-4 into two groups, 0 and 1-4 years, to facilitate comparison. If we include the cohort born in 1785-1789, we secure data from Mission Santa Clara as well as the two older missions and reach 711 baptisms. Unfortunately, we then deal both with the losses due to disappearance of Indians during the mission period and the considerably larger number of survivors in 1834. We are able to trace 479, or 67.4%, a distinctly lower proportion, with corresponding distortion in the higher ages of survival. We nevertheless have included a second life table of the three cohorts in Table 3.7 for purposes of comparison. We have also included life tables for individual missions for the varying spans of years that data permitted. The nearer those spans approach 1834, the more dubious the validity of the life tables.

TABLE 3.7

Life Table Constructed for Two Cohorts, Consolidated, of 1775-79 and 1780-84
The age group 0-4 has been split to show the values
for the first year of life. The data are from Table 3.6.

(SAN CARLOS BORROMEO AND SAN LUIS OBISPO)

Age Group	D_x	d_x	l_x	q_x	L_x	T_x	e_x
0	79	300	1,000	0.30000	8,520	136,130	13.61
1-4	62	236	700	0.33714	23,280	127,610	18.23
5-9	19	72	464	0.15517	21,400	104,330	22.48
10-14	9	34	392	0.08673	18,750	82,930	21.16
15-19	13	49	358	0.13687	16,675	64,180	17.93
20-24	17	65	309	0.21035	13,825	47,505	15.37
25-29	15	57	244	0.23360	10,755	33,680	13.80
30-34	15	57	187	0.30481	7,925	22,925	12.26
35-39	6	23	130	0.17692	5,925	15,000	11.54
40-44	11	42	107	0.39252	4,300	9,075	8.48
45-49	6	23	65	0.35384	2,675	4,775	7.35
50-54	11	42	42	1.00000	2,100	2,100	5.00

Life Table Constructed for Three Cohorts, Consolidated,
of 1775-79, 1780-84, 1784-89

The age group 0-4 has been split to show the values
for the first year of life. The data are from Table 3.6.

SAN CARLOS BORROMEO, SANTA CLARA, AND SAN LUIS OBISPO

Age Group	D_x	d_x	l_x	q_x	L_x	T_x	e_x
0	147	307	1,000	0.30688	8,465	123,980	12.40
1-4	117	244	693	0.35209	22,840	115,515	16.67
5-9	35	73	449	0.16258	20,625	92,675	20.64
10-14	16	33	376	0.08776	17,975	72,050	19.16
15-19	27	56	343	0.16326	15,750	54,075	15.76
20-24	32	67	287	0.23344	12,675	38,325	13.35
25-29	32	67	220	0.30454	9,325	25,650	11.66
30-34	25	52	153	0.33986	6,350	16,325	10.67
35-39	9	19	101	0.18811	4,575	9,975	9.88
40-44	19	40	82	0.48780	3,100	5,400	6.59
45-49	8	17	42	0.40476	1,675	2,300	5.48
50-54	12	25	25	1.00000	625	625	5.00

TABLE 3.7 (continued)

Life Table for Two Cohorts, Consolidated, of 1785-89 and 1790-94

The age group 0-4 has been split to show the values
for the first year of life.   The data are from Table 3.6.

SANTA CLARA

Age Group	D_x	d_x	l_x	q_x	L_x	T_x	e_x
0	41	380	1,000	0.38000	8,100	56,705	5.67
1-4	46	426	620	0.68710	16,280	48,605	7.84
5-9	4	37	194	0.19072	8,775	32,325	16.66
10-14	1	9	157	0.05732	7,625	23,550	15.00
15-19	5	46	148	0.31081	6,250	15,925	10.76
20-24	3	28	102	0.27450	4,400	9,675	9.49
25-29	4	37	74	0.50000	2,775	5,275	7.13
30-34	2	19	37	0.51351	1,375	2,500	6.76
35-39	1	9	18	0.50000	675	1,125	6.25
40-44	1	9	9	1.00000	450	450	5.00

Life Table for Two Cohorts, Consolidated, of 1791-94 and 1795-99

The age group 0-4 has been split to show the values
for the first year of life.   The data are from Table 3.6.

SANTA CRUZ

Age Group	D_x	d_x	l_x	q_x	L_x	T_x	e_x
0	34	453	1,000	0.45300	7,735	41,540	4.15
1-4	34	453	597	0.82815	20,555	32,805	6.18
5-9	2	26	94	0.27650	4,050	13,250	14.10
10-14	--	--	68	--	3,400	9,200	13.53
15-19	1	14	68	0.20588	3,050	5,800	8.53
20-24	3	40	54	0.74074	1,700	2,750	5.09
25-29	--	--	14	--	700	1,050	7.50
30-34	1	14	14	1.00000	350	350	5.00

TABLE 3.7 (continued)

Life Table for Two Cohorts, Consolidated, of 1797-99 and 1800-04
The age group 0-4 has been split to show the values
for the first year of life. The data are from Table 3.6.

SAN JUAN BAUTISTA

Age Group	D_x	d_x	l_x	q_x	L_x	T_x	e_x
0	55	387	1,000	0.38700	8,065	37,275	3.73
1-4	60	423	613	0.69000	16,060	29,210	4.77
5-9	17	120	190	0.63157	6,500	13,150	6.92
10-14	3	21	70	0.30000	2,975	6,650	9.50
15-19	3	21	49	0.42857	1,925	3,675	7.50
20-24	2	14	28	0.50000	1,050	1,750	6.25
25-29	2	14	14	1.00000	700	700	5.00

Life Table for Two Cohorts, Consolidated, of 1775-79 and 1780-84
The age group 0-4 has been split to show the values
for the first year of life. The data are from Table 3.6.

SAN CARLOS BORROMEO

Age Group	D_x	d_x	l_x	q_x	L_x	T_x	e_x
0	41	308	1,000	0.30800	8,460	115,070	11.51
1-4	38	286	692	0.41329	21,960	106,610	15.41
5-9	12	90	406	0.22167	18,050	84,650	20.85
10-14	5	38	316	0.12025	14,850	66,600	21.08
15-19	3	23	278	0.08273	13,325	51,750	18.62
20-24	6	45	255	0.17647	11,625	38,425	15.07
25-29	5	38	210	0.18095	9,550	26,800	12.76
30-34	8	60	172	0.34883	7,100	17,250	10.03
35-39	3	23	112	0.20535	5,025	10,150	9.06
40-44	6	45	89	0.50561	3,325	5,125	5.76
45-49	4	30	44	0.68181	1,450	1,800	4.09
50-54	2	14	14	1.00000	350	350	5.00

TABLE 3.7 (continued)

Life Table for Two Cohorts, Consolidated, of 1797-99 and 1800-04
*The age group 0-4 has been split to show the values
for the first year of life. The data are from Table 3.6.*

SAN MIGUEL ARCÁNGEL

Age Group	D_x	d_x	l_x	q_x	L_x	T_x	e_x
0	57	4,791	10,000	0.47910	76,045	780,405	7.80
1-4	26	2,185	5,209	0.41946	164,660	704,360	13.52
5-9	4	336	3,024	0.11111	142,800	539,700	17.85
10-14	3	252	2,688	0.09375	128,100	396,900	14.77
15-19	6	504	2,436	0.20689	109,200	268,800	11.03
20-24	6	504	1,932	0.26086	84,000	159,600	8.26
25-29	11	924	1,428	0.64705	48,300	75,600	5.29
30-34	4	336	504	0.66666	16,800	27,300	5.42
35-39	1	84	168	0.50000	6,300	10,500	6.25
40-44	1	84	84	1.00000	4,200	4,200	5.00

Life Table for Two Cohorts, Consolidated, of 1775-79 and 1780-84
*The age group 0-4 has been split to show the values
for the first year of life. The data are from Table 3.6.*

SAN LUIS OBISPO

Age Group	D_x	d_x	l_x	q_x	L_x	T_x	e_x
0	38	290	1,000	0.29000	8,550	158,265	15.83
1-4	24	183	710	0.25774	24,740	149,715	21.09
5-9	7	53	527	0.10056	25,025	124,975	23.71
10-14	4	31	474	0.06540	22,925	99,950	21.09
15-19	10	76	443	0.17155	20,250	80,025	18.06
20-24	11	85	367	0.23160	16,225	56,725	15.46
25-29	10	76	282	0.26950	12,200	40,550	14.38
30-34	7	53	206	0.25728	8,975	28,350	13.76
35-39	3	23	153	0.15032	7,075	19,375	12.66
40-44	5	38	130	0.29230	5,550	12,300	9.46
45-49	2	15	92	0.16304	4,225	6,750	7.34
50-54	9	69	77	0.89610	2,125	2,525	3.28
55-59	1	8	8	1.00000	400	400	5.00

As is evident from both Tables 3.6 and 3.7, the crude death rate of young children was enormous and the expectation of life exceedingly low. After completion of 5 years of life—i.e., at age 5 by European counting—there was some improvement, but the vital indices of those born in the missions remained lower than, and the probability of a continued existence much inferior to, that of the heathen brought into the missions subsequent to birth. Thus the value of q_x for age group 0-4 with the converts is 0.078 (see Table 3.3), while that for the corresponding mission-born may be calculated as 0.536, for the two cohorts of 1775-1779 and 1780-1784, and 0.551 for the three cohorts including that of 1785-1789. The value of e_x at birth is 35.43 for the local gentile converts, whereas for the mission-born the corresponding values in the two consolidated life tables are 14.09 and 12.89. Even if we concede that these values are severely distorted by inadequate control of age at death within the group 0-4, the difference is enormous. Our data do not permit a firm judgment whether or not the same condition persisted with the cohorts born after 1789, but little improvement is indicated by the recorded deaths at 0 and 1-4 years of age. What we lack most of all for comparison, and probably will never get, is the behavior in terms of mortality and survival of gentile infants and children as they existed in their native habitat prior to the coming of the missionaries and other Europeans.

Our data taken from the mission registers do not permit direct calculations of rates and indices on natality at the missions among the local Indians resident there. We may obtain an idea of the conditions surrounding natality from the reports sent back to Mexico City annually by the resident friars. A centralized set of copies retained by the Franciscan province was destroyed in the great San Francisco fire of 1906, but fortunately not before they had been copied in turn for Hubert Howe Bancroft a century ago. Those transcripts are now in the Bancroft Library at the University of California, Berkeley. Their present form, that in which Cook consulted them in the past, is a series of sheets which may be referred to as the Bancroft Transcripts.[34] For each mission there is shown the total popula-

34. The catalogue entry in the Bancroft Library is: "California–Statistics, vital [California Mission Statistics, 1769–1834]. Lists of population, births, marriages, deaths, livestock and crops for each mission, the Presidios of San Diego, Monterey, San Francisco, and Santa Barbara, the pueblos of San Jose and Los Angeles, and the Villa Branciforte, with analyses by place and overall statistics."

tion in each year as well as the number of male and female adults together with the children, each category being itemized. With these values, plus the number of births derived from the registers of baptism, we can arrive at some idea of the rate of live births at the missions.

The crude birth rate, or the simple ratio of births to total population, is probably the least desirable index to natality where complete censuses are to be found. In their absence, the gross rate may be determined, even if it lacks complete precision. Additionally, in the present instance, it is possible to compute the ratio of births to adult women. The term here does not mean women of reproductive age, for an adult in the California missions was anyone of either sex above the approximate age of 7-8 years, the division being that customary in much of the reporting of the time in the Spanish world. Unfortunately, therefore, we cannot compute the fertility ratio or the ratio of births to women 15 to 45 years of age.

When the rates, or ratios, are determined for each year from 1776 to 1832, the data are best presented in the form of graphs. Figure 3.1 depicts the ratios of births to adult females (in the special California definition), the values for all missions combined being given first and then those for each individual mission. The ratios of births to total population are shown in Figure 3.2, arranged in the same order. A striking feature of these two sets of graphs is the wide dispersion of the points for the individual missions, only those for Mission Santa Clara showing a fair measure of regularity. This dispersion is considerably reduced in the summary parts of the two sets of graphs, for some of the variation, although not all, tends to cancel out. The defect is inherent in the original numbers, particularly those for mission births, which show especially wide variation. There is less wide variation in the populations reported, but even they rose to a maximum at different times in the different missions and then fell fairly steadily until the end of the mission period. The causes for these fluctuations are manifold and cannot be discussed at the present juncture, although some of them have been indicated already in this essay. The basic questions to which answers are now sought are: (1) what were the birth rates? and (2) was there any change?

We can reduce the variability of the data by calculating moving averages for the 5 years surrounding each consecutive calendar year, except for the first and last 5-year periods, for

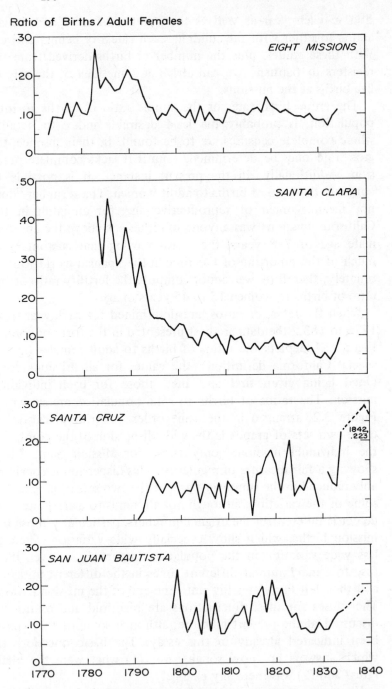

Figure 3.1   Ratio of births to adult female population. The line is based
              upon ratios for each calendar year. The ratios are plotted on
              the ordinate; the abscissa gives the calendar year.

Ratio of Births/Adult Females

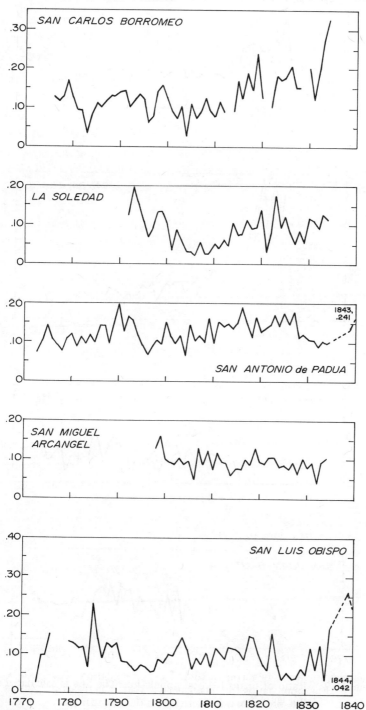

Ratio of Births/Total Population

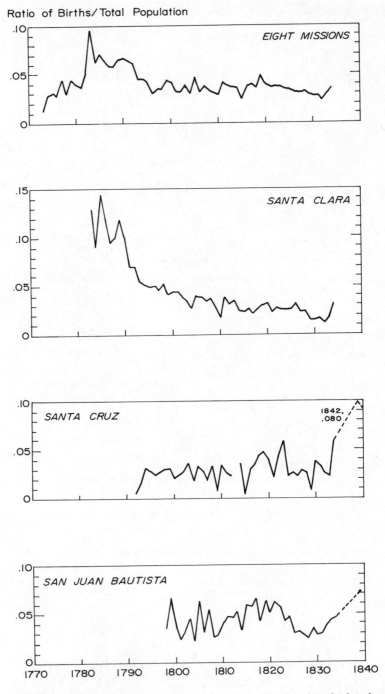

Figure 3.2   Ratio of births to total population. The line is calculated as
             in Figure 3.1.

Ratio of Births / Total Population

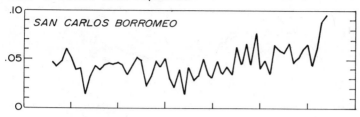

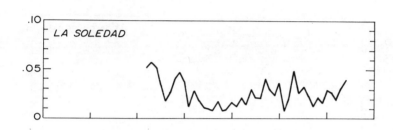

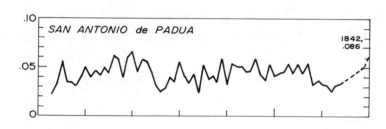

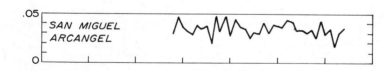

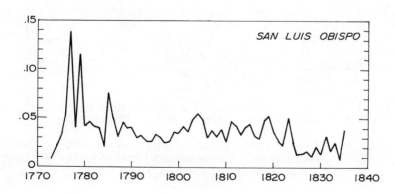

Ratio of Births / Adult Females — 5 Year Moving Averages

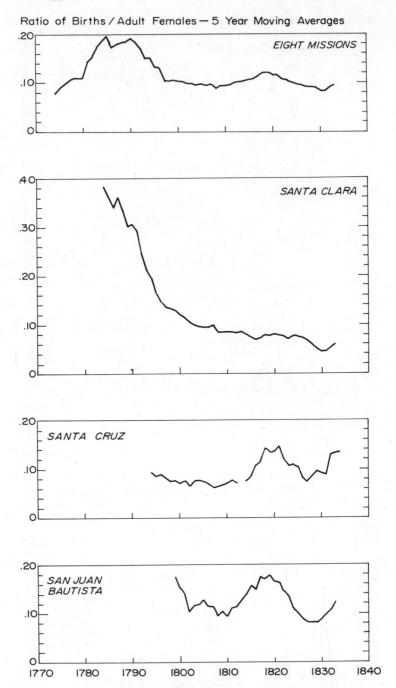

Figure 3.3   Ratio of births to adult female population. The line is based
              upon five-year moving averages of the ratios used in Figure
              3.1; the ordinate and abscissa as in that figure.

Ratio of Births / Adult Females — 5 Year Moving Averages

SAN CARLOS BORROMEO

LA SOLEDAD

SAN ANTONIO de PADUA

1842,
.245

SAN MIGUEL
ARCANGEL

SAN LUIS OBISPO

1770   1780   1790   1800   1810   1820   1830   1840

Ratio of Births / Total Population— 5 Year Moving Averages

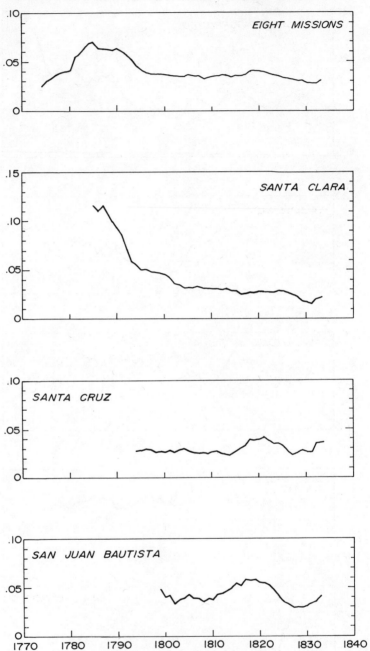

Figure 3.4   Ratio of births to total population. The line is based upon
five-year moving averages of the ratios used in Figure 3.2; the
ordinate and abscissa as in that figure.

Ratio of Births / Total Population-5 Year Moving Averages

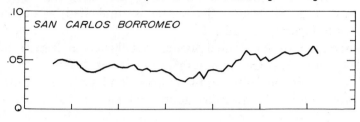

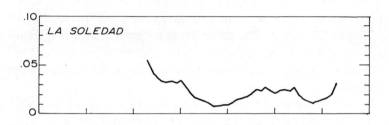

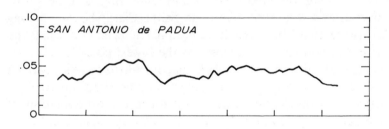

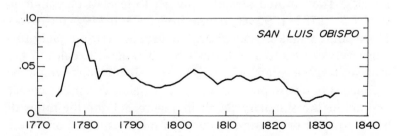

which 3-year averages are used. When these averaged points are graphed, a good deal of the scatter is eliminated, as demonstrated in Figures 3.3 and 3.4.

Inspection of the annual figures as adjusted in Figures 3.3 and 3.4 indicates that there remain very great differences from mission to mission. Initially, the individual missions show ranges for the ratio of births to adult women on the order of 0.38–0.37 to 0.05 or less, that is, from 380–370 births per 1,000 adult females down to 50 or less births. At the same time, the ratio of births to population ranged from near 0.130 down to 0.020 and 0.028, or from 130 births per 1,000 persons down to 20 and 28 births. The variation is so great that it is difficult to use the initial values for the individual missions as the basis for a guess at what the ratio was before the Indians entered the missions.

At each mission, except Santa Clara, the course of the ratios during the mission period was so irregular that it is again difficult to make generalizations. The ratios fell, at some missions reaching low points earlier and recovering, at others hovering around a central point, at Santa Clara showing a long downward trend that may have been reaching an end just as the mission period came to a close. At the lowest point for each set of ratios at Mission La Soledad, that for births to adult women was near 0.03 and births to population near 0.008, that is, 30 births per 1,000 adult females and 8 per 1,000 population. If such ratios had continued long and been characteristic of the other missions, as they were not, the neophyte population would have become extinct with rapidity in the face of the high death rate.

The two summary graphs represent a reconciliation of the highly divergent courses at the individual missions. In the summary graph for Figure 3.3, ratios of births to adult females, based on 5-year moving averages, the initial values fell between 0.075 and 0.1, that is, from 75 to 100 births per 1,000 adult females. They moved steadily upward to reach a maximum in the years 1783–1792 at values from 173 to 193 births per 1,000 adult females. Thereafter they dropped fairly rapidly to a range between 83 to 119 births per 1,000 adult females. A fair average for the years 1797–1834 for all missions would be around 100 births per 1,000 adult females. A similar course appears in the summary graph in Figure 3.4 for the ratios of births to total population at the eight missions, based on 5-year moving averages. The initial values averaged approximately 30 births per 1,000 population. The values rose to a maximum in the years 1781-1793, with an average of approximately 60 births per 1,000 total population, the peak year being 1785 with 70 births. Thereafter the values fell to a plateau, with an average of approximately 35 births per 1,000 population. The lower parts of this range would be considered a fairly high birth rate today; the higher parts approximate the highest values reported for present-day populations.

Let us return to some of the individual missions. The oldest mission was San Carlos Borromeo. The two graphs for it that are based on 5-year moving averages may reflect long-term trends better than at the others, except for San Antonio de Padua and San Luis Obispo, which were almost as old. That is particularly so if we are trying to lay bare the action of factors which might run a long-term course but stop before the Indians became extinct. If the corresponding graphs for San Antonio de Padua and San Luis Obispo tend to confirm the course of those at San Carlos Borromeo, then any conclusion as to longer-term trend would be strengthened. Initially, the ratio of births to adult women at San Carlos was near the level of 120. At the same time, the ratio of births to population was near 47. If a range is desired, we might think of 108 to 132 births per 1,000 adult women, and of 43 to 53 births per 1,000 persons. These are fairly high rates, which may be taken as probably somewhat lower than but close to those characteristic of the pre-mission aboriginal population.

Whether the course was linear or curved at Mission San Carlos is difficult to tell, but the ratios fell until at about 1805 a minimum was reached at values of approximately 100 births to 1,000 adult women and 34 births to 1,000 total population. Then improvement began. The ratios rose continuously until the end of the mission period. At about 1830 the values were 192 and 58 respectively. Those figures should be regarded as the central points of substantial ranges, as should all on the graphs.

The history of the birth rate at Mission San Carlos Borromeo, therefore, is reasonably clear. After a start at quite a high value, approximating the aboriginal one, it fell to a minimum after the rush of conversions in the 1790's and the epidemics of 1802. Thereafter it rose steadily and conclusively as long as the mission lasted. At the end, it was higher than at the beginning.

Experience at Mission San Antonio de Padua was different,

with the trend reversing direction a number of times. Initially
the ratios of births to women ranged between 100 and 120 per
1,000 women, and that of births to total population fell in
ranges from 37 to 40 per 1,000 population. Thereafter, the
ratios increased and decreased over periods of time. The ratio of
births to women reached peaks in the early 1790's and early
1820's at levels ranging from 150 to 160, while that for births
to total population ranged from 51 to 57 in the years
1785–1792, and in the years from 1817 to 1827 from 42 to 51.
In the last years of the mission period both ratios fell steadily,
reaching levels approximately as low as previous minima. This
decrease after a long period of relative stability may be due to
the bringing in of Tulares, whose presence meant that the ratios
became a reconciliation of two divergent tendencies.

For Mission San Luis Obispo, the graphs also show a more
irregular course than for Mission San Carlos, with a greater
initial variation. The ratio of births to adult women initially
may be set at an average of close to 170 births per 1,000 adult
women, and that of births to population at 55 births per 1,000
population, truly high values that may be the aboriginal ones.
The subsequent change in the ratios, although irregular, was one
of slow decline until the middle 1820's, when it reached bottom
at 45 for births to women and 15 for births to total population.
Thereafter the course of both was upward; in the early 1830's
they reached 100 to 150 births per 1,000 women and 40 to 42
births per 1,000 population.

The implications of the graphs are difficult to unravel. Mission San Antonio de Padua received contingents of Tulares;
Missions San Carlos de Borromeo and San Luis Obispo did not.
Part of the difficulty may lie there. One may hold that the
graphs support the view that once the native population had
become adapted and adjusted to mission life, the natural procre-
ative activity of the people asserted itself. In spite of disease
vectors and social restraints, the Indians were beginning to show
signs of demographic recovery, although the signs were still
faint at the end of the mission period. If so, the missions were
bringing their Indians through the shock of meeting the white
man with his new ways and new diseases in something less than
the 80 to 100 years that elsewhere in America seem to intervene
between first contact and the beginnings of demographic recovery. It is unfortunate that political developments cut short this
interesting human and biological experiment.

4. THE NON-INDIAN POPULATION

Accompanying the missionaries at the beginning of Christianization came numerous military and civilian personnel: the officials of the civil government, the garrisons of the missions and presidios, the artisans who helped the missionaries teach the Indians new crafts, settlers in the new land, and their families. A few of these individuals migrated from Spain, mostly army officers and administrators. The majority were of Mexican origin and already the products of the very considerable mixing of races in central and northern Mexico. They were known collectively as the *gente de razón,* a term which set them apart from the native Indian population. The process of mestization should be regarded as an ongoing one, for with the Hispanic gente de razón there also arrived a small number of Indians from the missions of Baja California, who might be counted among the Indians or among the gente de razón and increasingly moved into the gente de razón. Later in the nineteenth century there began a new stream of immigration, at first very small in comparison with the continuing one from Mexico, but by the later 1840's becoming a torrent. This new group was, for the area of the eight missions, almost entirely white and predominantly British, Irish, and Anglo-American, but had contingents from France, Germany, Portugal, and Italy. Despite some immigration from Mexico, Latin America, and Spain during the years of the Gold Rush, which tended to reinforce the existing Hispanic population, the new immigration quickly submerged the Indian and the Hispanic components both socially and demographically. After the missions disintegrated, there comes a time when it is difficult if not impossible to follow the fortunes of the Indians in the era of American settlement until the emergence of the Federal reservation system again provides information. The Hispanic population, on the other hand, may be studied to some extent by means of Church records throughout the nineteenth century and until the introduction of the California state registration system.

We make no attempt here to pursue the Mexican Californians through the nineteenth century, except insofar as information concerning them may be obtained from mission registers. Some data are available because all baptisms, burials, and marriages which involved the gente de razón were entered in the mission registers. Until after 1834 there were no secular priests or parishes in a province that, as far as the gente de razón were concerned, was completely Catholic. Even after 1834 the erection of new parishes came slowly. Two missions of the eight here under study have the bulk of entries on the gente de razón. They are San Carlos Borromeo and Santa Clara. Mission San Carlos has more than half the entries for gente de razón down to 1834, because its priests ministered to the spiritual needs of the military at the presidio of Monterey, the administrative staff at the provincial capital, and the citizens of the growing community that formed around the presidio, the capital, and the port. Mission Santa Clara ministered to the Hispanic population at the pueblo of San Jose, a short distance away. Registers at other missions have few entries; those that there are arose from the presence of the garrisons and artisans, increasingly of Mexican settlers on ranches, and, in the instance of Mission Santa Cruz, the existence of the small Mexican settlement of Branciforte. Begun in 1797 with 9 settlers and their families, 17 persons in all,[35] it remained minute for some decades and generated few entries in the Santa Cruz mission registers.

Entries for the gente de razón in the mission registers resemble those made for the Indians, but tend to be more extensive. For baptisms, in the earlier years, the missionary included, if he knew, the names and places of origin of the parents along with the name and birthplace of the infant. For many individuals a small family history is to be found. Ages frequently are not given, even for deaths and marriages. We must keep in mind that initially deaths and marriages were recorded for all the gente de razón, since all were Catholic, but that baptisms would be only of the newborn, for everyone else among the gente de razón had already been baptized. When Anglo-American and European immigrants began to arrive, there were Protestants among them, to be sure. During the Mexican period, they had to become Catholics in order to secure permission to remain, to become Mexican citizens, or to marry. The baptismal registers record these conversions. With the opening of the American period, the coverage of the Catholic parish registry rapidly became less than universal.

The facts that ages are frequently not given and that some mission registers are deficient in cross-references, such as those

---

35. Bancroft, *History of California,* I, p. 560, esp. n. 44.

of San Carlos Borromeo, in which no baptismal numbers occur in the death notices prior to 1830, make it difficult to evaluate the relationship between births and deaths among the gente de razón. There is also the additional complication that most deaths in the early years were of adults who had migrated to California. On the other hand, almost all the baptisms were of newborn. A schedule may be formulated, but it is very rough, as may be appreciated by examining Table 3.8A. Here the births and deaths of the gente de razón are summarized by decades from 1774 to 1834 for the two missions of San Carlos de Borromeo and Santa Clara. We have also incorporated a tabulation of such data for Mission Santa Cruz, but have not included it in the summary, since the data are too meager for any meaningful analysis. Information on numbers of baptisms for gente de razón at the other missions, but not on numbers of deaths, may be found by 5-year periods in Table 3.8B. The categories for age at death consist only of division into the two broad categories of *párvulo* and *adulto*. We cannot go beyond 1834, because thereafter the priests at Mission San Carlos condensed the death records to a mere notation of the name and omitted any reference to age, even the broad categories of párvulo and adulto.

TABLE 3.8A

Births and Deaths among the Gente de Razón
SANTA CLARA AND SAN CARLOS BORROMEO, 1774–1834[a]

Period	Births	Total deaths	Birth/ death ratio	Deaths of párvulos	Párvulo deaths per 1,000 births
1774–1784	89	35	2.54	15	169
1785–1794	124	40	3.10	21	169
1795–1804	228	82	2.78	33	145
1805–1814	244	103	2.37	43	176
1815–1824	383	143	2.68	49	128
1825–1834	710	245	2.90	120	169
Totals	1,778	648	2.74	281	158

[a] Information on the other missions pertaining to births and deaths among gente de razón is either incomplete or non-existent and therefore not included in this summary.

TABLE 3.8A (continued)

SANTA CLARA, 1777–1834

Period	Births	Total deaths	Birth/ death ratio	Deaths of párvulos	Párvulo deaths per 1,000 births
1777–1784	41	11	3.73	5	122
1785–1794	51	16	3.19	8	157
1795–1804	133	39	3.41	18	135
1805–1814	121	55	2.20	24	198
1815–1824	194	71	2.73	26	134
1825–1834	322	96	3.35	44	137
Totals	862	288	2.99	125	145

SANTA CRUZ, 1791–1834

1795–1804	5	2	2.50	1	200
1805–1814					
1815–1824					
1825–1834	6	9	0.67	5	833
Totals	11	11	1.00	6	545

SAN CARLOS BORROMEO, 1774–1834

Period	Births	Total deaths	Birth/ death ratio	Deaths of párvulos	Párvulo deaths per 1,000 births
1774–1784	48	24	2.00	10	208
1785–1794	73	24	3.29	13	178
1795–1804	95	43	2.21	15	158
1805–1814	123	48	2.56	19	154
1815–1824	189	72	2.62	23	122
1825–1834	388	149	2.60	76	196
Totals	916	360	2.54	156	170

From Table 3.8A we see that in the jurisdiction of the two missions of San Carlos and Santa Clara, during the decades up to 1835, there had been baptized 1,778 members of the gente de razón, almost exclusively of Hispano-Mexican descent. Because of the proximity of the Hispanic population to the mission, the baptisms are likely to be close to the number of actual births, although we cannot be sure that they coincide with that number. The Hispanic population was under somewhat looser control than the Indians, so that the delay between birth and baptism may have been somewhat longer and the chance of death in the intervening period, with its need for hasty baptism by any Christian, somewhat greater. Despite this lack of complete coincidence, we shall consider that baptisms do equal births for the purposes of our discussion. During the years covered in the table, there died 648 members of the gente de razón. The gross ratio of births to deaths is 2.74; that at Santa Clara 2.99, and that at San Carlos 2.54. The ratios by decade are also shown in the table, in the summary sheet and those for each mission. Although there is a good deal of variation, the range is not extreme and the ratios show a steady rise in population through natural increase. Similar data for Mission Santa Cruz show a level of unity but cover only a few individuals (11 baptisms and 11 deaths). We are unable to link the 372 recorded births of gente de razón at the remaining missions with deaths of gente de razón for any meaningful analysis, but suggest that the fairly steady rise in births with passage of time must have come at least in part from natural increase as well as immigration. The values we have for ratios of births to deaths are in marked contrast to the ratios for movement of population among the mission Indians. For the latter, there was a consistent excess of deaths over births.

Of the recorded deaths at the two missions, 281 are designated párvulos. A párvulo was a person up to the age of 7 or 8 years and is the nearest we can approach numerically to an infant in the data as they come to us. We tried to relate the párvulo deaths to the baptisms, but found that a check by name in the records of Mission San Carlos Borromeo indicated that only about 60% of the children who died had been born in the mission jurisdiction. It follows that the closest we can come to establishing an infant death rate is to equate the deaths of

párvulos to the total baptisms of gente de razón. The ratios by
decade for the two missions are shown in the summary of Table
3.8A and for the three missions—that is, including the meager
data for Santa Cruz—in the individual tabulations that follow.
They indicate for the two missions a range of 128 to 176
párvulo deaths per 1,000 baptisms. Those are averages of somewhat greater variation in the two missions, for which the range
is from 122 to 208. Mission Santa Clara, which had somewhat
higher ratios of baptisms to burials than Mission San Carlos—
that is, a more favorable ratio of net increase—also shows lower,
i.e., more favorable, ratios of párvulo deaths to 1,000 births.
Since it is clear from an examination of individual cases that
most, but not all, of the párvulos actually died in the first year
of existence, the probability is high that the true infant mortality lay somewhere between 100 to 150 deaths per 1,000 births.
That range is far below the range of rates demonstrated by the
mission-born Indians. It compares most favorably with the rates
calculated for the Mexico of the Diaz regime, already benefitting
from some influence of the new medical knowledge. (See the
discussion on the neophytes born in the missions, in Part 3 of
this essay.)

We may also compare the experience of the Hispanic population as recorded at the two missions with the data afforded by
the excellent historical demographic studies for France which
show infant mortality rates for localities in southwestern
France, western France, and the Beauvaisis ranging from 156 to
288 per 1,000 births. They cover periods of time of variable
length from the seventeenth to the end of the eighteenth century. Further, although the Spanish definition of parvulo
does not cover years of age 8-9, relatively few deaths usually
occur in those years, so that we may compare the rates for
párvulo deaths per 1,000 baptisms directly to the rates com-
puted in the French studies for deaths before age 10, that is, for
ages 0-9. For the localities studied in Brittany, as we have
already mentioned, roughly half of the children did not reach
their tenth year. Similarly, for the Beauvaisis, during the period
1656-1735, 47.1% of children died before age 10, a rate of 471
child deaths per 1,000 births. For localities in the southwest of
France and in Normandy, French experience was better in that
nearly two-thirds of the children reached their tenth year—that

is, slightly more than one-third died.[36] Studies of English parishes show rates of mortality even more favorable than those of eighteenth-century France. For one of the most thoroughly studied towns, Colyton, life-table treatment indicates that in the years from 1538 to 1837, of 1,000 people born, from 175 to 258 would die before their tenth year. The most favorable values are for 1750–1837 (175) and 1700–1749 (203), the least favorable one for 1650–1699 (258).[37] These proportions should be compared with the average rate of 158 párvulo deaths per 1,000 baptisms for the Hispanic population at the two missions during the years 1774–1834. Even with adjustment for deaths in ages 8–9, the average of the rates for the entire period would not reach 170 deaths per 1,000 births, that is, 83% of those born survived to the tenth year of life. Clearly the environment of Alta California was extraordinarily favorable to the Hispanic population.

Let us turn now to interethnic and interracial marriage as it shows up in the mission registers. The aggregate number of non-Indians who were born under mission auspices is found in Table 3.8B. From the foundation of the missions until 1855, some 5,354 infants were baptized. Of these, 4,726 were the children of parents of Spanish or Mexican stock. For varying periods of years it is possible to segregate the infants baptized into three categories, according to the birthplace of the parents. In the first years, all the gente de razón had been born in Mexico or had come through Mexico from Spain; we designate these people M. They gave way statistically to persons born in California (C) as migration attenuated and births increased in the new colony. For periods of years between 1818 and 1834, some missionaries designated the parents as *californios*. After 1834 the failure of the priests at some missions to include information on locality of origin of the parents—a failure that varies in highly erratic fashion from mission to mission—makes it necessary to indicate only the general Hispanic ancestry, regardless of birthplace; that is, we revert to classification M in Table 3.8B. Accordingly, the classification C in the table covers only a fraction of the Californio parents, so that only the

36. Goubert, "Legitimate Fecundity," pp. 599–600, and Henry, "Historical Demography," pp. 392–393; Pierre Goubert, *Beauvais et le Beauvaisis,* pp. 39–41.
37. E. A. Wrigley, "Mortality in Pre-Industrial England," pp. 552–560.

TABLE 3.8B

Children Born in the Missions Whose Parents Were Mexican Born (M), California Born of Mexican Born (M), California Born of Mexican Ancestry (C), California Indian (N), or Northern European or Anglo-Saxon (A)

EIGHT MISSIONS

Period	M M	M C	C C	Sub-total	A M or A C	A M as percent of combined A M and subtotal M	A A	M N	A N	Total
1770-1779	46			46				13		59
1780-1784	52			52				4		56
1785-1789	70			70				6		76
1790-1794	81	2		83				4		87
1795-1799	117	6	4	127				8		135
1800-1804	101	11	7	119				5		124
1805-1809	107	26	9	142				3		145
1810-1814	85	36	25	146				4		150
1815-1819	104	40	51	195				5		200
1820-1824	68	67	139	274	2	0.7		3		279
1825-1829	71	73	230	374	16	4.1		1		391
1830-1834	84	56	282	422	32	7.0	2	3		459
1835-1839				530	40	7.0	4	2		576
1840-1844				637	74	10.4	7	4	1	723
1845-1849				725	106	12.8	19	7	1	858
1850-1854				784	170	17.8	65	11	6	1,036
Totals				4,726	440	8.5	97	83	8	5,354

268

TABLE 3.8B (continued)

SANTA CLARA

Period	M M	M C	C C	Sub-total	A M or A C	A M as percent of combined A M and subtotal M	A A	M N	A N	Total
1777-1779	15			15						15
1780-1784	26			26						26
1785-1789	24			24				1		25
1790-94	26			26						26
1795-1799	70			70				1		71
1800-1804	59	1		60				2		62
1805-1809	60			60						60
1810-1814	61			61						61
1815-1819	56	3	12	71				4		75
1820-1824	9	37	71	117	1	0.8		1		119
1825-1829	8	16	112	136	4	2.9				140
1830-1834	2	16	155	173	9	4.9				182
1835-1839				186	11	5.6				197
1840-1844				239	18	7.0				257
1845-1849				273	38	12.2	9		1	321
1850-1854				140	29	17.2	27	2		198
Totals				1,677	110	6.2	36	11	1	1,835

TABLE 3.8B (continued)

SANTA CRUZ

Period	M M	M C	C C	Sub-total	A M or A C	A M as percent of combined A M and subtotal M	A A	M N	A N	Total
1791–1794										
1795–1799	5			5						5
1800–1804										
1805–1809										
1810–1814										
1815–1819										
1820–1824										
1825–1829										
1830–1834	6			6						6
1835–1839	57			57	7	10.9				64[a]
1840–1844	64			64	17	21.0		1		81
1845–1849	71			71	20	22.0				92
1850–1854	123			123	38	23.6	2		2	165
Totals	326			326	82	20.1	2	1	2	413

[a] The mission baptized few gente de razón until 1834 when secularization occurred. Branciforte began as a very small Hispanic settlement and grew slowly until the end of the mission period.

270

TABLE 3.8B (continued.)

Period	M M	M C	C C	Sub-Total	A M or A C	A M as percent of combined A M and subtotal M	A A	M N	A N	Total
SAN JUAN BAUTISTA										
1797-1799	2			2						2
1800-1804	4			4						4
1805-1809	10			10				1		11
1810-1814	8			8						8
1815-1819	29			29						29
1820-1824	33			33	1	3.0		1		35
1825-1829	47			47	5	9.6				52
1830-1834	59			59	8	11.9		1		68
1835-1839	104			104	9	8.0		1		114
1840-1844	110			110	14	11.3	1			125
1845-1849	115			115	6	5.0	1	2		124
1850-1854	212			212	19	8.2	11	2		244
Totals	733			733	62	7.8	13	8		816

TABLE 3.8B (continued)

Period	M M	M C	C C	Sub-Total	A M or A C	A M as percent of combined A M and subtotal M	A A	M N	A N	Total
SAN CARLOS BORROMEO										
1774–1779	19			19				10		29
1780–1784	16			16				3		19
1785–1789	29			29				4		33
1790–1794	34	2		36				4		40
1795–1799	31	6	4	41				6		47
1800–1804	30	10	7	47				1		48
1805–1809	19	26	9	54				1		55
1810–1814	6	36	25	67				1		68
1815–1819	2	37	39	78						78
1820–1824	13	30	68	111						111
1825–1829	8	57	118	183	7	3.7		2		192
1830–1834	10	40	127	177	15	7.8	2	2		196
1835–1839				176	13	6.9	4			193
1840–1844				195	22	10.1	6	3	1	227
1845–1849				217	29	11.8	9	4		259
1850–1854				232	54	18.9	24	7	4	321
Totals				1,678	140	7.7	45	48	5	1,916

TABLE 3.8B (continued)

Period	M M	M C	C C	Sub-Total	A M or A C	A M as percent of combined A M and subtotal M	A A	M N	A N	Total
						LA SOLEDAD				
1791–1794										
1795–1799	4			4						4
1800–1804	4			4				2		6
1805–1809	13			13						13
1810–1814	3			3				1		4
1815–1819	12			12				3		15
1820–1824	7			7				1		8
1825–1829	6			6				1		7
1830–1834	6			6				1		7
1835–1839										
1840–1844										
1845–1849										
1850–1854										
Totals	55							9		64

TABLE 3.8B (continued)

Period	M M	M C	C C	Sub-total	A M or A C	A M as percent of combined A M and subtotal M	A A	M N	A N	Total
					SAN ANTONIO DE PADUA					
1771–1774	1			1				1		2
1775–1779	4			4						4
1780–1784	6			6				2		8
1785–1789	6			6				1		7
1790–1794	11			11				1		12
1795–1799	4			4						4
1800–1804	1			1				1		2
1805–1809	1			1						1
1810–1814	5			5						5
1815–1819	3			3						3
1820–1824	2			2						2
1825–1829										
1830–1834	1			1						1
1835–1839	2			2				1		3
1840–1844	4			4				1		5
1845–1849	2			2						2
1850–1854	4			4			1			5
Totals	57			57			1	8		66

TABLE 3.8B (continued)

Period	M M	M C	C C	Sub-total	A M or A C	A M as percent of combined A M and subtotal M	A A	M N	A N	Total
				SAN MIGUEL ARCÁNGEL						
1770–1779										
1780–1784										
1785–1789										
1790–1794										
1795–1799										
1800–1804	2			2						2
1805–1809	2			2						2
1810–1814	6			6						6
1815–1819	5			5						5
1820–1824	3			3						3
1825–1829	3			3						3
1830–1834	2			2						2
1835–1839	4			4						4
1840–1844	2			2						2
1845–1849										
1850–1854	4			4						4
Totals	33			33						33

TABLE 3.8B (continued)

Period	M M	M C	C C	Sub-total	A M or A C	A M as percent of combined A M and subtotal M	A A	M N	A N	Total
SAN LUIS OBISPO										
1770–1779	7			7						7
1780–1784	4			4						4
1785–1789	11			11						11
1790–1794	10			10						10
1795–1799	6			6						6
1800–1804	3			3						3
1805–1809	4			4						4
1810–1814	2			2						2
1815–1819	2			2						2
1820–1824	4			4						4
1825–1829	2			2						2
1830–1834										
1835–1839	1			1						1
1840–1844	23			23	3	11.5				26
1845–1849	47			47	13	21.7				60
1850–1854	69			69	30	30.3				99
Totals	195			195	46	19.1				241

subtotal for all infants born to parents of Hispanic culture is accurate. We should also warn that in terms of our classification a parent of Portuguese origin would not count as M, but that a parent of Spanish or Latin American origin would, regardless of the year of migration to California.[38]

In the 1820's the first non-Spanish-speaking immigrants arrived in California. Some were Catholics; all who wished to settle and become Mexican citizens were required to convert to the Catholic form of Christianity. Many, if not most, men coming in the years of the Mexican period married California women. We have designated this group of immigrants A. In the years 1820–1824, 2 children of such couples were baptized; in 1825–1829, 16. In general, in the succeeding 5-year periods the number rose steadily. Up to the end of 1854, the total number was 440. Their weight among the newly-born can be appreciated if we express their number as a percentage of the total children born to all parents who were both of M and C culture, plus those who are listed as AM. (We omit AA, MN, and AN—that is, children of European and Anglo-American parents on both sides, and the product of unions in which one parent was a California Indian.) This value is shown in Table 3.8B and is seen to increase from 0.7% in 1820–1824 to 17.8% in 1850–1854. In other words, by 1854 close to one-fifth of the gente de razón infants baptized at the parish churches directly succeeding the eight missions were derived from mixed Mexican or Californio parentage on one side and non-Hispanic parentage of Caucasian stock on the other. The latter were predominantly Anglo-American, British, and Irish, and almost invariably the fathers. Again, there was wide variation from mission to mission, the highest proportion of such mixing being evident at Santa Cruz and the next highest at San Carlos Borromeo.

At the same time, there was considerable mixing between the Hispanic and the native Indian components, and later between the new migrants and the Indians. Some of the effects can be localized in the mission registers. We have found 83 children of mixed MN parentage and 8 children of AN parentage. These children were the offspring of marriages; invariably the mother was N. They represent 1.7% of the gente de razón births. There

38. By accident, we are following here the idea of Hispano in the general Latin American usage of Hispanoamericano, which includes only people from Spanish-speaking countries of Latin America but excludes Brazilians.

must have taken place, in addition, a great deal of less formal mixing in which men of Hispanic or other European stock begot children upon native women. Extramarital coupling of native men with women of Hispanic, European, or Anglo-American origin would have been exceedingly rare, as was marriage. The mission registers give us almost no direct data on illegitimate children of such mixed origin, nor are clues easy to find. The mission registers do record a small number of baptisms of illegitimate and abandoned (*exposito*) infants among the gente de razón. For San Jose (i.e., registers of Mission Santa Clara), the baptisms are largely associated with certain mothers, who may have been genuinely promiscuous or in the later years may have been living in common-law unions with long-term partners. We have carried such children as M on the assumption that the father was almost certainly M or C. That assumption is fully justified for the earlier years, but less so after 1846–1848.

5. THE MARRIAGE RECORDS

The mission books of marriages carry the entries, for both Indians and gente de razón, of all legal unions in their territories down to 1846. Even secularization did not at once change this situation in the territory of the eight missions. The opening of the Anglo-American period brought clergymen of other denominations and new justices of the peace, who under the new system of law were equally able to perform marriages recognized as legal, but Roman Catholics continued to marry in a religious ceremony performed by a priest and registered in the parish registers. By the 1850's the parish system began to be extended, so that the mission registers no longer contained all entries for Roman Catholic marriages performed in the former territories of the eight missions. Accordingly, we have chosen 1854 as the cut-off date for selection of data on gente de razón—or in the Anglo-American usage, the whites.

In the entries of the marriage registers of the missions may be found at maximum for each couple the ethnic affiliation of bride and groom, the birthplaces of both, in many instances the birthplaces of the parents, and the previous marital status. The most important evidence provided is that on ethnic origin or affiliation, which immediately sets off the Indians from the gente de razón. For the latter, the evidence in the marriage entries too may serve as a complement to data in the baptismal entries. Comparison is simple if the person had been born in the territory of the same mission in which he was married. It would be more difficult, but possible, if the person had been born elsewhere in California, and increasingly difficult, but not impossible, with greater distance of the parish of birth in Mexico or Spain, if the parish or birthplace is known. This kind of examination, however, lies beyond the scope of our present study.

We shall discuss certain data which are provided in the marriage entries for both the Indians and the gente de razón, and which are not available in the entries of the baptismal and burial registers. One problem which faced the missionaries when they were converting the California Indians was that many of the new converts had been living in what Indian custom and rite recognized as marriage. The problem was not a new one; it appeared almost at the inception of Christianity, and the first rules for dealing with it emanated from St. Paul, including what is called the Pauline Dispensation. A new marriage is necessary between the former partners even if both convert to Christianity. Should one of the former partners remain heathen, the other partner is free, under certain conditions, to marry another person, provided that person is Christian. The rules were further refined in the discussions within the Mexican Church during the sixteenth century and in the regulations adopted by the first three Mexican Church councils. These regulations attempted to specify the conditions in which renewal of the heathen marriage by Christian rite was necessary or obligatory, the conditions in which unions with new partners were to be permitted or required, and the way in which previously polygamous arrangements were to be brought to Christian monogamy. This last led to a great deal of difficulty in Mexico, since the husband, on being faced with a requirement to declare who was his first wife so that he might be united with her in Christian marriage, frequently developed a poor memory in the hope of being allowed to select a younger and more attractive woman from among his previous spouses. There may well have been similar problems in California, for the California Indians were hardly invariably monogamous, but the marriage entries are mute on this point. The rules of the Church, then, as they came to the Franciscans in Alta California, via the Bishopric of Sonora and the Archbishopric of Mexico, required them to see that Indians who converted married their spouses in Christian ceremony if both became Christian; to permit them, under carefully laid-out conditions, to choose a new Christian partner if the former spouse by Indian rite or custom did not become Christian; and to marry only a Christian if they had not been married previously by heathen rite or custom. The position of the Church then and now is an interesting one of not recognizing Indian custom as providing a proper basis for marriage, but, on the other hand, of agreeing that it has a measure of validity.[39]

It is difficult to judge from the marriage entries in the mission registers the details of policies followed by the missionaries in dealing with the numerous questions that must have arisen, for most decisions would be made in advance of the marriage and would be recorded only if required by Church regulations. Accordingly, we are led to a series of inferences. Basically, the friars appear to have taken the position that baptism wiped out all previous marriage ties as though they had not been, but that if both partners became Christian, there was an obligation for them to marry each other by Christian ceremony. The first part of this policy appears in the entries in the application of the Spanish terms for unmarried man and woman, *soltero* and *soltera*, to Indians of seasoned years who were frequently but not invariably marrying former marriage partners. One also encounters solteros and solteras of 40, 50, and 60 years of age marrying partners of ages as low as 13 or 14. The marriages were by no means all of old men with very young women, but often of old women with mere boys. It is difficult to believe that many men or women aged 18 to 25 remained unmarried in aboriginal society. We are obviously

39. The literature on validity of marriages entered into prior to conversion to Roman Catholic Christianity and the marital obligations and privileges of converts is extensive and complex. An urbane and informed discussion, with particular references to the archdiocese of Mexico, may be found in John T. Noonan, Jr., *Power to Dissolve: Lawyers and Marriages in the Courts of the Roman Curia*, pp. 263–266, 343–363, 394–399, and the appropriate pages of notes. The prevailing rules, as they were understood in eighteenth- and early nineteenth-century California and Mexico, are laid out in a pamphlet by Tadeo Amat, Bishop of Monterey, in *A Treatise on Matrimony*. The discussions and resulting rules in sixteenth-century Mexico may be traced in José A. Llaguno, *La personalidad jurídica del indio y el III Concilio Provincial Mexicano (1585)*, pp. 11, 21–22, 32, 122–123, 127–128, and 281; Joaquín García Icazbalceta, *Don Fray Juan de Zumárraga*, I, pp. 142–146; Gerónimo de Mendieta, *Historia eclesiástica indiana*, pp. 301–306; and John T. Noonan, Jr., "Marriage in Michoacan."

meeting in the entries a convention resulting from conversion to Christianity.

The second part of the policy stated above appears also in the marriage entries in a substantial number of Indian marriages, through the notation by the recording priest that the couple had been married previously in heathen existence. In a very rare number of entries the priest recorded that the couple had had other spouses by Indian rite but preferred their new partners for Christian marriage. From the scarcity of such entries, we infer that in a very few instances, because of special circumstances not noted, converts whose previous spouses also converted were allowed to choose new marriage partners, but that in general the missionaries did insist that, if both spouses converted, they remarry their old partners by Christian ceremony. The data, in both absolute and relative terms, are presented in Table 3.9. There we show data from seven of our eight missions. Since the comparison of marriages throughout the history of each mission is somewhat misleading, in that the confirmation of Indian-rite marriages by Christian ceremony would happen only during the years of active conversion and would decline as the mission population increasingly consisted of Indians born there, we give for each mission a subtotal of data at the end of the years of active conversion. For Mission Santa Clara and in the summary, no such treatment is possible. At Santa Clara the Tulares arrived soon enough to continue the active conversion of adult gentiles so that there is no break, but rather an increase in the proportion of marriages by Christian rite of partners previously living as man and wife in heathen society. In the summary, the fact that the years of active conversion came at different times makes it impossible to mark off any term of years.

It is evident from the summary sheet that during the peak

The specific Mexican Church legislation is in the proceedings of the Primera Junta Apóstolica, 1524–1525; the papal bull in answer, Rome, 10 July 1537; Constituciones de el arzobispado y provincia de la muy insigne, y muy leal ciudad de Temextitlan, México de la Nueva España; Concilio Primero, 1556; and Privilegios de indios, n. d. but ca. 1765, this last forbidding marriages among Indians only to and including the second degree of consanguinity—all in *Concilios provinciales primero y segundo*, pp. 6–7, 31, 88–89, 98–100, and 391–392; and decrees of the Third Mexican Church Council, 1585, in *Concilium mexicanum provinciale III*, pp. 269–288. The solutions are essentially those indicated by Father Juan Focher, O.F.M., in his *Itinerarium catholicum proficiscentium ad infideles convertendos,* 1574, consulted in bilingual text, *Itinerario del misionero en América*, pp. 161–212.

years of conversion, 1770 to 1809, more than one-third of the marriages at the missions reunited couples who had been living together according to Indian law and custom. The summary tends to smooth out a great deal of variation from mission to mission. For some 5-year periods and at some missions, the proportion of such unions to total Indian marriages ran more than half, and at San Antonio de Padua for the years 1773–1774 reached the value of 73.7%. In each mission the proportion would trail off unless there was a renewed injection of adult gentile converts through the importation of Tulares from the Central Valley. Their presence may be found in the data presented in Tables 3.1 and 3.2, which should be examined in conjunction with Table 3.9.

TABLE 3.9

Marriages of Converts Who Had Previously Been Married by Indian Custom

Period	Total Marriages	Unions of Persons Previously Married as Gentiles	Percent of Such Unions
SEVEN MISSIONS[a]			
1770–1774[b]	51	28	54.9
1775–1779	236	109	46.2
1780–1784	361	125	34.6
1785–1789	345	88	25.5
1790–1794	692	329	47.5
1795–1799	948	288	30.4
1800–1804	1,219	472	38.7
1805–1809	922	314	34.1
1810–1814	559	149	26.7
1815–1819	506	101	20.0
1820–1824	787	284	36.1
1825–1829	491	72	14.7
1830–1834	423	15	3.5
Totals	7,540	2,374	31.4

[a] No data available for San Miguel Arcángel, since the marriage register is lost, nor for San Luis Obispo, 1771–1774.

[b] Six missions, since no data for San Luis Obispo.

TABLE 3.9 (continued)

Period	Total Marriages	Unions of Persons Previously Married as Gentiles	Percent of Such Unions
		SANTA CLARA	
1778-1779	11	4	36.4
1780-1784	72	19	26.4
1785-1789	87	28	32.2
1790-1794	293	192	65.5
1795-1799	296	78	26.4
1800-1804	313	121	38.7
1805-1809	335	156	46.6
1810-1814	193	77	39.9
1815-1819	188	79	42.0
1820-1824	223	99	44.4
1825-1829	235	58	24.7
1830-1834	137	1	0.1
Totals	2,383	912	38.3

Period	Total Marriages	Unions of Persons Previously Married as Gentiles	Percent of Such Unions
		SANTA CRUZ	
1791-1794	74	45	60.8
1795-1799	180	94	52.2
1800-1804	91	17	18.7
1805-1809	129	44	34.1
1810-1814	76	39	51.5
1815-1819	68	3	4.4
1820-1824	99	26	26.3
Subtotals 1791-1824	717	268	37.4
1825-1829	48		
1830-1834	37		
Totals	802	268	33.4

TABLE 3.9 (continued)

Period	Total Marriages	Unions of Persons Previously Married as Gentiles	Percent of Such Unions
		SAN JUAN BAUTISTA	
1797-1799	75	42	56.0
1800-1804	256	147	57.4
1805-1809	128	33	25.8
1810-1804	63	--	0.0
1815-1819	70	2	2.9
1820-1824	273	129	47.3
1825-1829	71	8	11.3
1830-1834	91	3	3.3
Totals	1,027	364	35.4

Period	Total Marriages	Unions of Persons Previously Married as Gentiles	Percent of Such Unions
		SAN CARLOS BORROMEO	
1770-1774	32	14	43.8
1775-1779	106	49	46.2
1780-1784	110	32	29.1
1785-1789	100	27	27.0
1790-1794	108	26	24.1
1795-1799	65	3	4.6
Subtotals 1770-1799	521	151	29.0
1800-1804	68	--	--
1805-1809	84	5	6.0
1810-1814	51	--	--
1815-1819	32	--	--
1820-1824	29	--	--
1825-1829	21	--	--
1830-1834	32	--	--
Totals	838	156	18.6

TABLE 3.9 (continued)

Period	Total Marriages	Unions of Persons Previously Married as Gentiles	Percent of Such Unions
		LA SOLEDAD	
1792-1794	49	27	55.1
1795-1799	87	35	40.2
1800-1804	141	50	35.5
1805-1809	81	33	40.8
1810-1814	77	21	27.3
1815-1819	58	8	13.8
1820-1824	85	30	35.3
1825-1829	30	--	--
1830-1834	50	11	22.0
Totals	658	215	32.7

Period	Total Marriages	Unions of Persons Previously Married as Gentiles	Percent of Such Unions
		SAN ANTONIO DE PADUA	
1773-1774	19	14	73.7
1775-1779	79	38	48.2
1780-1784	124	62	50.0
1785-1789	106	27	25.5
1790-1794	75	10	13.3
1795-1799	126	21	16.7
1800-1804	198	61	30.8
1805-1809	115	37	32.2
1810-1814	72	7	9.7
1815-1819	61	9	14.8
Subtotals 1773-1819	975	286	29.3
1820-1824	53	--	--
1825-1829	63	--	--
1830-1834	49	--	--
Totals	1,140	286	25.1

TABLE 3.9 (continued)

Period	Total Marriages	Unions of Persons Previously Married as Gentiles	Percent of Such Unions
		SAN LUIS OBISPO	
1771-1775	(45)^c	--	--
1776-1779	40	18	45.0
1780-1784	55	12	21.8
1785-1789	52	6	11.5
1790-1794	93	29	31.2
1795-1799	119	15	12.6
1800-1804	152	76	50.0
1805-1809	48	6	12.5
1810-1814	27	5	18.5
Subtotals 1771-1814	586	167	28.5
1815-1819	29	--	--
1820-1824	25	--	--
1825-1829	23	--	--
1830-1834	27	6	27.2
Totals	690	173	25.1

^{c} Marriage register burned for this period; replacement by Father Serra has inadequate data for use here.

Once a Christian ceremony of marriage had taken place, the partners of that ceremony were not free to remarry so long as both lived, except under unusual conditions requiring judgment by an ecclesiastical court such as did not exist within California within the mission years, but some of whose powers were delegated to the provincial President. If one of the partners to the marriage died, the other was free to remarry. The marriage entries carefully specify for each individual to a marriage cere- mony whether he or she had been previously married in the Christian Church. For both Indians and gente de razón, there- fore, we get some indication through the marriage entries of the severity of mortality. In the case of the Indians, however, it is necessary to delete from the count those marriages which were, in effect, a repetition of an Indian ceremony, for unions which occurred prior to the first Christian marriage are otherwise never recorded. With this adjustment, if the number of remarried widows and widowers is large, then we must conclude that the death rate was high among young adults in order to free these marriageable persons. The converse must be true if the number is small.

Table 3.10A gives data for seven of the eight missions on remarriage among the Indians down to 1834. For the years after 1834, we have taken off data only for some of the missions. Accordingly, the summary gives the number of missions from which data are made available in each semi-decade. Differences in the earlier years are due to dates of founding. The subtotals for data down to 1834 are the most reliable; subsequent adduction of data should be considered a series of samples of lessening reliability. Two items in Table 3.10A are of significance. The first is that the average for all seven missions down to 1834 is 35.7%—i.e., 35.7% of those men and women entering wedlock had already been married in the Christian faith. Their previous spouses must have died, for there was no divorce nor were they likely to have available to them other avenues of dissolution of marriage ties. The second feature is that the proportion of those remarrying rose steadily until it reached maxima in the years 1805- 1814 and 1825- 1829. Equally high values are shown for 1840- 1844 and 1850- 1854, but are based upon data from fewer missions. They also occur in years when many Indians, presumably a larger proportion of the young, had abandoned the missions and left behind older adults. The explanation of the maxima in the years 1805- 1814 and 1825- 1829 is that in the early years most of the brides and grooms were converted gentiles. These, however, were replaced by mission-born Indians until the latter group, subsequent to about 1810, exclusively constituted the newlyweds at most missions. We have already found from inspection of baptism and burial records that the mission-born component suffered from a very high rate of mortality. The marriage records, which show increased remarriage, substantiate this finding. Further, there was a marked difference between men and women in the proportion of second and later marriages. In the aggregate, over 40% of the marriages involved remarriage by men, whereas only approximately 30% involved remarriages by women.

TABLE 3.10A

Gentile and Mission Born Widows and Widowers Who Remarried
Indians Not Previously Married by Indian Custom

Period	Number of Missions Furnishing Data	Total Indians Married	Widowers		Widows		Both Sexes	
			Number	Percent of Men	Number	Percent of Women	Number	Percent of Total
SEVEN MISSIONS[a]								
1770-1774	3	136						
1775-1779	4	254	23	18.1	25	19.7	48	18.9
1780-1784	4	470	47	20.0	61	26.0	108	23.0
1785-1789	4	516	79	30.6	57	22.1	136	26.4
1790-1794	6	724	84	23.2	65	18.0	149	20.6
1795-1799	7	1,322	230	34.8	164	24.8	394	29.8
1800-1804	7	1,504	339	45.1	231	30.7	570	37.9
1805-1809	7	1,230	337	54.8	247	40.2	584	47.5
1810-1814	7	820	204	49.8	169	41.2	373	45.5
1815-1819	7	828	171	41.3	142	34.3	313	37.8
1820-1824	7	1,006	205	40.8	166	33.0	371	36.9
1825-1829	7	850	242	56.9	141	33.2	383	45.1
1830-1834	7	804	194	48.3	110	27.4	304	37.8
Subtotals		10,464	2,155	41.1	1,578	30.2	3,733	35.7

TABLE 3.10A (continued)

Period	Number of Missions Furnishing Data	Total Indians Married	Widowers		Widows		Both Sexes	
			Number	Percent of Men	Number	Percent of Women	Number	Percent of Total
1835–1839	4	212	45	42.5	34	32.1	79	37.3
1840–1844	2	142	34	47.9	28	39.4	62	43.7
1845–1849	1	68	17	50.0	8	23.5	25	36.8
1850–1854	1	20	7	70.0	2	20.0	9	45.0
Totals		10,906	2,258	41.4	1,650	30.3	3,908	35.8

a Data for San Miguel Arcángel not available, since registers lost.

TABLE 3.10A (continued)

SANTA CLARA

Period	Total Indians Married	Widowers		Widows		Both Sexes	
		Number	Percent of Men	Number	Percent of Women	Number	Percent of Total
1778–1779	14						
1780–1784	106	7	13.2	13	24.5	20	18.9
1785–1789	118	33	55.9	20	33.9	53	44.9
1790–1794	202	35	34.7	22	21.8	57	28.2
1795–1799	436	96	44.0	73	33.5	169	38.8
1800–1804	384	110	57.3	85	44.3	195	50.8
1805–1809	358	100	55.7	68	38.0	168	46.9
1810–1814	232	64	55.2	42	36.2	106	45.7
1815–1819	218	54	49.5	42	38.5	96	44.0
1820–1824	248	60	48.4	39	31.5	99	39.9
1825–1829	354	98	55.4	46	26.0	144	40.7
1830–1834	272	68	50.0	39	28.7	107	38.2
Subtotals	2,942	725	49.3	489	33.2	1,214	41.3

TABLE 3.10A (continued)

Period	Total Indians Married	Widowers		Widows		Both Sexes	
		Number	Percent of Men	Number	Percent of Women	Number	Percent of Total
1835–1839	158	39	49.4	25	31.6	64	40.5
1840–1844	142	34	47.9	28	39.4	62	43.7
1845–1849	68	17	50.0	8	23.5	25	36.8
1850–1854	20	7	70.0	2	20.0	9	45.0
Totals	3,330	822	49.4	552	33.2	1,374	41.3

TABLE 3.10A (continued)

Period	Total Indians Married	Widowers Number	Widowers Percent of Men	Widows Number	Widows Percent of Women	Both Sexes Number	Both Sexes Percent of Total
SANTA CRUZ							
1791-1794	58	2	6.9	31	36.1	2	3.4
1795-1799	172	45	52.3	31	36.1	76	44.2
1800-1804	148	20	27.0	21	28.4	41	27.7
1805-1809	170	25	29.4	24	28.2	49	28.8
1810-1814	74	17	46.0	17	46.0	34	46.0
1815-1819	130	18	27.7	15	23.1	33	25.4
1820-1824	146	29	39.8	9	12.3	38	26.6
1825-1829	96	28	58.4	9	18.8	37	38.6
1830-1834	74	20	54.1	9	24.3	29	39.1
Subtotals	1,068	204	38.2	135	25.3	339	31.7
1835-1839	38	5	26.3	7	36.8	12	31.6
Totals	1,106	209	37.8	142	25.7	351	31.7

TABLE 3.10A (continued)

SAN JUAN BAUTISTA

Period	Total Indians Married	Widowers		Widows		Both Sexes	
		Number	Percent of Men	Number	Percent of Women	Number	Percent of Total
1797–1799	66			1	3.0	1	1.5
1800–1804	218	21	19.3	15	13.8	36	16.5
1805–1809	190	32	33.7	29	30.5	61	32.1
1810–1814	126	30	47.7	34	54.0	64	50.8
1815–1819	136	20	29.4	18	26.5	38	28.0
1820–1824	288	40	27.7	45	31.2	85	29.5
1825–1829	126	40	63.5	21	33.3	61	48.4
1830–1834	176	35	39.8	17	19.3	52	29.5
Totals	1,326	218	32.9	180	27.2	398	30.0

293

TABLE 3.10A (continued)

SAN CARLOS BORROMEO

Period	Total Indians Married	Widowers		Widows		Both Sexes	
		Number	Percent of Men	Number	Percent of Women	Number	Percent of Total
1770–1774	36						
1775–1779	114	15	26.3	20	35.1	35	30.7
1780–1784	156	26	33.4	34	43.6	60	38.5
1785–1789	146	24	32.9	18	24.7	42	28.8
1790–1794	164	25	30.5	24	29.3	49	29.9
1795–1799	124	14	22.6	7	11.3	21	17.0
1800–1804	136	31	45.5	23	33.9	54	39.7
1805–1809	150	54	72.0	39	52.0	93	62.0
1810–1814	102	31	60.8	25	49.0	56	54.9
1815–1819	64	13	40.6	15	46.9	28	43.8
1820–1824	58	17	58.6	20	69.0	37	63.8
1825–1829	42	11	52.4	10	47.6	21	50.0
1830–1834	64	13	40.6	7	21.8	20	31.2
Subtotals	1,356	274	40.4	242	35.7	516	38.1
1835–1839	16	1	12.5	2	25.0	3	18.7
Totals	1,372	275	40.1	244	35.6	519	37.8

TABLE 3.10A (continued)

Period	Total Indians Married	Widowers		Widows		Both Sexes	
		Number	Percent of Men	Number	Percent of Women	Number	Percent of Total
LA SOLEDAD							
1791–1794	44	2	9.1			2	4.5
1795–1799	106	13	24.5	3	5.7	16	15.1
1800–1804	192	46	48.0	22	22.8	68	35.4
1805–1809	96	33	68.8	16	33.3	49	51.1
1810–1814	112	28	50.0	26	46.4	54	48.2
1815–1819	100	16	32.0	9	18.0	25	25.0
1820–1824	110	23	41.8	13	23.6	36	32.7
1825–1829	60	22	73.4	9	30.0	31	51.7
1830–1834	78	18	46.2	3	7.7	21	26.9
Totals	898	201	40.3	101	20.2	302	33.6

TABLE 3.10A (continued)

SAN ANTONIO DE PADUA

Period	Total Indians Married	Widowers		Widows		Both Sexes	
		Number	Percent of Men	Number	Percent of Women	Number	Percent of Total
1771–1774	10						
1775–1779	82	8	19.5	4	9.7	12	14.6
1780–1784	122	14	23.0	14	23.0	28	23.0
1785–1789	160	19	23.7	16	20.0	35	21.9
1790–1794	128	10	15.6	11	17.2	21	16.4
1795–1799	210	38	36.2	33	31.4	71	33.8
1800–1804	274	74	54.0	46	33.6	120	43.8
1805–1809	182	63	69.3	49	53.9	112	61.6
1810–1814	130	23	32.9	16	22.9	39	30.0
1815–1819	122	30	49.2	28	45.9	58	47.5
1820–1824	106	26	49.1	29	54.7	55	51.9
1825–1829	126	28	44.4	31	49.2	59	46.8
1830–1834	98	32	65.3	27	55.1	59	60.3
Subtotals	1,750	365	41.7	304	34.7	669	38.2
1835–1839	128	29	45.3	21	32.8	50	39.0
1840–1844	80	25	62.5	15	37.5	40	50.0
Totals	1,958	419	42.8	340	34.7	759	38.8

TABLE 3.10A (continued)

Period	Total Indians Married	Widowers		Widows		Both Sexes	
		Number	Percent of Men	Number	Percent of Women	Number	Percent of Total
				SAN LUIS OBISPO			
1771-1775[b]	(90)			1	4.5	1	2.3
1776-1779	44						
1780-1784	86						
1785-1789	92	3	6.5	3	6.5	6	6.5
1790-1794	128	10	14.8	8	12.5	18	14.1
1795-1799	208	24	23.1	16	15.4	40	19.2
1800-1804	152	37	48.2	19	25.0	56	36.8
1805-1809	84	30	71.4	22	52.4	52	62.0
1810-1814	44	11	50.0	9	40.9	20	45.5
1815-1819	58	20	69.0	15	51.8	35	60.4
1820-1824	50	10	40.0	11	44.0	21	42.0
1825-1829	46	15	65.2	15	65.2	30	65.2
1830-1834	42	8	38.1	8	38.1	16	38.1
Totals	1,034	168	32.5	127	24.5	295	28.5

[b] Book burned for this period; replacement does not give adequate data.

In Table 3.10B we present data on remarriages among the gente de razón. Our data are from three missions, but they cover the overwhelming bulk of the non-Indians in the territory of the eight missions down to 1834, and a steadily lessening but still considerable proportion of Catholic marriages down to 1854. The data are organized by 10-year periods centered upon the last year of each calendar decade, except for the first period, 1770–1784. For the gente de razón, the rate of remarriage was reasonably constant from 1770 to 1834 at Monterey (Mission San Carlos Borromeo) and much more variable at the two other missions. The rates in the summary reflect the preponderance of the non-Indian population in San Jose, which resorted to Mission Santa Clara. In general, the rates of remarriage fell sharply with the new immigration after 1835. During the mission period the values of all three missions combined held to a mean of 12.7% for both sexes, slightly more than one-third of the mean rate for the Indians of both sexes in the same span of time. This difference further supports the finding, based upon the baptismal and burial records, that mortality among the mission Indians far exceeded that among the neighboring population of European culture. Another difference between Indians and non-Indians that shows up in Table 3.10B is that the proportion of gente de razón widows was slightly higher among people marrying than that of widowers, and so comes closer to present-day experience in the differential survival of the sexes. In sharp contrast, among the Indians, the proportion of widowers remarrying was markedly higher than that of widows. Lastly, the drop in the proportion of widowers as against widows among the gente de razón who married between 1835 and 1854 may be testimony to the presence of a large surplus of bachelors among the new immigrants, and their search for wives.

Yet another aspect of gente de razón marriage that may be studied through the marriage entries is the racial origin and ethnic affiliation of each participant, for these are either explicitly stated for each spouse, or may be inferred from the name and circumstances recorded. It becomes possible, therefore, to construct a chart showing for each decade of mission activity the number of marriages performed and the combinations of racial and ethnic affiliation involved. In Table 3.11 we give the data on 912 marriages celebrated between 1770 and 1834 at the

TABLE 3.10B

Widowers and Widows Who Remarried
Gente de Razón

Period	Total Persons Married	Widowers		Widows		Both Sexes	
		Number	Percent of Men	Number	Percent of Women	Number	Percent of Total
THREE MISSIONS[a]							
1770–1784	60	3	10.0	2	6.7	5	8.3
1785–1794	64	2	6.3	5	15.6	7	10.9
1795–1804	116	12	20.7	11	19.0	23	19.8
1805–1814	116	8	13.8	11	19.0	19	16.4
1815–1824	198	12	12.1	11	11.1	23	11.6
1825–1834	298	15	10.1	16	10.7	31	10.4
Subtotals	852	52	12.2	56	13.1	108	12.7
1835–1844	348	15	8.6	15	8.6	30	8.6
1845–1854	668	21	6.3	40	12.0	61	9.1
Totals	1,868	88	9.4	111	11.9	199	10.1

TABLE 3.10B (continued)

Period	Total Persons Married	Widowers		Widows		Both Sexes	
		Number	Percent of Men	Number	Percent of Women	Number	Percent of Total
			SANTA CLARA				
1778-1784	26	3	23.1	1	7.8	4	15.4
1785-1794	34	2	11.8	1	5.9	3	8.8
1795-1804	64	8	25.0	8	25.0	16	25.0
1805-1814	60	7	23.3	7	23.3	14	23.3
1815-1824	96	5	10.4	6	12.5	11	11.5
1825-1834	100	5	10.0	2	4.0	7	7.0
Subtotals	380	30	15.8	25	13.2	55	14.5
1835-1844	128	7	10.9	6	9.4	13	10.2
1845-1854	234	10	8.5	23	19.7	33	14.1
Totals	742	47	12.7	54	14.6	101	13.6

TABLE 3.10B (continued)

SAN JUAN BAUTISTA

Period	Total Persons Married	Widowers		Widows		Both Sexes	
		Number	Percent of Men	Number	Percent of Women	Number	Percent of Total
1797–1804	4	1	50.0			1	25.0
1805–1814	10						
1815–1824	22	1	9.1	1	9.1	2	9.1
1825–1834	40	2	10.0	1	5.0	3	7.5
Subtotals	76	4	10.5	2	5.3	6	7.9
1835–1844	86	5	11.6	4	9.3	9	10.5
1845–1854	178	8	9.0	11	12.4	19	10.7
Totals	340	17	10.0	17	10.0	34	10.0

TABLE 3.10B (continued)

SAN CARLOS BORROMEO

Period	Total Persons Married	Widowers		Widows		Both Sexes	
		Number	Percent of Men	Number	Percent of Women	Number	Percent of Total
1770–1784	34			1	5.9	1	2.9
1785–1794	30			4	26.6	4	13.3
1795–1804	48	3	12.5	3	12.5	6	12.5
1805–1814	46	1	4.4	4	17.4	5	10.9
1815–1824	80	6	15.0	4	10.0	10	12.5
1825–1834	158	8	10.1	13	16.5	21	13.3
Subtotals	396	18	9.1	29	14.7	47	11.9
1835–1844	134	3	4.5	5	7.5	8	6.0
1845–1854	256	3	2.3	6	4.7	9	3.5
Totals	786	24	6.1	40	10.2	64	8.1

Note to Table 3.10B

a Data are for Santa Clara, San Juan Bautista, and San Carlos Borromeo. The marriage register for San Miguel is lost. That for Santa Cruz does not indicate whether the parties had been married previously (for gente de razón). That for La Soledad indicates 10 marriages of gente de razón, without indication of previous marital status. That for San Antonio de Padua shows 9, of which 7 were between Mexicans and mission neophytes; several of the former were widowers, but otherwise there is no statement. The register for San Luis Obispo shows 9 marriages of gente de razón, of which 5 were between Mexicans and mission neophytes, but there is no indication of previous marital status.

same three missions covered in Table 3.10B. Marriages in which both partners were Indian are, of course, excluded. The categories are the same as those used in Table 3.8B and the problems of application, in general, the same. The data from the three missions (Santa Clara, San Juan Bautista, and San Carlos Borromeo) cover the overwhelming majority of the non-Indian population. Addition of marriage data from four of the remaining five missions, the only ones for which marriage registers are extant, would add data on 32 marriages down to 1834 to the 423 in the summary table for the same term of years. The proportions would be very different in those 32 marriages, in that 14 fell in our subtotal designated M and 18 in the category of MN, that is, with one partner an Indian.

At the three missions, the early years showed a predictable course in that the first marriages involved adults immigrating from Spain and Mexico. As the children born in California grew to maturity and married, there came into being a Californio component which gradually became dominant. The flaws in the data on exact affiliation within subcomponents of the general category M probably have placed many more marriages in MM in the later years than there should be, for we have counted cases of doubt as MM. The subtotal M, however, is reliable.

Until the period 1815–1824 there were no marriages of non-Hispanic gente de razón. Even the 3 marriages in that 10-year period (2 AM and 1 AA) took place in the 1820's. Thereafter such marriages, particularly those of a non-Hispanic but gente de razón male with a woman of Hispanic affiliation, show up as a steadily rising proportion of combined M and AM marriages. (Proportions based on total marriages would be slightly lower, but follow the same course.) Our value for the last 10-year period for the eight missions is 20.3, somewhat higher than the corresponding value for gente de razón baptisms for the same years. The table does not go farther, and the data after 1846–1848 already are less inclusive, since new elements of Protestant and civil marriages had come into being but lie outside our sources. As far as our data go, we may conclude that by the 1850's ethnic fusion between the Hispanic people of California and the new immigration, despite new migration from Mexico, other countries of Latin America, and Spain, was proceeding at the rate of one-fifth the Hispanic stock per generation. If, as seems likely, some of the marriages took place

TABLE 3.11

Marriages Showing Interethnic and Interracial Unions

Marriages between Indians not included. Symbols as in Table 3.8B.

THREE MISSIONS[a]

Period	M M	M C	C C	Sub-total	A M or A C	Percent of Combined A M/A C plus Subtotal M	M N	A N	A A	Total
1770–1784	15			15			10			25
1785–1794	21	8		29			2			31
1795–1804	31	15	8	54			4			58
1805–1814	16	11	31	58						58
1815–1824	10	20	63	93	2	2.1	3			99
1825–1834	22	36	73	131	19	12.7	2		1	152
1835–1844	29	15	87	131	24	15.5	9			164
1845–1854	82	18	148	248	63	20.3	9	1	4	326
Totals	226	123	410	759	108	12.5	39	1	5	912

TABLE 3.11 (continued)

Period	M M	M C	C C	Sub-total	A M or A C	Percent of Combined A M/A C plus Subtotal M	M N	A N	A A	Total
SANTA CLARA										
1778–1784	7			7			1			8
1785–1794	14	2		16						16
1795–1804	19	5	7	31			1			32
1805–1814	7	7	16	30						30
1815–1824		3	42	45			2		1	48
1825–1834		5	41	46	6	11.5				52
1835–1844	1	6	49	56	5	8.2	3			64
1845–1854	10	18	57	85	28	24.8	1		4	118
Totals	58	46	212	316	39	11.0	8		5	368

TABLE 3.11 (continued)

Period	M M	M C	C C	Sub-total	A M or A C	Percent of Combined A M/A C plus Subtotal M	M N	A N	A A	Total
				SAN JUAN BAUTISTA						
1795–1804	2			2						2
1805–1814	5			5						5
1815–1824	9			9	2	18.2				11
1825–1834	19			19	1	5.0				20
1835–1844	37			37	5	11.9	1			43
1845–1854	72			72	12	14.3	5			89
Totals	144			144	20	12.2	6			170

TABLE 3.11 (continued)

Period	M M	M C	C C	Sub-total	A M or A C	Percent of Combined A M/A C plus Subtotal M	M N	A N	A A	Total
				SAN CARLOS BORROMEO						
1770–1784	8			8			9			17
1785–1794	7	6		13			2			15
1795–1804	10	10	1	21			3			24
1805–1814	4	4	15	23						23
1815–1824	1	17	21	39			1			40
1825–1834	3	31	32	66	12	15.4	1			79
1835–1844	1	9	38	48	14	22.6	5			67
1845–1854			91	91	23	20.2	3	1		118
Totals	34	77	198	309	49	13.7	24	1		383

TABLE 3.11 (continued)

[a] The marriage register for San Miguel Arcángel has been lost. Those for the other four missions give sparse data, which we tabulate in briefer form:

Mission	MM	MN	Total
Santa Cruz			
to 1834	2	2	4) 13
to 1839	9		9)
La Soledad			
to 1834	6	4	10
San Antonio de Padua			
to 1834	2	7	9
San Luis Obispo			
to 1834	4	5	9

by civil or Protestant ceremony, fusion would have been proceeding that much faster.

The data in Table 3.11 also cover marriages of gente de razón
with California Indians. They represent a small proportion of
total marriages of gente de razón. Even if we add the data for
the four other missions, we find that down to 1834, of a total
of 455 marriages, only 39, or 8.6%, involved marriage with a
California Indian. The proportion of such marriages was far
higher among the gente de razón scattered in garrisons and
ranches in the territories of the four missions that had no
Hispanic pueblo. Only in the territory of Mission San Juan
Bautista was the rural Hispanic population sufficiently numerous to provide marriage partners among the gente de razón.
We are not entitled, however, to conclude from these data that
we here have the true rate of racial fusion between people of
Hispanic culture and California Indians, for much of the procre-
ation of children probably proceeded without religious marriage
or any formal legal union, just as *unión libre* is an important
form of sexual association in Mexico today. The children of
such unions more likely would be counted as Indians, since the
mother would be an Indian, and with the collapse of the mission
system might never enter the white man's records. Futhermore,
in the last years of our study, 1835- 1854, a process was taking
place that is also characteristic of Hispanic culture. Indian
neophytes, who may have been Christian for as many as three
generations, were settling among the gente de razon in San Jose
and other Hispanic settlements and were winning acceptance, as
is shown in the marginal entries for baptisms and marriages,
which begin to use the terms *vecino* and *vecina* (also employed
increasingly for the gente de razon) in place of *indigena*, that is
to say, Indian. How many people were involved in this kind of
passing, how far acceptance went, what the end results might
have been, we are unable to state. The first years of the
American period unleashed a series of new forces of violent
impact that changed the demographic history of California even
more completely than had the coming of the missionaries.

6. SOME COMMENTS

Our essay basically has attempted to apply the techniques of
examination of vital registers as they have been worked out by
students of historical demography on two continents. We have,

we think, shed new light upon a series of facts of the experience of Indian and Hispanic populations during the California mission period. Considerably more probably can be done. Much studied as the California missions have been, and voluminous the publications in existence, we have been forced repeatedly to point to questions we cannot answer at this time and suggest that more research is needed with the specific question in mind. Our essay, furthermore, covers only the registers of eight missions. There were twenty-three missions in all in Alta California, every one of them keeping the same kind of registers. Remarkably few of such registers have been mislaid or lost, so that the same kind of techniques, perhaps even in improved form, can be applied to this mass of raw data, with yield that is certain to be rich but whose ultimate dimension one can foresee only dimly. The Indians of Southern California, even after missionization, remained in rancherías. Their type of mission settlement should yield information on yet other kinds of reactions and adaptations.

The Hispanic population, with fuller entries in the mission registers and control over the entire number, can probably be traced through what is at this point the ultimate in satisfactory reconstruction from vital registers, the reconstitution of families. We guess that the mission registers of all California, supplemented by other materials, should permit tracing the Hispanic immigrants and their children for at least a century and a quarter. From the data available in the registers of the eight missions we have studied, we suspect further that the Hispanic population should turn out to be as robust, as long-lived, and as fecund as the *habitants* of French Canada. Presumably they should show the same rapid multiplication of numbers until they met some check. That might have come either through filling up the vital space available to them or the entrance of a more formidable competing group. We know that the latter occurred. They and their descendants were rapidly absorbed by the newcomers.

To what extent similar studies of American Indians, Hispanos, and others can be carried on for the Southwest of the United States and the North of Mexico, we do not yet know. A series of surveys will have to locate the materials that survive and determine the extent of analysis possible. By and large, they have yet to be made.

Works Cited
or Consulted

MANUSCRIPTS

Mexico

Archivo General de la Nación, Mexico City (abbreviated in the text as AGN)

Historia,

    vols. 522–523. Summaries by intendancies and provinces of incomplete censuses taken during the administration of Viceroy Revillagigedo II, 1789–1794.

Padrones,

    108 vols. Returns of the military census (i.e., counts of non-Indian population), 1791–1793.

Archivo Municipal, Guadalajara

    legajos 273 and 276. Sheets of the city census of 1838.

Spain

Archivo de los Duques del Infantado, Madrid

    vol. 54, ff. 148–180. Report of Juan de Cervantes Casaus on the royal finances, Mexico City, 4 September 1646. 32 ff.

Archivo General de Indias, Seville (abbreviated in the text as AGI)

Audiencia de Méjico,

    legajos 2578–2581 and 2589–2591. Portions of 1777 census reports from the bishoprics of Puebla and Oaxaca.

Indiferente General,

    legajos 102 and 1526. Portions of the 1777 census for the bishopric of Durango.

United States

Bancroft Library, University of California, Berkeley

    California–Statistics, vital [California Mission Statistics 1769–1834].

Lists of population, births, marriages, deaths, livestock and crops for each mission, the Presidios of San Diego, Monterey, San Francisco, and Santa Barbara, the pueblos of San Jose and Los Angeles, and the Villa Branciforte, with analyses by place and overall statistics. 32 folders. (Call number C–C 64.)

    Palafox y Mendoza, Juan de. Instrucción reservada. n.d., but 1643–1647. In Mexican Manuscript 162, ff. 7v–46v.

Archive of the Diocese of Monterey-Salinas, Monterey, California

Mission Registers of   San Juan Bautista
   Nuestra Señora de la Soledad   San Luis Obispo
   San Antonio de Padua   San Miguel Arcángel
   San Carlos Borromeo   Santa Cruz

Library of the University of Santa Clara, Santa Clara, California
    Mission Registers of Santa Clara
Library of the Genealogical Society of Utah, Salt Lake City
    Card catalogue. Consulted on film at the branch of the Genealogical
    Society in Oakland, California.
    Mission Registers of the Diocese of Monterey-Salinas, California, in
    microfilm. Consulted at the branch of the Genealogical Society in
    Oakland, California.
Library of the University of Texas at Austin
    Relaciones Geográficas, in the García Icazbalceta Collection.

PRINTED MATERIALS

Aguirre Beltrán, Gonzalo. "Cultura y nutrición," In *Estudios antro-
    pológicos publicados en homenaje al doctor Manuel Gamio* (Mexico
    City, 1956), pp. 227–249.
Amat, Tadeo. *A Treatise on Matrimony*. San Francisco, 1864.
Anderson, Richmond K., José Calvo, Gloria Serrano, and George C. Payne.
    "A Study of the Nutritional Status and Food Habits of Otomí Indians
    in the Mezquital Valley of Mexico," *American Journal of Public Health
    and the Nation's Health*, XXXVI (1946): 883–903.
[Anonymous Conqueror]. *Relación de algunas cosas de la Nueva España y
    de la gran ciudad de Temestitan, Mexico, hecha por un gentilhombre
    del señor Fernando Cortes*. Ed. by Jorge Gurría Lacroix. Mexico City,
    1961.
Armillas, Pedro. "Gardens on Swamps." *Science,* 169 (Nov. 12, 1971):
    633–661.
Arriaga, Eduardo E. *New Life Tables for Latin American Populations in
    the Nineteenth and Twentieth Centuries*. Population Monograph Series,
    no. 3. University of California, Berkeley, Institute of International
    Studies, 1968.
Aschmann, Homer. *The Central Desert of Baja California: Demography
    and Ecology*. (*Ibero-Americana*: 42.) Berkeley and Los Angeles, 1959.
Ashtor, E. "Essai sur l'alimentation des diverses classes sociales dans
    l'Orient médiéval," *Annales: Économies, sociétés, civilisations*, XXIII
    (1968): 1017–1053.
Bancroft, Hubert Howe. *History of California*. 7 vols. San Francisco,
    1884–1890.
——. *History of Mexico*. 6 vols. San Francisco, 1883–1888.
——. *History of the North Mexican States and Texas*. 2 vols. San Fran-
    cisco, 1883–1889.
Bard, Philip, ed. *Medical Physiology*, 10th ed. St. Louis, 1961.
Barrett, Ellen C. *Baja California, 1535–1956: A Bibliography of Historical,
    Geographical and Scientific Literature*. Los Angeles, 1957.
——. *Baja California II, 1535–1964: A Bibliography of Historical, Geo-
    graphical and Scientific Literature*. Los Angeles, 1967.
Beltrán, Enrique. "Plantas usadas en la alimentación por los antiguos
    mexicanos," *America Indígena*, IX (1949): 195–204.
Bennassar, B., and J. Goy, eds. "Dossier: Histoire de la consommation.
    Contribution à l'histoire de la consommation alimentaire du XIVe au
    XIXe siècle," *Annales: économies, sociétés, civilisations*, XXX (1975):
    402–632.

Boas, Franz. "Physical Characteristics of the Indians of the North Pacific Coast," *American Anthropologist*, old series, IV (1891): 25–32.

Bonfil Batalla, Guillermo. *Diagnóstico sobre el hambre en Sudzal, Yucatán.* Publication no. 11. Instituto Nacional de Antropología e Historia, Departamento de Investigaciones Antropólogicas, Mexico City, 1962.

Borah, Woodrow. *New Spain's Century of Depression. (Ibero-Americana:* 35.) Berkeley and Los Angeles, 1951.

———. "Reflections on the Demographic History of the Peninsula of Baja California, 1534–1910," a paper prepared for the Segunda Reunión sobre Antropología e Historia del Noroeste, Ensenada, Baja California Norte, October 1976; to be published in the proceedings.

———. "Los tributos y su recaudación en la Audiencia de la Nueva Galicia durante el siglo XVI," Bernardo García Martinez et al., eds., *Historia y sociedad en el mundo de habla española: Homenaje a José Miranda* (Mexico City, 1970), pp. 27–47.

———, and Sherburne F. Cook. *The Aboriginal Population of Central Mexico on the Eve of the Spanish Conquest. (Ibero-Americana:* 45.) Berkeley and Los Angeles, 1963.

———. *The Population of Central Mexico in 1548: An Analysis of the Suma de visitas de pueblos. (Ibero-Americana:* 43.) Berkeley and Los Angeles, 1960.

———. *Price Trends of Some Basic Commodities in Central Mexico, 1531–1570. (Ibero-Americana:* 40.) Berkeley and Los Angeles, 1960.

Boserup, Ester. *The Conditions of Agricultural Growth: The Economics of Agrarian Change Under Population Pressure.* Chicago, 1965.

Bowman, J. N. "The Parochial Books of the California Missions: 1961," *Historical Society of Southern California Quarterly*, XLIII (1961): 303–315.

Braudel, Fernand. *Civilisation matérielle et capitalisme (XVe–XVIIIe siècles)*, vol. 1. Paris, 1967.

Brooks, Richard H., Lawrence Kaplan, Hugh C. Cutler, and Thomas W. Whitaker. "Plant Material from a Cave on the Rio Zape, Durango, Mexico," *American Antiquity*, XXVII (1961–1962): 356–369.

Byers, Douglas, and Richard S. MacNeish, eds. *The Prehistory of the Tehuacan Valley.* 5 vols. to date. Austin, 1967–1972.

Calnek, Edward E. "Settlement Pattern and Chinampa Agriculture at Tenochtitlán," *American Antiquity*, XXXVII (1972–1973): 104–115.

Cárcer Disdier, M. de. "Los pavos," *Homenaje a Rafael García Granados* (Mexico City, 1960), pp. 89–111.

Carrión, Juan de. *Descripción del pueblo de Guaytlalpan.* Ed. by José García Payón. Jalapa, 1965.

Chávez, Angélico. *Archives of the Archdiocese of Santa Fe, 1678–1900.* Bibliographical Series, vol. 3. Academy of American Franciscan History, Washington, D.C., 1957.

Clark, James Cooper, ed. and trans. *Codex Mendoza, the Mexican Manuscript Known as the Collection of Mendoza and Preserved in the Bodleian Library, Oxford.* 3 vols. London, 1938.

Clavijero, Francisco Javier. *Historia antigua de México,* 2nd ed. Ed. by Mariano Cuevas. 4 vols. Mexico City, 1938.

Coahuila, Gobernador. *Memoria,* 1824/25, 1831/32, 1851.

Colección de documentos inéditos para la historia de España. 112 vols. Madrid, 1842–1895.

Concilios provinciales primero, y segundo, celebrados en ... México. Mexico City, 1769.

Concilium mexicanum provinciale III. Mexico City, 1770.

Cook, Sherburne F. *The Aboriginal Population of the San Joaquin Valley, California.* (*Anthropological Records,* XVI, no. 2: 31–78.) Berkeley and Los Angeles, 1955.

———. *The Conflict Between the California Indian and White Civilization.* (*Ibero-Americana:* 21–24.) 4 vols. Berkeley and Los Angeles, 1943.

———. *The Conflict Between the California Indian and White Civilization.* Berkeley and Los Angeles, 1976.

———. *The Historical Demography and Ecology of the Teotlalpan.* (*Ibero-Americana:* 33.) Berkeley and Los Angeles, 1949.

———. *The Population of the California Indians, 1769–1970.* Berkeley and Los Angeles, 1976.

———. *Population Trends Among the California Mission Indians.* (*Ibero-Americana:* 17.) Berkeley and Los Angeles, 1940.

———. *Santa María Ixcatlán: Habitat, Population, Subsistence.* (*Ibero-Americana:* 41.) Berkeley and Los Angeles, 1958.

———. *Soil Erosion and Population in Central Mexico.* (*Ibero-Americana:* 34.) Berkeley and Los Angeles, 1949.

———, and Woodrow Borah. *Essays in Population History: Mexico and the Caribbean.* 2 vols. Berkeley and Los Angeles, 1971–1974.

———. *The Indian Population of Central Mexico, 1531–1610.* (*Ibero-Americana:* 44.) Berkeley and Los Angeles, 1960.

———. "On the Credibility of Contemporary Testimony on the Population of Mexico in the Sixteenth Century," *Summa antropologica en homenaje a Roberto J. Weitlaner* (Mexico City, 1966), pp. 229–239.

———. *The Population of the Mixteca Alta, 1520–1960.* (*Ibero-Americana:* 50.) Berkeley and Los Angeles, 1968.

———. "Quelle fut la stratification sociale au centre du Mexique durant la première moitié du XVIᵉ siècle?," *Annales: Économies, sociétés, civilisations,* XVIII (1963): 226–258.

———, and Lesley Byrd Simpson. *The Population of Central Mexico in the Sixteenth Century.* (*Ibero-Americana:* 31.) Berkeley and Los Angeles, 1948.

Cordero, Enrique. "La subestimación de la mortalidad infantil en México," *Demografía y economía,* II, no. 1 (or no. 4 in count by numbers) (1968): 44–62.

Cortés, Hernán. *Cartas y documentos.* Ed. by Mario Hernández Sánchez-Barba. Mexico City, 1963.

Cravioto, René O. "Nutritive Value of the Mexican Tortilla," *Science,* 102, no. 2639 (July 27, 1945): 91-93.

Cuevas, Mariano. *Historia de la iglesia en México,* 5th ed. 5 vols. Mexico City, 1946–1947.

Dávalos Hurtado, Eusebio. "La alimentación entre los mexicas," *Revista mexicana de estudios antropológicos,* XIV (1954–1955): 113–118.

Deevey, Edward S., Jr. "Limnologic Studies in Middle America, with a Chapter on Aztec Limnology," *Transactions of the Connecticut Academy of Arts and Sciences,* XXXIX (1957): 213–328.

Denevan, William M. "Aboriginal Drained-Field Cultivation in the Americas," *Science,* 169 (Aug. 14, 1970): 647–654.

Díaz del Castillo, Bernal. *Historia verdadera de la conquista de la Nueva España,* 5th ed. Ed. by Joaquín Ramírez Cabañas. 2 vols. Mexico City, 1960.

Dressler, Robert L. "The Pre-Columbian Cultivated Plants of Mexico,"

Harvard University *Botanical Museum Leaflets*, XVI, no. 6 (December 1953): 115–173.

Dupâquier, Jacques. "Villages et petites villes de la généralité de Paris; Introduction," *Annales de démographie historique* (1969): 11–13.

El Colegio de México, Centro de Estudios Económicos y Demográficos. *Dinámica de la población de México.* Mexico City, 1970.

Engelhardt, Zephyrin. *Mission Nuestra Señora de la Soledad.* Santa Barbara, 1929.

——. *Mission San Carlos Borromeo (Carmelo).* Santa Barbara, 1934.

——. *Mission San Juan Bautista, a School of Church Music.* Santa Barbara, 1931.

——. *Mission San Luis Obispo in the Valley of the Bears.* Santa Barbara, 1933.

——. *The Missions and Missionaries of California.* 4 vols. San Francisco, 1908–1914. (2nd ed. of Vol. I, rev. [Santa Barbara, 1929], used in preference to 1st ed.)

——. *San Antonio de Padua, the Mission in the Sierras.* Santa Barbara, 1929.

——. *San Miguel Arcángel, the Mission on the Highway.* Santa Barbara, 1929.

——. *San Francisco or Mission Dolores.* Chicago, 1924.

Ensayo de una memoria estadística del distrito de Tulancingo. Mexico City, 1825.

Farrar, W. V. "Tecuitlatl: A Glimpse of Aztec Food Technology," *Nature*, 211 (1966): 341–342.

Fernández Duro, Cesáreo. *La armada invencible.* 2 vols. Madrid, 1884–1885.

Filippini, J.-P. "Le régime alimentaire des soldats et des miliciens pris en charge par la marine française au XVIIIᵉ siècle," *Annales: Economies, sociétés, civilisations*, XX (1965): 1157–1162.

Flannery, Kent V., Anne V. T. Kirkby, Michael J. Kirkby, and Aubrey W. Williams, Jr. "Farming Systems and Political Growth in Ancient Oaxaca," *Science*, 158 (Oct. 27, 1967): 445–454.

Flores, Ana María. *La magnitud del hambre en México,* 2nd ed. Mexico City, 1973.

Focher, Juan. *Itinerario del misionero en América.* (Latin text with Castilian translation.) Introduction and notes by P. Antonio Eguiluz, O.F.M. Madrid, 1960.

Fonseca, Fabián de, and Carlos de Urrutia. *Historia general de real hacienda.* 6 vols. Mexico City, 1845–1853.

Gabel, Norman E. *A Comparative Racial Study of the Papago.* University of New Mexico Publications in Anthropology, no. 4. Albuquerque, 1949.

García Icazbalceta, Joaquín. *Don Fray Juan de Zumárraga, primer obispo y arzobispo de México,* 2nd ed. 4 vols. Mexico City, 1947.

——. *Nueva colección de documentos para la historia de México.* 2d ed. 3 vols. Mexico City, 1941.

Gerhard, Peter. *A Guide to the Historical Geography of New Spain.* Cambridge, 1972.

Gibson, Charles. *The Aztecs Under Spanish Rule: A History of the Indians of the Valley of Mexico, 1519–1810.* Stanford, 1964.

—— *Tlaxcala in the Sixteenth Century.* New Haven, 1952.

Gómara, Francisco López de. *Historia general de las Indias,* "Hispania *victrix,"* cuya segunda parte corresponde a la Conquista de Méjico, new ed. 2 vols. Barcelona, 1954.

Goubert, Pierre. *Beauvais et le Beauvaisis de 1600 à 1730. Contribution à l'histoire sociale de la France du XVIIe siècle.* Paris, 1960.

———. "Legitimate Fecundity and Infant Mortality During the Eighteenth Century: A Comparison," *Daedalus,* XCVII, no. 1 (Winter 1968): 593–603.

Hammond, George P., ed. *A Guide to the Manuscript Collections of the Bancroft Library. Volume II. Mexican and Central American Manuscripts.* Berkeley and Los Angeles, 1972.

Handbook of Middle American Indians (abbreviated in the text as *HMAI*). General editor, Robert Wauchope, 16 vols. Austin, Texas, 1964–1976.

Harner, Michael. "The Ecological Basis for Aztec Sacrifice," *American Ethnologist,* IV, no. 1 (February 1977): 117–135.

Harris, Reginald G. "The San Blas Indians," *American Journal of Physical Anthropology,* old series, IX (1926): 17–63.

Havard, V. "Food Plants of the North American Indians," *Bulletin of the Torrey Botanical Club,* XXII (1895): 98–123.

Hémardinquer, Jean-Jacques. "A propos de l'alimentation des marins. a) Sur les galères de Toscane au XVIe siècle," *Annales: Économies, sociétés, civilisations,* XVIII (1963): 1141–1149.

Henry, Louis. "Historical Demography," *Daedalus,* XCVII, no. 1 (Winter 1968): 385–396.

Hérnández, Francisco. *Historia natural de Nueva España* (vols. 2 and 3 of *Obras completas*). Mexico City, 1959.

Hérnández, Mercedes, Adolfo Chávez V., and Hector Bourges. *Valor nutritivo de los alimentos mexicanos; Tables de uso practico,* 6th ed. Mexico City, 1974.

Horacasitas de Pozas, Isabel. "Estudio sobre la alimentación en el poblado de Acacoyahua," *Anales del Instituto Nacional de Antropología e Historia* [6a ép. of whole series] V (1951): 153–176.

Hrdlička, Aleš. "The Pueblos," *American Journal of Physical Anthropology,* old series, XX (1935): 235–460.

Ibero-Americana (abbreviated in the text as IA). University of California Publications, Berkeley and Los Angeles.

No.

17 Cook, Sherburne F. *Population Trends Among the California Mission Indians.* 1940.

21–24 ———. *The Conflict Between the California Indian and White Civilization.* 1943.

31 ———, and Lesley Byrd Simpson. *The Population of Central Mexico in the Sixteenth Century.* 1948.

33 ———. *The Historical Demography and Ecology of the Teotlalpan.* 1949.

34 ———. *Soil Erosion and Population in Central Mexico.* 1949.

35 Borah, Woodrow. *New Spain's Century of Depression.* 1951.

36 Simpson, Lesley Byrd. *Exploitation of Land in Central Mexico in the Sixteenth Century.* 1952.

40 Borah, Woodrow, and Sherburne F. Cook. *Price Trends of Some Basic Commodities in Central Mexico, 1531–1570.* 1958.

41 Cook, Sherburne F. *Santa María Ixcatlán: Habitat, Population, Subsistence.* 1958.

42 Aschmann, Homer. *The Central Desert of Baja California: Demography and Ecology.* 1959.

43 Borah, Woodrow, and Sherburne F. Cook. *The Population of Central Mexico in 1548: An Analysis of the* Suma de visitas de pueblos. 1960.

44 Cook, Sherburne F., and Woodrow Borah. *The Indian Population of Central Mexico, 1531–1610.* 1960.

45 Borah, Woodrow, and Sherburne F. Cook. *The Aboriginal Population of Central Mexico on the Eve of the Spanish Conquest.* 1963.

50 Cook, Sherburne F., and Woodrow Borah. *The Population of the Mixteca Alta, 1520–1960.* 1968.

Israel, J. I. *Race, Class and Politics in Colonial Mexico, 1610–1670.* Oxford, 1975.

Ivanovsky, Alexis. "Physical Modifications of the Population of Russia Under Famine," *American Journal of Physical Anthropology,* old series, VI (1923): 331–353.

Jacobson, Paul H. "Cohort Survival for Generations Since 1840," *Milbank Memorial Fund Quarterly,* XLII, no. 1 (July 1964), part 1: 36–53.

Johnston, Richard E., Patricia S. Gindhart, Richard L. Jantz, Kenneth M. Kensinger, and Geoffrey F. Walker. "The Anthropometric Determination of Body Composition Among the Peruvian Cashinahua," *American Journal of Physical Anthropology,* new series, XXXIV (1971): 409–415.

Keys, Ancel, Josef Brožek, Austin Henschel, Olaf Mickelsen, Henry Longstreet Taylor, et al. *The Biology of Human Starvation.* 2 vols. Minneapolis, 1950.

Kleiber, Max. "Body Size and Metabolic Rate," *Physiological Reviews,* XXVII (1947): 511–541.

Kroeber, Alfred L. *Handbook of the Indians of California.* (Photolithographic facsimile of 1st ed., 1925.) Berkeley, 1970.

Lane, Frederick C. "Salaires et régime alimentaire des marins au debut du XIVᵉ siècle," *Annales: Économies, sociètès, civilisations,* XVIII (1963): 133–138.

Lasker, Gabriel Ward. "The Age Factor in Bodily Measurements of Adult Male and Female Mexicans," *Human Biology,* XXV (1953): 50–63.

LeGoff, A. "Bilan d'une étude de démographie historique: Auray au XVIIIe siècle (vers 1740–1789)," *Annales de démographie historique* (1974): 197–229.

Llaguno, José A. *La personalidad jurídica del indio y el III Concilio Provincial Mexicano (1585). Ensayo histórico-jurídico de los documentos originales.* Mexico City, 1963.

Llamas, Roberto. "La alimentación de los antiguos mexicanos," Mexico, Universidad Nacional Autónoma, Instituto de Biología, *Anales,* VI (1936): 245–258.

Lohmann Villena, Guillermo. *Los americanos en las órdenes nobiliarias (1529–1900).* 2 vols. Madrid, 1947.

López de Gómara, Francisco. See Gómara, Francisco López de.

Martínez, Pedro. *Descripción de la villa de Pánuco. (1612.)* Ed. by Leonardo Pasquel. Mexico City, 1944.

Meigs, Peveril, III. *The Dominican Mission Frontier of Lower California.* (University of California Publications in Geography, vol. 7.) Berkeley, 1935.

Méndez, José, and Carrol Behrhorst. "The Anthropometric Characteristics of Indian and Urban Guatemalans," *Human Biology*, XXXV (1963): 457–469.

Mendieta, Gerónimo de. *Historia eclesiástica indiana*. (Facsimile of 1st ed.) Mexico City, 1971.

Mendizábal, Miguel Othon de. *Obras completas*. 6 vols. Mexico City, 1946–1947.

Mexico (City). *Actas de cabildo del ayuntamiento de México*. 54 vols. Mexico City, 1859–1914.

Mexico (State), Gobernador. *Memoria*, 1878/79.

Mexico, Archivo General de la Nación (AGN). *Boletín*. 1a ép., 30 vols., 1930–1959. 2a ép., 13 vols, 1960–1972.

———. *El libro de las tasaciones de pueblos de la Nueva España, Siglo XVI*. Mexico City, 1952.

Mexico, Dirección General de Estadística. *Anuario estadistico de los Estados Unidos Mexicanos, 1970–1971*. Mexico City, 1973.

———. *Censos agropecuarios. 1. Totales comparativos en 1930, 1940 y 1950. 2. Por entidades y distritos económico-agrícolas en 1950*. Mexico City, 1959.

———. Censos generales:

1895 *Censo general de la República Mexicana verificado el 20 de octubre de 1895*. 31 parts. Mexico City, 1897–1899.

1900 *Censo general de la República Mexicana . . . verificado en 1900*. 34 parts. Mexico City, 1901–1907.

1910 *Tercer censo [de] población de los Estados Unidos Mexicanos . . . 1910*. 12 parts in 3 vols. Mexico City, 1918–1920.

1921 *Censo general de habitantes. 30 de noviembre de 1921*. 30 parts. Mexico City, 1925–1928.

1930 *Quinto censo de población, 15 de mayo 1930*. 34 parts. Mexico City, 1932–1936.

1940 *6° censo de población, 1940*. 30 parts. Mexico City, 1943–1948.

1950 *Séptimo censo general de población, 6 de junio de 1950*. 33 parts. Mexico City, 1952–1953.

1960 *VIII censo general de población, 1960*. 35 parts. Mexico City, 1962–1964.

1970 *IX censo general de población, 1970*. 35 parts. Mexico City, 1971–1973.

———. *Primer censo agrícola-ganadero, 1930. Resumen general*. Mexico City, 1936.

———. *Segundo censo agrícola-ganadero de los Estados Unidos Mexicanos, 1940. Resumen general*. Mexico City, 1951.

Mexico, Secretaría de Agricultura y Fomento. *Memoria . . . septiembre de 1937–agosto de 1938*. 2 vols. Mexico City, 1938.

Miranda, José. "La población indígena de Ixmiquilpan y su distrito en la época colonial," *Estudios de historia novohispana*, I (1966): 121–130.

———. "La población indígena de México en el siglo XVII," *Historia mexicana*, XII (or no. 46; October-December 1962): 181–189.

———. *El tributo indigena en la Nueva España durante el siglo XVI*. Mexico City, 1952.

Morin, Claude. "Population ét épidémies dans une paroisse mexicaine: Santa Inés Zacatelco, XVIIe–XIXe siècles," *Cahiers des Amériques Latines, Serie sciences de l'homme*, no. 6 (2nd half of 1972): 43–73.

Morineau, Michel. "Rations de marine (Angleterre, Hollande, Suède et Russie)," *Annales: Économies, sociétés, civilisations*, XX (1965):

1150-1157.

Motolinía, Toribio de Benavente. *Historia de los indios de la Nueva España*, new ed. Mexico City, 1941.

———. *Memoriales*. Mexico City, 1903.

National Academy of Sciences—National Research Council, Division of Biology and Agriculture, Food and Nutrition Board, Committee on Amino Acids. *Evaluation of Protein Nutrition*. Publication no. 711. Washington, D.C., 1959.

Newman, Marshall T. "Adaptations in the Physique of American Aborigines to Nutritional Factors," *Human Biology*, XXXII (1960): 288-313.

———. "Ecology and Nutritional Stress in Man," *American Anthropologist*, LXIV (1962): 22-34.

Noonan, John T., Jr. "Marriage in Michoacán," in Chiappelli, Fredi, Michael J. B. Allen, and Robert L. Benson, eds., *First Images of America: The Impact of the New World on the Old* (2 vols., Berkeley and Los Angeles, 1976), I: 351-362.

———. *Power to Dissolve: Lawyers and Marriages in the Courts of the Roman Curia*. Cambridge, Mass., 1972.

Nuevo Léon, Gobernador. *Memoria*, 1891.

Oviedo y Valdés, Gonzalo Fernández de. *Historia general y natural de las Indias*. Ed. by Juan Pérez de Tudela Bueso. 5 vols. Madrid, 1959. Biblioteca de autores españoles.

———. *Sumario de la natural historia de las Indias*. Ed. by José Miranda. México City and Buenos Aires, 1950.

Palerm, Angel. *Obras hidráulicas prehispánicas en el sistema lacustre del valle de Mexico*. Mexico City, 1973.

———, and Eric Wolf. *Agricultura y civilización en Mesoamérica*. Mexico City, 1972.

Parsons, James J., and William M. Denavan. "Pre-Columbian Ridged Fields," *Scientific American*, vol. 217 (1967): 93-100.

Paso y Troncoso, Francisco del, comp. *Epistolario de Nueva España, 1505-1818*. 16 vols. Mexico City, 1939-1942.

———. *Papeles de Nueva España: Segunda serie, geografía y estadística* (abbreviated in the text as *PNE*). 6 vols. Mexico City, 1905-1906. Plus appendixes and additional volumes published by Vargas Rea, Mexico City, 1944-1948.

———. *Papeles de la Nueva España: Relaciones geográficas de la diócesis de Michoacán, 1579-1580*. (The remainder of vol. 7, as planned by Paso y Troncoso.) 2 vols. Guadalajara, 1958.

Pérez de Arteaga, Diego. *Relación de Misantla*. Revisión y notas de David Ramírez Lavoignet. Jalapa, 1962.

Pérez Hidalgo, Carlos, Adolfo Chávez V., and Herlindo Madrigal. "Recopilación sobre el consumo de nutritivos en diferentes zonas de México. 1. Consumo calórico-proteico. 2. Consumo de vitaminas y minerales," *Archivos latinoamericanos de nutrición*, XX (1970): 367-381, and XXIII (1973): 293-294.

Pomar, Juan Bautista. *Relación de Texcoco*. In Joaquín García Icazbalceta, ed. *Nueva colección de documentos para la historia de México*, 2nd ed. (Mexico City, 1941), III: 1-64.

[Ponce, Fray Alonso]. *Relación breve y verdadera de algunas cosas de las muchas que suciederon al padre Fray Alonso Ponce en las provincias de la Nueva España*. 2 vols. Madrid, 1873.

Radding de Murrieta, Cynthia. "Problemática histórica para estudios de población de la subregión de Alamos, Sonora." Draft for the Centro Regional del Noroeste (INAH), Hermosillo.

———. *Catálogo del Archivo de la Parroquía de la Purísima Concepción de los Álamos, 1685–1900.* (Instituto Nacional de Antropología e Historia, Dirección de Centros Regionales, *Cuadernos,* No. 22.) Hermosillo, 1976.

Ramírez Cabañas, Joaquín, ed. *La ciudad de Veracruz en el siglo XVI.* Mexico City, 1943.

Rendón, Silvia. "La alimentación tarasca," *Anales del Instituto Nacional de Antropología e Historia,* [6a ép. of whole series] II (1941–1946): 207–288.

Revista mexicana de estudios antropológicos [históricos]. 22 vols. (Vols. 1 and 2 publish the text of many of the Relaciones Geográficas in manuscript at the University of Texas Library.) Mexico City, 1927–1973.

Río, Ignacio del, comp. *A Guide to the Archivo Franciscano of the National Library of Mexico . . . with an Introduction by Lino Gómez Canedo.* Mexico City and Washington, D.C., 1975.

Roca, Juan, and Roberto Llamas. "Consideraciones sobre el valor alimenticio del pulque," Mexico, Universidad Nacional Autónoma, Instituto de Biología, *Anales,* XI (1940), pp. 363–371.

———. "Régimen alimenticio de los habitantes de la región de Izúcar de Matamoros (Puebla)," Mexico, Universidad Nacional Autónoma, Instituto de Biología, *Anales,* XII (1942): 583–609.

Round, F. E. *The Biology of the Algae.* London, 1965.

Ruch, Theodore C., and Harry D. Patton. *Physiology and Biophysics,* 19th ed. Philadelphia, 1965.

Sahagún, Bernardino de. *Historia general de las cosas de Nueva España.* Ed. by Miguel Acosta Saignes. 3 vols. Mexico City, 1955.

Salinas Meza, René. "Raciones alimenticias en Chile colonial," *Historia* (Santiago, Chile), XII (1974–1975): 57–76.

Salomon, Noël. *La campagne de Nouvelle Castille à la fin du XVIᵉ siècle d'après les* Relaciones Topográficas. Paris, 1964.

Sánchez-Albornoz, Nicolás. *Gastos y alimentación de un ejército en el siglo XVI según un presupuesto de la época.* (Offprint with new numbering of pages from *Cuadernos de historia de España,* 1950, Universidad de Buenos Aires, Instituto de Investigaciones Históricas.) Buenos Aires, 1950.

Sauer, Jonathan D. "The Grain Amaranths: A Survey of Their History and Classification," St. Louis, Missouri, Botanical Garden, *Annals,* XXXVII (1950): 561–632.

Sherman, Henry C. *Chemistry of Food and Nutrition,* 7th ed. New York, 1946.

Silva, José Gentil da. *Desarrollo económico, subsistencia y decadencia en España, con representación gráfica de las informaciones por Jacques Bertin.* (Translation of *En Espagne. Développement économique, subsistance, déclin.*) Madrid, 1967.

Silveira, Maria Cristina, and Carlos Silveira. "A alimentacão na 'Armada Invencível'," *Revista de história* (São Paulo), XXXVI, no. 74, April–June 1968: 301–312.

Silvera, Katharine M. *Baja California Bibliography, 1965–1966: A Supplement.* La Jolla, 1968.

Simpson, Lesley Byrd. *The Encomienda in New Spain: The Beginnings of*

Spanish Mexico, 2nd rev. ed. Berkeley and Los Angeles, 1950.
———. *Exploitation of Land in Central Mexico in the Sixteenth Century.* (*Ibero-Americana*: 36.) Berkeley and Los Angeles, 1952.
Slicher van Bath, B. H. *The Agrarian History of Western Europe, A. D. 500–1850.* Trans. by Olive Ordish. London, 1963.
Spain, Dirección General de Archivos y Bibliotecas. *Guía de fuentes para la historia de Ibero-América conservadas en España.* 2 vols. Madrid, 1966–1969.
Spain, Real Academia Española. *Diccionario de la lengua española,* 16th ed. Madrid, 1939.
Spooner, Frank. "Régimes alimentaires d'autrefois: proportions et calculs en calories," *Annales: Économies, sociétés, civilisations,* XVI (1961): 568–574.
Standley, Paul C. *Trees and Shrubs of Mexico.* (Contributions from the United States National Herbarium, vol. 23). 5 parts. Washington, D.C., 1920–1926.
Stoudt, Howard W., Albert Damon, and Ross A. McFarland. "Heights and Weights of White Americans," *Human Biology* XXXII (1960): 331–341.
Taylor, William B. *Landlord and Peasant in Colonial Oaxaca.* Stanford, 1972.
Thompson, J. Eric S., ed. and trans. "The Relacion de Tecuanapa, Guerrero." *Tlalocan,* V (1965): 85–96.
Tlalocan. 6 vols. 1943–1971.
United States Department of Commerce, Bureau of the Census. *The Eighteenth Decennial Census of the United States, Census of Population: 1960. Volume I.* Washington, D.C., 1964.
———. *1970 Census of Population. Volume I. General Population Characteristics. Part I. United States Summary.* 2 sections. Washington, D.C., 1973.
———. *Historical Statistics of the United States, Colonial Times to 1957.* Washington, D.C., 1960.
United States Department of Health, Education and Welfare, Public Health Service, National Vital Statistics Division. *Vital Statistics of the United States, 1960.* 3 vols. Washington, D.C., 1963.
Veracruz (State). *Estadística del estado libre y soberano de Veracruz.* Jalapa, 1831–1832.
Vollmer, Günter. "La evolución cuantitativa de la población indígena en la región de Puebla (1570–1810)," *Historia mexicana,* XXIII, no. 1 (or no. 89; July–September 1973): 43–51. Also published in abbreviated form in Fundación Alemana para la Investigación Científica, Proyecto Puebla-Tlaxcala, *Comunicaciones,* no. 8 (1973): pp. 37–39.
Weitlaner, Robert J. "Sobre la alimentación chinanteca," *Anales del Instituto Nacional de Antropología e Historia* [6a ép. of whole series], V (1951): 177–195.
West, Robert C., and Pedro Armillas. "Las chinampas de México: Poesía y realidad de los 'Jardines Flotantes'," *Cuadernos americanos,* L (1950): 165–182.
Whetten, Nathaniel. *Rural Mexico.* Chicago, 1948.
Wimmer, Larry T., and Clayne L. Pope. "The Genealogical Society Library of Salt Lake City: A Source of Data for Economic and Social Historians," *Historical Methods Newsletter,* VIII, no. 2 (March 1975): 51–58.

Wohl, Michael G., and Robert S. Goodhart, eds. *Modern Nutrition in Health and Disease: Dietotherapy*, 4th ed. Philadelphia, 1968.

World Health Organization. "Special Subject: Infant Mortality," *World Health Statistics Report*, XXIII, no. 9 (1970): 777-837.

Wrigley, E. A. "Mortality in Pre-Industrial England: The Example of Colyton, Devon, over Three Centuries." *Daedalus*, XCVII, no. 1 (Winter 1968): 546-580.

Zavala, Silvio A. *La encomienda indiana*, 2nd rev. ed. Mexico City, 1973.

Zubirán, Salvador, and Adolfo Chávez V. "Algunos datos sobre la situación nutricional en México," *Boletín de la Oficina Sanitaria Panamericana*, LIV (1963): 101-113.

Index

Acorns: neglected as food source in pre-Conquest Mexico, 136-138
Adult: use of term in California mission registers, 249
Age distribution: of converts in California missions, Table 3.2, 197-204; age at death of converts, Table 3.3, 206-209; survival of converts, 210-229, Tables 3.4A, 3.4B, 3.5 and passim; baptisms and deaths of mission-born Indians, by cohorts, Table 3.6, 232-238; life tables for selected cohorts, Table 3.7, 244-247
Agriculture: pre-Conquest Indian agricultural system, 133-135; major aboriginal crops, 134-135; physical labor requirements, 153-158; pre-Conquest maize productivity, 165-167; agricultural census of 1930, 166; agricultural census of 1940, 166; agricultural census of 1950, 166n; digging stick vs. plow yields, 167, 171; introduction of new crops by Spanish, 167-168; and post-Conquest Indian population decline, 168-173; Indian resistance to adoption of wheat, 169-170; widespread Indian adoption of bananas and sugarcane, 170; Indian resistance to adoption of plow, 171-172; rise in per capita output in 16th century, 172-173; increasing specialization, 16th century, 173
Álamos, 179n
Alcabala: see Taxes
Algae: use of as food in pre-Conquest Valley of Mexico, 136
Almojarifazgo: see Taxes
Alta California: see California
Amat, Tadeo (Bishop of Monterey), 280n
Amatlán (town), Table 1.3n, 115
Amozoc (town), Table 1.4A, 118
Analco, 105

Anderson, Richmond K., 163n
Animal foods: types consumed by pre-Conquest Indians, 135; adoption of Spanish-introduced animals by Indians, 170-171
Anonymous Conqueror, 141, 162
Archivo General de Indias, Seville, 2, 4
Archivo General de la Nación, Mexico City, 4
Armada de Barlovento: see Taxes
Arriaga, Eduardo E., 241, 242
Arteaga, Reverend Mother Cristina de la Cruz de, 5
Atitalaquía (town), 140n
Atlatlauca (town), 139n
Atlixco, Valley of: alcabala farm, 1646, Table 1.4A, 118

Baja California: mission records, 179; Indian immigrants from, 261
Bananas, 170 and note
Bancroft, Hubert Howe, 190n, 248
Bancroft Library, 180, 248
Bancroft Transcripts, 248
Baptism: of Indian gentiles in California missions, Tables 3.1, 3.2, 193-204; survival of converts, 210-229, Tables 3.4A, 3.4B, 3.5 and passim; survival of mission-born Indians, Table 3.6, 232-238; records on non-Indians, 262-265
Bard, Philip, 151
Beauvaisis, 266
Birth rate: see Natality
Body size: pre-Conquest Indians, contemporary statements, 141-142; anthropometry of skeletal remains, 142; derived from present-day conditions, 142-150; average height and weight of Indian tribes, North and South America, Table 2.1, 143-147; height of males and females, Indian tribes and other ethnic groups, Table 2.2, 148; height differences between

328

Index

Gerhard, Peter, 12
Gibson, Charles, 4-5, 130n, 165 and
  note, 171n, 174-175
Goats: adoption of by Indians, 171, 172
Gold: see Taxes
Gómez Canedo, Father Lino, O.F.M.,
  179n
Goodhart, Robert S., 152-153
Grande, Francisco, 160
Great Armada, 164n
Green Revolution, 164n, 165
Guadalajara (city): *alcabala* farm, 1646,
  Table 1.4A, 118 and 122n
Guatemala, 149
Guatemala, Audiencia of, 126

Haciendas: resident families' rations, 175
Havard, V., 137n
Hernández, Francisco, 135
Hernández, Mercedes, 164n
Huapanapa (town), 106
Huatenicamanes (Oaxaca), 65, 116
Huatulco (town): customs, 1646, Table
  1.4A, 120
Huaxteca (province), 105
Huayacocotla (town), Table 1.3n, 115
Huipiles: see Cloth

Indian population: increase, 1644-1698,
  2; in Mixteca Alta, pre-Conquest to
  1620, 2-3; in west-central Mexico,
  1548-1650, 3; in Puebla region,
  1570-1650, 3; in central Mexico,
  1650, 3; demographic transition, 13,
  101; pre-Columbian central Mexico,
  132; Central Plateau (Region I),
  1568, 1646, and ratio 1646/1568,
  16; 1646, 23; 1620-1625, 28; 1568,
  24; 1595, 28; Valles-Pánuco (Region
  II), 1568, 1646, 34; 1595, 35; Central Veracruz (Region IIA), 1568,
  1620-1625, 42; 1595, 42; Alvarado-
  Coatzacoalcos (Region III), 1568,
  1646, 1620-1625, 46; 1595, 50;
  Northwestern Oaxaca (Region IV),
  1568, 1646, 1620-1625, 51; 1595,
  56; the Zapotecas (Region V), 1568,
  1646, 59; 1620-1625, 64; 1595, 65;
  Oaxaca Coast (Region VI), 1568,
  1646, 67; 1620-1625, 70; 1595, 71;
  1646, 71; Zacatula-Guerrero (Region
  VII), 1568, 1646, 73; 1620-1625, 78;
  1595, 78; 1646, 78; Michoacán
  (Region VIII), 1568, 1646, 80;
  1620-1625, 82; 1595, 1646, 83; Eastern Jalisco-Zacatecas (Region IX),
  1568, 1646, 85; 1620-1625, 1646,
  1595, 87; Colima-Nayarit (Region
  X), 1568, 1646, 89; 1620-1625,

1646, 1595, 93; central Mexico
  entire, 1568, 1595, 1620-1625,
  1646, 95-99, 100; differences with
  earlier figures explained, 100; Sinaloa
  (Nueva Galicia), 17th century, 100;
  regional variations in decline, to
  1620-1625, 101, 168; low point in
  central Mexico, 1620-1625, 101-102,
  168; density, central Mexico, pre-
  Conquest, 132; proportion children,
  1518, 152; post-Conquest decline
  and Indian agriculture, 168-173; ratio
  of converted to non-mission Indians
  in California, 193-194; total gentile
  baptisms in missions, Table 3.1, 195;
  age of gentiles at baptism, Table 3.2,
  197-204; age at death of Indian gentiles, Table 3.3, 206-209; survival of
  converted gentiles, Tables 3.4A,
  3.4B, 3.5, 210-229; baptisms and
  deaths of mission-born Indians, by
  cohorts, Table 3.6, 232-238; infant
  mortality in missions, 239-243; life
  tables for selected cohorts, Table 3.7,
  244-247; life expectancy of mission-
  born Indians compared to gentile
  converts, 248; birth rates in missions,
  248-260; ratio of births to adult female and total populations, Figures
  3.1, 3.2, 3.3, 3.4, 250-257; and interethnic mixture with non-Indians,
  267-278; marriage in missions,
  278-310; remarriage and mortality in
  missions, 287-298, Table 3.10A and
  passim
Indian towns: changes in, 1568-1646,
  8-9; identification of, 12
Infant mortality: see Mortality
Infantado, Duques del, 5
Israel, J. I., 3 and note
Ivanovsky, Alexis, 160
Ixmiquilpan, Table 1.3n, 115

Jacona: *alcabala* farm, 1646, Table 1.4A,
  118
Jalapa (Province), Table 1.3n, 115; 138n
Jilotepec de Abasolo (town), Table 1.3n,
  115
Jowdy, E. William, 4-5

Keys, Ancel, 160
Kleiber, Max, 150
Kroeber, Alfred E., 182
Labor: daily activity schedule of pre-
  Conquest central Mexican Indian
  male adults, 155-158; hypothetical
  day of average Aztec male *macehual*,
  156-157; adjusted for yerly rest-days,
  157; Aztec women, 157-158; chil-